FREEZE

For Jess and Emily

First published in Great Britain in 2013
by Weidenfeld & Nicolson

1 3 5 7 9 10 8 6 4 2

A CIP catalogue record for this book is available from the
British Library.

ISBN: 978 0 297 86516 2

Printed and bound in China

Photographer: Cristian Barnett
Stylist: Claire Bignell
Designers: Andy Campling and Loulou Clark
Editors: Sally Coleman and Jillian Young
Proofreader: Elise See Tai
Indexer: Rosemary Dear

The Orion Publishing Group's policy is to use papers that are natural,
renewable and recyclable and made from wood grown in sustainable
forests. The logging and manufacturing processes are expected to
conform to the environmental regulations of the country of origin.

Weidenfeld & Nicolson
Orion Publishing Group Ltd
Orion House
5 Upper Saint Martin's Lane
London, WC2H 9EA

An Hachette UK Company

www.orionbooks.co.uk

FREEZE

JUSTINE PATTISON

With 120 delicious recipes and
fantastic new ways to use your freezer
and make life just that bit easier

WEIDENFELD & NICOLSON

CONTENTS

Introduction

The chances are you've bought or borrowed this book because you are looking for a bit of advice on how to use your freezer more effectively. And when I started writing *Freeze* I probably needed just the same thing. I didn't begin the book thinking I was an expert but as the months went by, I managed to work out – by trial and error and a few spectacular successes and failures – what worked for me.

I spoke to lots of women – and some men. How did they use their freezers? The findings weren't much of a surprise. Most people seemed to use them as a storage space for the odd loaf of bread, fish fingers, maybe a couple of pizzas, an unidentifiable collection of leftovers that they felt too guilty to bin – and of course, frozen peas. Every freezer contains them. Perhaps freezer manufacturers should provide free peas with every freezer – just to get you started.

What I found surprising though, is that without exception, all these people, cooks and non-cooks alike, wanted to know how they could make better use of the freezer and would it really make life easier. They didn't use the freezer to its maximum capability because they didn't want to, but because they didn't know how to.

Revolutionising the way you *Freeze*

When I was growing up in the 1970s it seemed that every other mum had a huge chest freezer in the garage, utility room or shed. (My brothers and I were always being told not to climb inside when playing hide and seek, which made us somewhat wary.) And they'd all be off to Bejam, cash and carry or the butcher, stocking up with Findus crispy pancakes, arctic rolls and beef burgers or bulk cooking massive casseroles and meat pies.

There were a great many freezer cookbooks written in the Seventies and Eighties. Some of them offered sensible advice on freezing vegetables and fruit from the garden – this being the era of recession and 'The Good Life'. Other books were packed full of recipes for dishes that could be frozen and then whipped out when unexpected guests appeared and needed to be fed. Is it just me, or is the chance of unexpected guests suddenly turning up the most ridiculous reason to stock your freezer full of rustic pâtés and fancy canapés?

Even contemporary freezer cookbooks – and there are a few – seem to be written for women who either have the time to spend a whole weekend sweating over the stove batch cooking, or contain recipes that you could find in lots of other books and just happen to freeze. Most of the time these recipes require thorough and lengthy defrosting before reheating, which means you have to plan your weekly meals well ahead of time. I don't cook like that. No one I know cooks like that. I'm taking a guess that you probably don't either. And that's the point of this book. To show you how to use your freezer for the way we cook – and eat – today.

Flexible food

The possibility that the whole family is in the house at the same time and also ready to eat together remains a dream. That is not to say that I've given up on family meals, I certainly haven't. I just need my food to be flexible. Very flexible.

With a well stocked freezer you can have a variety of quick meals at your fingertips. Even if you aren't a brilliant cook, or if you work full time, have a family to look after and are still trying to have a bit of time for yourself, you can still produce a selection of homemade dishes that you will feel proud to put on the table.

How about a Thai chicken curry within 15 minutes and without spending a fortune on a ready meal? Or a chicken in a creamy tarragon sauce minutes after coming through the door yet not having to stop and shop on your way home. Your family could be sitting down together on a weekday night and tucking into proper family-sized fish pie – real food straight from the freezer. Dining in and entertaining could be a darn sight more relaxing and enjoyable when beef in Burgundy and lemon and raspberry pavlova are on the menu. You'll find all these recipes and a hundred more within the pages of this book.

Only dishes that made it through the cooking, freezing and reheating process with no compromise in quality or appearance are in this book. So whether it's a family favourite such as cottage pie, lasagne or my quick mix carrot cake, all have been freezer and kitchen triple tested.

It's not all about batch baking or bulk buying though, my contemporary take on freezer cooking takes into account those homes with only 2–3 freezer drawers as well as those with massive chest freezers in the garage. For me, freezer cooking in the 21st century can relate more to quick dishes that can be prepared in a flash – often using both fresh and frozen ingredients – and clever ways of maximising space.

I've come up with lots of new but very practical ways that I hope will make freezing work for you. From flat freezing to frozen super-quick strips, this book is bursting with ideas and innovations, tips and techniques to help you revolutionise the way you *Freeze*.

Recipe notes

All the recipes in this book have been carefully tested but by following a few simple tips, you can ensure perfect results. Before you start preparing any of the recipes, I recommend you read the back section of techniques first as it will help you understand how the book works and give you all the advice you need to guarantee success.

Weigh all the ingredients carefully – I rely on my digital scales for accuracy – and use proper 15ml tablespoon and 5ml teaspoon measures plus a measuring jug.

I've made cooking times and oven temperatures as accurate as I possibly can, but all ovens are different. Keep an eye on your food and be prepared to cook for a longer or shorter time if necessary.

Try to choose a dish or tin as close as possible to the one recommended in the recipe for best results for cooking or freezing.

All the onions and garlic used in my recipes are to be peeled, unless otherwise specified. All citrus fruit skins are unwaxed or well scrubbed for grating. Vegetables, such as peppers, should be cut into roughly the size stated – there is no need to be exact.

I always use free-range eggs. Use the size recommended in each recipe for the best results.

Microwave oven wattages vary hugely. My recipes have been tested using an 900W microwave, so you will need to adjust the timings if using an oven with a different wattage. Refer to the manufacturer's guidelines for details.

It's especially important to cook or reheat frozen food to a high enough temperature to ensure it is safe to eat. This is particularly important when cooking meat, poultry or fish from frozen. Invest in a digital food thermometer (see page 223).

Top reasons to freeze

Flexibility
With a well-stocked freezer you have access to a huge variety of meals without constant trips to the shops. It's also the perfect way of catering for fussy eaters while giving you the chance to feed family members at different times.

Convenience
Cooking from frozen saves time preparing meals when life is busy and also means you can get well ahead when there's a bit of spare time to hand.

Money saving
Freezing gives you the opportunity to buy in bulk or take advantage of price offers. You can also freeze your garden produce and enjoy it all year round.

Less waste
Freezing is the perfect way to preserve leftovers from one meal to make into another. It's also the best and quickest way of storing foods that you might have overbought.

You know what's in it
Making your own food for the freezer means you'll know exactly what is in each dish. The food doesn't need additional preservatives and will remain fresh as long as you wrap it well and freeze it quickly.

Effortless entertaining
Freeze-ahead meals take the hassle out of entertaining, leaving you happy and relaxed instead of hot and flustered.

Best nutrition
Freezing ensures foods remain closer to their natural state and retain more nutrients than other methods of preserving.

Most of the time, freezer cooking isn't about cooking at all. It's about reheating something that's already been cooked. This book is a bit different because I often use raw frozen ingredients and then cook them from frozen.

I realised when I came to write this book that I had been cooking from frozen for a while anyway. When desperate for something to cook for supper, I would chase hard blocks of frozen mince around the saucepan, squishing off chunks with a spatula whenever they became soft enough. I've even cooked a block of eight lamb chops, carefully prying them apart with a knife as they thawed in the pan. None of this unusual activity gave rise to food poisoning, the food didn't taste spoiled and no one noticed that their Bolognese or lamb casserole wasn't cooked in exactly the same way as usual.

It got me wondering how I could make cooking from frozen easier. After all, 500g blocks of frozen mince do take a while to thaw, even if you are chipping away at them like a mountain climber attempting to reach the summit by nightfall. I soon worked out that the shape of the food made all the difference. Food that is frozen in large, solid masses not only takes longer to freeze, which will affect the texture and overall quality, but also takes longer to cook or reheat from frozen.

My solution was to cut meat, poultry and fish into thin strips for freezing and then cook them from frozen. I'll often buy a large pack of free-range chicken breasts, at a good price, cook a couple that evening and slice up the rest for the freezer. I do exactly the same with steaks, pork fillet, fish and even sausages – basically any lean cut that's sure to cook fast and will be used within a month or so. I call them my super-quick strips and you can find out how to prepare them on page 200. Using additional improvised ingredients from the store cupboard, freezer or fridge, they offer the answer to a myriad of lovely meals.

QUICK FIXES

Thai chicken and coconut curry

Serves 2

A delicious Thai-style green or red chicken curry with fragrant spices, tender strips of chicken and colourful vegetables. This is enough chicken for two servings, but you could easily add more and stretch the curry to serve three to four people instead. I've given the weights for chicken and vegetables but a generous handful of each will do fine. Serve with rice and prawn crackers and don't forget to remove the kaffir lime leaves after cooking.

2 tbsp sunflower oil

200g frozen super-quick chicken strips (see page 200)

400ml can coconut milk

2 heaped tbsp Thai green or red curry paste

5 kaffir lime leaves (fresh or frozen, see page 208)

1 tsp caster sugar

1½ tbsp nam pla (Thai fish sauce)

100g frozen or fresh green beans, trimmed

125g mixed frozen peppers or 1 red or yellow pepper, deseeded and cut into thin strips or chunks

2–3 tbsp chopped fresh or frozen coriander (optional)

Heat the oil in a large non-stick saucepan or deep frying pan. Add the frozen super-quick chicken strips and fry for 2 minutes until lightly coloured on all sides, turning regularly. Pour over the coconut milk and add the curry paste, lime leaves, caster sugar and fish sauce. Bring to a gentle simmer and cook for 5 minutes.

Add the fresh or frozen vegetables and return to a gentle simmer. Cook for a further 5 minutes until the chicken is thoroughly cooked, vegetables are tender and the coconut milk has slightly thickened, stirring regularly. Remove the lime leaves and scatter the curry with chopped coriander, if using. Serve in deep bowls.

Fast fish stew

Serves 3–4

This is a really easy one-pot supper that can be ready in just 25 minutes. Add extra fish for very hungry people, or decrease the amount if cooking for two. If you don't have any potatoes to hand, stir in some freshly cooked pasta or rice. This speedy stew makes use of lots frozen foods: fish chunks, mixed seafood and green beans. To make things even faster you can also use frozen onion and garlic (see page 208).

1 tbsp olive oil	2 tsp caster sugar
1 medium onion, finely sliced	3 medium potatoes (roughly 375g),
2 large garlic cloves, finely sliced	peeled and cut into 2cm chunks
1 heaped tsp ground coriander	150g frozen green beans
good pinch saffron strands	400g frozen chunks of cod, haddock or
2 bay leaves	salmon or a mixture (see page 198),
150ml white wine	plus frozen prawns if you like
400g can chopped tomatoes	flaked sea salt
1 tbsp tomato purée	freshly ground black pepper
350ml cold water	freshly chopped flat-leaf parsley (optional)

Heat the oil in a large flame-proof casserole dish or non-stick saucepan and gently fry the onion and garlic for 5 minutes until well softened, stirring occasionally. Stir in the ground coriander, saffron and bay leaves. Cook for a couple of minutes, stirring occasionally. Season with a good pinch of salt and plenty of ground black pepper.

Pour over the wine and bubble for a few seconds before adding the tomatoes, tomato purée, water, sugar and potatoes. Increase the heat a little, bring to a gentle simmer and cook for 15 minutes, stirring occasionally until the potatoes are softened but not breaking apart. Add the frozen green beans and return to a simmer.

Drop the frozen fish pieces or mixed seafood on top of the bubbling liquid and cover with a lid. Poach over a medium heat for 8–10 minutes or until the fish and seafood is cooked (it should be firm but not dry). Carefully hold the lid in place and shake the pan gently a couple of times as the fish cooks. Add frozen prawns, if using, for the last 5 minutes of the cooking time.

Ladle into warmed deep plates or bowls and scatter with flat-leaf parsley, if using. Serve with spoonfuls of garlic mayonnaise and toasted French bread.

Warm chicken salad with lemon and herb dressing

Serves 3–4

This delicious warm chicken salad is made with tender chicken breast escalopes cooked from frozen and can be ready in less than 10 minutes. For a super-fast salad, use a ready-made dressing – Caesar is good or even just a drizzle of olive oil and balsamic vinegar. Romaine lettuce has a lovely crisp texture but any variety will be fine and if you have extra salad ingredients to hand, toss in some cucumber, celery, fennel or peppers for extra crunch.

1 tbsp sunflower oil
4 frozen chicken escalopes
  (see Clever idea)
1 romaine lettuce, leaves separated,
  washed and drained
12 cherry tomatoes, halved
handful frozen croutons (see page 184)
40g fresh or frozen Parmesan cheese,
  shaved with a peeler or grated

Lemon and herb dressing
4 tbsp mayonnaise
2–3 tsp fresh lemon juice
1 tbsp cold water
1 tsp finely chopped parsley, tarragon
  or young thyme leaves (fresh or
  frozen) or ½ tsp dried mixed herbs
freshly ground black pepper

Clever idea

Chicken escalopes are easy to prepare and are a great way to cook quickly from frozen. To prepare them, cut boneless, skinless chicken breasts in half horizontally through the middle. Rub both sides of the escalopes with sunflower oil – one tablespoon should be enough for 8 escalopes. Season well with freshly ground black pepper and flaked sea salt. Place on a lined baking tray and open freeze for 2 hours. Take the escalopes off the tray and pop them into a freezer bag. Label, seal and freeze for up to one month.

Heat the oil in a large non-stick frying pan. Fry the frozen chicken over a medium-high heat for 3–4 minutes on each side until golden brown and cooked through. There should be no pink remaining. Don't be tempted to turn the chicken too early or it could stick.

While the chicken is cooking, make the dressing. Put the mayonnaise in a small bowl and stir in the lemon juice, to taste, and water until smooth. Add the finely chopped herbs and stir well.

Tear the lettuce leaves and arrange in deep plates or bowls (or one big dish if you prefer). Scatter with the cherry tomatoes. Take the chicken out of the pan and put on a board to rest for a couple of minutes. Put the croutons in the frying pan and toast lightly from frozen for 1–2 minutes, turning occasionally until hot.

Slice the chicken and place it on the lettuce leaves. Scatter with the Parmesan cheese and croutons. Drizzle over the dressing and serve.

Easy chicken and mushroom risotto

Serves 4

This delicious and creamy risotto uses frozen super-quick chicken strips and the staple for any freezer – frozen peas. The only effort involved is to be sure to stir the risotto regularly for a creamy texture. Use home-made chicken stock from the freezer or good-quality chicken stock cubes. If you have some Parmesan in the freezer it can be grated into the risotto straight from frozen. Serve with rocket leaves, drizzled with a little olive oil and some good-quality balsamic vinegar.

25g butter
1 medium onion, finely chopped
2 garlic cloves, crushed
1 large bay leaf
1 tbsp olive oil
300g frozen super-quick chicken strips (see page 200)
150g fresh or frozen chestnut mushrooms, sliced

250g Arborio (risotto) rice
100ml dry white wine
1 litre hot chicken stock (home-made or made from 1½ chicken stock cubes)
150g frozen peas
25g fresh or frozen Parmesan cheese, finely grated
freshly ground black pepper

Melt the butter in a large non-stick saucepan over a medium heat. Fry the onion, garlic and bay leaf for 2–3 minutes or until they begin to soften, stirring occasionally.

Add the oil, frozen super-quick chicken strips and mushrooms. Season with lots of freshly ground black pepper. Increase the heat a little and continue cooking for a further 6–8 minutes or until the chicken is lightly coloured and the mushrooms are pale-golden.

Add the rice and stir around for a few seconds before pouring over the wine. Allow to bubble for a few seconds more then add all the stock. Stir well and bring to the boil.

Reduce the heat to a fast simmer and cook uncovered for a further 12 minutes, or until the rice is almost tender and the risotto is creamy, stirring regularly, especially towards the end of the cooking time. Often with risotto, the stock is added a ladleful at a time, but this method is a lot less bother and gives great results.

Add the frozen peas and Parmesan to the risotto and cook for 4–5 minutes more until the peas are hot and the cheese has melted. Adjust the seasoning to taste before serving in warmed bowls topped with a rocket salad if you like.

30-minute meatballs

Serves 6

When you are next in the supermarket, pop a couple packs of meatballs in the trolley and freeze them when you get home. As with all the recipes in this Quick Fix chapter, they can be cooked straight from frozen. I've also given a recipe for my easy parsley and lemon meatballs below so you can always give them a go if you have a bit more time.

1 tbsp sunflower oil	150ml water
2 x packs of 12 frozen meatballs	1 tbsp tomato purée
1 medium onion, chopped	1 tsp dried oregano
2 garlic cloves, crushed	flaked sea salt
400g can chopped tomatoes	freshly ground black pepper

Heat the oil in a large, deep non-stick frying pan over a medium-high heat and fry the frozen meatballs for 8–10 minutes, turning regularly until lightly browned. Add the onion and cook with the meatballs for 5 minutes, stirring often and adding the garlic after 3 minutes.

Tip the tomatoes into the pan and add the water, tomato purée, oregano, a good pinch of salt and plenty of ground black pepper. Bring to a simmerand cook, stirring regularly for 15 minutes or until the sauce is thick and the meatballs are thoroughly cooked. If in doubt, cut one of the meatballs open – there should be no pink remaining.

Meatballs with parsley and lemon

Put one finely chopped onion, 3 crushed garlic cloves, 250g each lean minced beef and pork, 2 teaspoons dried oregano, 6 heaped tablespoons finely chopped fresh parsley, the finely grated zest of one lemon and 20g fresh white breadcrumbs in a large bowl. Season well with 1 teaspoon flaked sea salt and lots of ground black pepper. Mix with your hands until thoroughly combined.

Roll into 24 walnut-sized small balls and open freeze on 2 lined trays (see page 214). Pack into labelled freezer bags. Seal and freeze for up to 3 months. Thaw or cook from frozen. Makes 24.

Super-quick beef and noodle stir-fry

Serves 2

This recipe uses frozen super-quick beef steak strips straight from the freezer, stir-fried in a lovely rich sauce flavoured with ginger and garlic. If you've previously frozen a quantity of beef steak strips then a handful taken from the bag is all you need for this recipe. The beef stays really succulent and the noodles make it go a long way. Using ready prepared stir-fry vegetables will make this super-super quick but you can also chop or slice anything that you may have in the fridge.

125g dried medium egg noodles
1½ tbsp dark soy sauce
2 tsp cornflour
100ml fresh orange juice
    (or from a carton)
1 large garlic clove, crushed (or 1
    heaped tsp frozen chopped garlic)
20g chunk fresh root ginger, peeled
    and finely grated (or 2 tsp frozen
    chopped ginger)

2 tbsp sunflower oil
150g frozen super-quick beef steak
    strips (see page 200)
300g pack fresh mixed stir-fry
    vegetables
freshly ground black pepper

Clever idea

This recipe is a good way to use up any vegetables you may have in the fridge. Always include a little onion; spring onions or sliced red onions are good. Cut peppers and carrots into thin strips, and top and tail mangetout. Sliced courgettes, runner beans, broccoli florets and shredded cabbage or kale all work well. You can also use frozen vegetables straight from the freezer but you will have to increase the cooking time by a minute or so.

Bring a medium pan of water to the boil. Add the noodles and return to the boil. Cook for 3 minutes or according to packet instructions then drain in a colander, rinse under cold water and leave to stand.

While the noodles are boiling, mix 1 tablespoon of the soy sauce with the cornflour in a small bowl until smooth. Stir in the remaining soy sauce, orange juice, garlic and ginger then set aside.

Heat the oil in a large non-stick frying pan or wok over a high heat. Add the frozen super-quick beef strips and stir-fry for 2 minutes until lightly browned. Remove the beef with a slotted spoon and put it on a plate. Add the stir-fry vegetables to the pan and cook for 2–3 minutes until they are just tender, adding an extra slurp of oil if the pan becomes a little dry.

Tip the drained noodles into the pan and add the beef and sauce. Stir-fry for a further 1–2 minutes until the noodles and beef are hot and sauce is glossy. Season with black pepper. Serve at once.

Very easy lamb with red wine gravy

Serves 4

This is a very simple supper that can be knocked together in no time. Cook as many chops as you need – cutlets will take a little less time. The red wine and redcurrant gravy is so easy that you might as well make the whole quantity even if you are serving fewer than four people. Delicious served with my dauphinoise potatoes (see page 165).

2 tbsp sunflower oil
8 frozen lamb loin chops or cutlets
   (ideally herb rubbed, see my tip
   below)
100ml red wine

½ lamb stock cube
150ml cold water, plus 2 tbsp
1 tbsp redcurrant jelly
1 tbsp cornflour

Heat the oil in a large non-stick frying pan and fry the frozen lamb for 8–10 minutes on each side, depending on thickness, until hot throughout. Keep the heat to a medium setting so the lamb sizzles without burning. Turn the lamb on to its side to brown the fat and continue cooking for a further 2–3 minutes until golden.

Remove the lamb to a plate and leave to rest. Spoon the fat out of the pan; discard and return the pan to the heat. Pour the wine into the pan and bring to a simmer. Drop the stock cube into the pan and break it up with a wooden spoon so that it dissolves into the wine. Add the water and redcurrant jelly and return to a simmer. Cook for 2–3 minutes until the stock cube dissolves and the jelly melts, stirring regularly.

Mix the cornflour with 2 tablespoons of cold water and stir into the sauce. Cook for 1–2 minutes more, stirring constantly until thickened and glossy. Return the chops to the pan and warm through gently in the sauce until hot throughout.

Clever idea

Lamb cutlets taste even better if you coat them lightly with fresh herbs before freezing. If freezing 8 lamb chops, simply rub all over with 1 tbsp sunflower oil and then coat in a mixture of 3 tbsp of finely chopped mint leaves, 2 tbsp of finely chopped fresh thyme leaves, 1 tsp of ground black pepper and ½ tsp of flaked sea salt. Open freeze on a lined tray for 2 hours then pack in a freezer bag or rigid container. Cover, label and freeze for up to 3 months. Cook from frozen or thaw first and shorten the cooking time by 4–5 minutes on each side.

Bangers with onion gravy

Serves 4

A family favourite that I now make with sausages I've previously frozen. Making this dish with frozen sausages means I can pick up good-quality sausages in the supermarket when they are on offer or when I'm at the butcher's or farmers' market. Team them with my cheesy mash (see page 164) for a quick midweek meal.

2 tbsp sunflower oil
8–12 good-quality frozen pork
    sausages
1 medium onion, finely sliced
1 tbsp plain flour
450ml pork or beef stock, made with
    1 stock cube

1 tbsp tomato ketchup
1 tsp Worcestershire sauce
flaked sea salt
freshly ground black pepper

Heat the oil in a large non-stick frying pan and fry the frozen sausages over a medium heat for 12 minutes, turning occasionally until nicely browned. Add the onion to the pan and cook with the sausages for a further 8 minutes, stirring every now and then until the sausages are cooked through and the onion is softened and deep golden brown. Keep an eye on the onion so it doesn't burn.

Transfer the sausages to a plate and stir the flour into the pan. Cook for 20–30 seconds, stirring constantly. Gradually start adding the stock to lift the juices and sediment from the bottom of the pan, stirring well in between each addition. Finally, add the ketchup and Worcestershire sauce to the pan and bring to a simmer. Cook the gravy for 2–3 minutes, stirring constantly. Season to taste.

Return the sausages to the pan and reheat them in the hot gravy for a couple of minutes until piping hot throughout. Serve with cheesy mashed potato and fresh or frozen vegetables.

Pasta with spicy sausage ragù

Serves 4–5

A full-flavoured supper dish that uses frozen bacon lardons and frozen sausage pieces to make a rich, tasty sauce for pasta. Onion, capers and olives can also be used straight from the freezer. If you like your food a little milder, reduce the quantity of chilli flakes.

1 tbsp olive oil
150g frozen diced smoked lardons
   or streaky bacon
250g frozen skinned sausage pieces
   or sausage meat (see page 196)
1 medium onion, finely chopped
3 large ripe tomatoes (roughly 350g)
   or 400g can chopped tomatoes
200g dried pasta shapes, such as
   penne
150ml red wine

2 tbsp tomato purée
1 tsp caster sugar
1 tsp dried chilli flakes
40g baby capers, drained and
   roughly chopped
50g good-quality pitted black
   or green olives
flaked sea salt
freshly ground black pepper
handful of fresh basil, roughly torn
   (optional)

Place a large non-stick frying pan over a medium heat. Add the oil, frozen lardons, frozen sausage pieces and onion. Cook together for about 20 minutes, until well browned, stirring regularly to break up the sausage meat. You want it to become quite sticky and to pick up lots of smoky flavours.

While the onion and sausage are cooking, half-fill a large saucepan with water and bring to the boil. Make a small cross in the bottom of each of the fresh tomatoes and add them to the water. Dunk for around 30 seconds, to allow the skins to wrinkle back. Remove with a slotted spoon and put the tomatoes on a chopping board to cool for a short while. Add the pasta to the same water and return to the boil. Cook for 10–12 minutes, or according to the packet instructions, until tender.

When the tomatoes are cool enough to handle, slip off the skins and discard. Roughly chop the flesh, throwing away any tough central cores but leaving the seeds. Pour the wine into the frying pan with the sausages and add the chopped tomatoes (and seeds), tomato purée, sugar, chillies and capers. Press the olives between your thumb and finger to roughly crush, add to the sauce and cook for a further 5 minutes or until rich and thick, stirring regularly. Season to taste.

Drain the cooked pasta and return to the saucepan. Tip the sausage ragù into the same pan and toss together. Spoon into warmed bowls and serve scattered with torn basil leaves if you have some handy.

Somerset pork with apples

Serves 2

I love the traditional combination of pork with apples. This recipe makes a regular appearance in my kitchen and makes the most of frozen pork loin steaks. Serve with my mashed or microwave jacket potatoes (see page 207) or freshly cooked rice.

2 tbsp sunflower oil
1 eating apple, quartered, cored
   and sliced
2 frozen pork loin steaks
½ medium onion, sliced
150ml dry cider or pork stock

1 tbsp finely shredded fresh sage leaves
   or ½ tsp dried sage
100ml double cream or crème fraîche
flaked sea salt
freshly ground black pepper

Heat 1 tablespoon of the oil in a large non-stick frying pan and fry the apple pieces over a high heat for 3–4 minutes until golden brown, turning once or twice. Transfer to a plate with a slotted spoon.

Return the pan to the heat, add the remaining oil and the frozen pork loin steaks. Cook for 5 minutes over a medium heat or until lightly browned then turn over and season with salt and ground black pepper.

Add the onion to the pan and cook with the pork for a further 10 minutes, stirring occasionally until the onion is softened and browned and the pork is cooked. If the pork steaks are particularly thick, you may need to cook them for up to 5 minutes more, turning a few times. The pork is cooked when it is no longer pink inside but remains juicy.

Turn the pork once more and season with more salt and pepper. Brown the sides of the pork by leaning it against the side of the pan. Cook for 2 minutes.

Transfer the pork to the plate with the apples and pour the cider or stock into the pan. Stir in the sage and bring to the boil. Cook until the liquid has reduced by half. Stir in the cream or crème fraîche and cook for 1–2 minutes more, stirring constantly. Season to taste.

Return the pork and apples along with any extra juices that may have collected on the plate to the pan and warm through in the bubbling cream sauce for a minute or so before serving.

This chapter is dedicated to complete meals in single portions. I've attempted to give you a simple selection of dishes that are easy to assemble and will suit those occasions when you are simply too tired to cook, too busy to start from scratch or need to leave something ready for the rest of the family to prepare.

Cooking individual meals from frozen takes a little more time than reheating a chilled ready-meal but the freezer offers more choice. There is no reason why any of these dishes can't be frozen in larger portions for family meals or likewise any of the family meals in the next chapter can't be adapted to freeze as meals for one. It's crucial to make your freezer work for you in order to get the most out of it.

I always think some chilli or spice really perks up a meal, so you'll find more than a fair share of Indian and Asian inspired dishes and curries here. Freeze the meals in foil containers or freezer-proof plastic ones and always put the reheating instructions on the label, that way there is no confusion when you are not around to take charge. Some of the recipes give an alternative number of servings, so you can adjust according to your family's appetite.

If reheating more than one portion, you will need to increase the time. Check your microwave manufacturer's instructions for details. Microwave ovens do vary so I advise you to check the internal temperatures of meat or chicken with a digital food thermometer so you can be sure the dish is hot throughout (see page 223).

I used to try and freeze my rice, pasta and mash alongside the main part of the meal but through testing several versions of each recipe I discovered that it made far more sense to freeze the parts separately so they are ready to reheat from frozen at the same time. The only exceptions to this are the noodle meals, which seem to lend themselves to freezing combined. You'll find out how to freeze accompaniments on page 206. I find that freezing cooked rice, pasta or mash in individual portions, flattened into zip-seal freezer bags, gives the best – and fastest – results. Either keep them in a different section of the freezer or place them on top of each main dish so it's simple to assemble a complete meal. Secure with freezer tape if you have some.

MEALS
FOR
ONE

Creamy smoked haddock and spinach bakes

Makes 4 servings

Like a pie but quicker. Toasted bread and cheese make a brilliant, quick and easy crunchy topping under which nestle tender pieces of fish and spinach in a lovely, velvety sauce. These bakes make a perfect supper or lunch dish – served just as they are or with an extra portion of vegetables.

500g smoked haddock fillet
½ medium onion, cut into 6 wedges
1 bay leaf
600ml full-fat or semi-skimmed milk
3 slices of thick white bread, crusts
    removed, torn into 2cm pieces
50g butter

50g plain flour
4 tbsp double cream or milk
medium bag of baby spinach leaves
    (roughly 150g)
50g mature Cheddar cheese,
    coarsely grated
freshly ground black pepper

To FREEZE (up to 3 months)
Allow the bread and cheese topped bakes to cool completely without baking in the oven. Cover, label and freeze.

To SERVE
Uncover as many bakes as you need and place on a baking tray. Cook from frozen in a preheated oven at 200°C/Fan 180°C/Gas 6 for 25–30 minutes or until piping hot throughout.

Put the haddock, onion and bay leaf in a large frying pan and pour over the milk. Bring to a gentle simmer and cook for just one minute. Remove from the heat and leave to stand for 15 minutes.

While the fish is standing, put the bread pieces in a large frying pan and toast over a medium-high heat for about 5 minutes until golden and crisp around the edges, turning regularly. Remove from the heat.

Strain the fish in a large colander, reserving the cooking liquor. Discard the onion wedges and bay leaf and peel off and discard the fish skin. Melt the butter in a large non-stick saucepan over a low heat. Add the flour and cook for 30 seconds. Gradually add the reserved cooking liquor and double cream or additional milk, stirring continuously. Bring to a gentle simmer and cook for 2–3 minutes until the sauce is thick and glossy, while stirring.

Add the baby spinach to the pan, it will look like a lot but will quickly wilt into the sauce. Cook for 2 minutes further, stirring constantly until the leaves soften. Flake the fish into chunky pieces and stir lightly into the sauce. Season with ground black pepper.

Divide the mixture between 4 individual shallow freezer-proof baking dishes or foil containers. Scatter the toasted bread pieces over the fish and sauce. Sprinkle with the cheese.

To cook now, place the containers on a baking tray and cook in a preheated oven at 200°C/Fan 180°C/Gas 6 for 15–20 minutes until golden brown and bubbling.

Moroccan chicken with apricots and almonds

Makes 6–8 servings

This mildly spiced casserole freezes well and heats up perfectly to make a comforting supper after a busy day. Scatter with a few sprigs of fresh coriander and serve alongside a large bowl of fluffy couscous or rice.

12 boneless, skinless chicken thighs
3 tbsp sunflower oil
2 medium onions, halved and thinly sliced
3 garlic cloves, thinly sliced
50g chunk fresh root ginger, peeled and finely chopped
2 heaped tsp ground cumin
2 heaped tsp ground coriander
1 tsp dried chilli flakes
generous pinch saffron
1 cinnamon stick
2 tbsp plain flour
2 x 400g cans chopped tomatoes

400ml chicken stock (made with 1 chicken stock cube)
3 tbsp runny honey
50g sultanas
75g ready-to-eat dried apricots, quartered
finely grated zest ½ lemon
50g blanched almonds (optional)
400g can chickpeas, drained and rinsed
small bunch fresh coriander, roughly chopped (or 3 tbsp frozen coriander)
flaked sea salt
freshly ground black pepper

Trim any excess fat from the chicken thighs and cut each one into 4 pieces. Season well with salt and freshly ground black pepper. Heat one tablespoon of the oil in a large non-stick frying pan. Fry the chicken in 2 batches over a medium-high heat for 3–4 minutes or until lightly coloured, turning every now and then. Transfer to a large non-stick saucepan or flameproof casserole and add a tablespoon of oil between batches.

Add the remaining oil, onions, garlic and ginger to the frying pan and cook over a medium heat for 6–8 minutes, stirring occasionally until softened and beginning to brown. Stir in the spices and fry for one minute. Sprinkle over the flour and stir well.

Tip the spiced onions into the pan with the chicken pieces and add the canned tomatoes, stock, honey, sultanas, apricots, lemon zest and almonds if using. Stir well and bring to a gentle simmer. Cover loosely with a lid and cook for 30 minutes, stirring occasionally.

Stir in the chickpeas, increase the heat and cook uncovered for 10 minutes more or until the sauce has thickened. Stir regularly so the sauce doesn't stick. Remove the cinnamon stick and stir in the coriander.

To FREEZE (up to 3 months)
Divide the chicken mixture between 8 freezer-proof containers. Cool. Cover, label and freeze.

To SERVE
Turn one portion of the frozen chicken mixture out of the container and into a wide microwave-proof bowl. Cover with cling film and microwave on HIGH for 5 minutes. Stand for 2 minutes. Press the chicken and vegetables with a spoon to separate into chunks. Microwave on HIGH for a further 2 minutes or until piping hot throughout. Stand for 2–3 minutes before serving.

Chinese ginger chilli chicken

Makes 6 servings

Chicken, ginger, chilli and peppers cooked in a delicious, slightly spicy sweet and sour sauce. Add some chunks of fresh pineapple or halved water chestnuts if you like. Freshly cooked noodles can be divided between the freezer-proof containers before spooning the chicken mixture on top ready to freeze (see page 206). Alternatively, serve with frozen rice that can be reheated while the chicken is resting.

4 boneless, skinless chicken breasts
3 tbsp sunflower oil
2 small onions, each cut into 12 wedges
4 peppers, red, green, orange and
   yellow for a colourful mix, deseeded

Sauce
2 tbsp cornflour
300ml pineapple juice (from a carton)
150ml water

3 garlic cloves, finely chopped
40g chunk fresh root ginger,
   peeled and finely chopped
2 tbsp dark soy sauce
2 tbsp white wine vinegar
3 tbsp soft light brown sugar
5 tbsp tomato ketchup
1–1½ tsp dried chilli flakes
freshly ground black pepper

To FREEZE (up to 2 months)
Divide the chicken mixture between 6 freezer-proof containers. Cool. Cover, label and freeze.

To SERVE
Turn one portion of the frozen chicken mixture out of the container and into a wide microwave-proof bowl. Cover with cling film and microwave on HIGH for 5 minutes. Stand for 2 minutes. Press the chicken and vegetables with a spoon to separate into chunks. Microwave on HIGH for a further 2 minutes or until piping hot throughout. Stand for 2–3 minutes before serving.

To make the sauce, put the cornflour in a large bowl and stir in 3 tablespoons of the pineapple juice to make a smooth paste. Add the remaining pineapple juice and water and stir in the garlic, ginger, soy sauce, vinegar, sugar, ketchup and chilli flakes until thoroughly combined. Set aside.

Cut each chicken breast into 7–9 even pieces, depending on size. Heat 2 tbsp of the oil in a large non-stick frying pan or wok and stir-fry the onion and peppers for 2 minutes over a high heat. Add the remaining oil and the chicken to the pan and stir-fry for 2 minutes until coloured on all sides.

Give the sauce a mix and add to the pan with the chicken and vegetables. Stir well, season with some ground black pepper and bring to a simmer. Cook for 5 minutes until the sauce is thickened and glossy and the chicken is cooked, turning the chicken and vegetables occasionally. Serve with rice or noodles.

Char siu pork with noodles

Makes 6 servings

Although not a strictly traditional recipe, this stir-fry is inspired by the sweet, spicy flavour of Chinese barbecue char siu pork. It's packed with flavour and miraculously it heats up brilliantly in the microwave. Be sure to get all of the ingredients prepared before you begin to stir-fry.

To FREEZE (up to 1 month)
Spread the pork, vegetables and noodles over 2 baking trays and leave to cool quickly. As soon as they are cold, divide them between 6 labelled zip-seal bags. Press out as much air as possible and seal. Place the bags on a baking tray and freeze until solid, then remove the baking tray.

To SERVE
Rinse a bag of the frozen pork and vegetables under a hot tap for a few seconds. Unseal and shake onto a microwave-proof plate. Cover with cling film and cook in the microwave on HIGH for 3 minutes. Stand for 60 seconds then cook for a further minute until piping hot throughout. Stand for 2 minutes before serving. You can also let the pork and noodles thaw in the fridge for a few hours and then reheat them in the microwave or a wok for 2–3 minutes until hot.

450g pork tenderloin, well trimmed
5 tbsp hoisin sauce
3 tbsp dry sherry
2 tbsp dark soy sauce
2 tbsp runny honey
1 tsp Chinese five-spice powder
3 tbsp sunflower oil
250g dried medium egg noodles
1 tsp cornflour
1 tbsp cold water

2 small red onions, cut into thin wedges
3 peppers (any colours), deseeded and sliced
100g small chestnut mushrooms, sliced
2 garlic cloves, finely chopped
25g chunk fresh root ginger, peeled and finely chopped
1 bunch spring onions (roughly 10), trimmed and diagonally sliced
freshly ground black pepper

Put the hoisin sauce, sherry and soy sauce in a large bowl and stir in the honey and five-spice powder. Add the pork and turn to coat in the sticky marinade. Cover and chill for 30–60 minutes, turning the pork in the marinade every 15 minutes or so.

Preheat the oven to 200°C/Fan 180°C/Gas 6. Drain the pork well, reserving the marinade. Place the pork on a small foil-lined tray. Roast in the centre of the oven for 20 minutes. Remove from the oven and leave to stand.

While the pork is roasting, cook the noodles in a large pan of boiling water for 3 minutes or according to the packet instructions until tender. Drain well in a colander. Rinse under running water until cold, then drain. Mix the cornflour with the water and stir into the reserved marinade. Cut the pork lengthways in half and then slice thinly.

Place a large non-stick frying pan or wok over a high heat. Add 2 tablespoons of the oil and stir-fry the onions, peppers and mushrooms for 3–4 minutes or until beginning to soften and lightly colour. Add the remaining oil and stir in the garlic and ginger.
Stir-fry with the vegetables for one minute more.

Tip the sliced pork into the hot pan and add the noodles, spring onions and reserved marinade. Toss together for 2–3 minutes until piping hot throughout. Serve hot.

To FREEZE (up to 1 month)
Divide the chicken and rice mixture
between 6 or 8 freezer-proof
containers. There should be enough
liquid to almost cover the chicken
and rice. Cool. Cover, label and
freeze.

To SERVE
Turn the frozen chicken and rice out
of the container and into a wide
microwave-proof bowl. Cover with
cling film and microwave on HIGH
for 5 minutes. Stand for 2 minutes.
Press the chicken and vegetables
with a spoon to separate into
chunks. Microwave on HIGH for a
further 2 minutes or until piping hot
throughout. Stand for 2–3 minutes
before serving.

Chicken with chorizo, peppers and rice

Makes 6–8 servings

A simple chicken and rice dish packed with robust Spanish flavours. It's a bit like paella but without the seafood. Feel free to chuck in a few frozen prawns before the end of the reheating time. You can add frozen peas rather than the beans if you like, just stir them into the chicken and rice five minutes before the end of the cooking time.

12 boneless, skinless chicken thighs
4 tbsp olive oil
150g chorizo (picante) sausage
2 medium onions, sliced
2 red peppers, deseeded
2 yellow peppers, deseeded
250g green beans, trimmed
2 garlic cloves, crushed
good pinch saffron strands

1 tsp dried chilli flakes
275g easy-cook long grain rice,
    such as Uncle Ben's
1.2 litres hot chicken stock
    (made with 1 chicken stock cube)
400g can chopped tomatoes
flaked sea salt
freshly ground black pepper

Trim any excess fat from the chicken thighs and cut each one into 4 pieces. Season well with salt and freshly ground black pepper. Pour 2 tablespoons of the oil into a large non-stick frying pan and place over a medium-high heat. Fry the chicken in 2 batches for 4–5 minutes, turning regularly until lightly coloured. Transfer to a large flameproof casserole or non-stick saucepan as soon as each batch is done.

Skin the chorizo and cut into 5mm slices. Add the chorizo to the frying pan and cook for 30 seconds until it begins to release oil but do not allow it to overcook or it could become tough. Scatter over the chicken and return the pan to the heat.

Add the onions to the pan and fry for 5 minutes until softened and very lightly browned, stirring occasionally. Add the remaining oil, peppers and green beans to the onions and cook for 2 minutes until they begin to soften. Stir in the garlic, saffron, chilli flakes and rice and cook for one minute more, stirring constantly.

Tip the rice mixture into the casserole with the chicken then pour over the chicken stock and canned tomatoes. Stir together well and bring to a gentle simmer. Cook uncovered for 12 minutes, stirring regularly until the rice is almost tender. Remove it from the heat immediately as it will continue to cook and absorb liquid as it stands. Season to taste with salt and pepper.

Extra special chilli con carne

Makes 6 servings

The secret to a decent chilli is a long slow simmer to help mellow the spices and enrich the sauce. I prefer to use a combination of hot chilli powder for heat and smoked chilli for a more authentic flavour although you can infuse the stew with a couple of halved chipotle chillies too. It's a perfect freeze-ahead meal for friends or family.

1kg braising steak (such as chuck steak)
4 tbsp sunflower oil
2 medium onions, chopped
2 garlic cloves, finely chopped
2 tsp hot chilli powder
2 tsp smoked paprika, preferably sweet
2 tsp ground cumin
2 tsp ground coriander
2 tbsp plain flour
150ml red wine or extra stock

600ml beef stock (made with 1 beef stock cube)
400g can chopped tomatoes
2 tsp caster sugar
1 tsp dried oregano
400g can red kidney beans, drained and rinsed
freshly squeezed juice 1 lime
flaked sea salt
freshly ground black pepper

Trim off any fat from the beef and cut the meat into roughly 3cm chunks. Heat 2 tablespoons of the oil in a large non-stick frying pan. Season the beef with salt and pepper and fry in 2 batches over a fairly high heat until browned on all sides. Tip into a large flameproof casserole dish and add a little extra oil to the frying pan to prevent the beef sticking. Preheat the oven to 180°C/Fan 160°C/Gas 4.

Return the frying pan to the heat and add 2 tablespoons more of the oil along with the onions. Cook over a medium heat for 5 minutes until softened, stirring regularly. Add the garlic, chilli powder, paprika, cumin and coriander. Fry for 2–3 minutes more, stirring constantly. Sprinkle over the flour and stir well.

Gradually stir in the wine and half of the beef stock. Bring to a simmer, stirring. Pour the onions and liquid over the beef in the casserole and add the tomatoes, remaining stock, sugar and oregano. Season with salt and plenty of freshly ground black pepper.

Bring the liquid to a simmer, then cover with a lid and transfer carefully to the oven. Cook for 1 hour. Remove from the oven and stir in the kidney beans. Return to the oven and cook for a further 45–60 minutes or until the beef is very tender and the sauce has thickened. Stir in the lime juice and serve.

To FREEZE (up to 3 months)
Divide the chilli con carne between
6 freezer-proof containers. Cool.
Cover, label and freeze.

To SERVE
Turn one portion of the frozen chilli
con carne out of the packaging
and into a wide microwave-proof
bowl. Cover with cling film and
microwave on HIGH for 5 minutes.
Stand for 2 minutes. Press with
a spoon to separate into chunks
and stir. Microwave on HIGH for a
further 2 minutes or until piping hot
throughout. Stand for 2–3 minutes
before serving.

Pasta Bolognese

Makes 8 servings

A rich, meaty Bolognese with a velvety cheese sauce and tender pasta makes a welcome meal. Pasta can become a little soft when frozen so choose a good quality pasta for the best results.

To FREEZE (up to 3 months)
Divide the pasta and Bolognese between 8 freezer-proof containers or individual foil dishes. Spoon the cheese sauce on top. Sprinkle with the remaining cheese. Cool. Cover, label and freeze.

To SERVE
Rinse the base of one of the containers with hot water for a few seconds. Remove the packaging and place the frozen pasta Bolognese in a microwave-proof dish, making sure the cheese sauce is on top. Cover with cling film and microwave on HIGH for 3 minutes. Stand for 2 minutes. Microwave on HIGH for a further 2–3 minutes or until piping hot throughout. Stand for 2–3 minutes before serving.

Alternatively, if using an individual foil dish, thaw completely in the fridge. Remove the lid. Bake in a preheated oven at 200°C/Fan 180°C/Gas 6 for 25–30 minutes until piping hot.

400g lean minced beef, or a mixture of pork and beef mince
2 medium onions, finely chopped
2 garlic cloves, finely chopped
2 tbsp plain flour
150ml red wine or extra stock
400g can chopped tomatoes
2 tbsp tomato purée
500ml beef stock (made with 1 beef stock cube)
1 tsp caster sugar
1 heaped tsp dried oregano
2 bay leaves

400g dried pasta shapes, such as penne, rigatoni or paccheri
flaked sea salt and freshly ground black pepper

Cheese sauce
50g butter
50g plain flour
600ml full-fat or semi-skimmed milk
150g mature Cheddar cheese, coarsely grated

Place a large non-stick saucepan or flameproof casserole over a medium heat and cook the mince with the onions and garlic for 10 minutes until lightly coloured. Use a wooden spoon to break up the meat as it cooks, squishing it against the base and sides of the pan.

Stir in the flour followed by the wine, tomatoes, tomato purée, beef stock, sugar, oregano and bay leaves. Season with a good pinch of salt and plenty of freshly ground black pepper. Bring to the boil, then reduce the heat and simmer gently for 40 minutes, stirring occasionally until the mince is tender. Remove from the heat.

To make the cheese sauce, melt the butter in a large non-stick saucepan and stir in the flour. Cook over a low heat for about 30 seconds. Gradually add the milk to the pan, stirring constantly between each addition. Increase the heat a little and bring to a gentle simmer. Cook for 3 minutes, stirring constantly. Stir in 100g of the cheese and simmer for 1–2 minutes more until melted. Season the sauce with salt and pepper.

While the sauce is being prepared, cook the pasta in a large pan of boiling water until almost tender. It is important not to overcook the pasta at this stage if freezing, as it will be cooked again when reheated. Drain in a colander and stir into the Bolognese.

To eat now, spoon the Bolognese and pasta into a warmed serving dish or divide between deep plates or bowls. Pour over the hot cheese sauce and serve sprinkled with the remaining cheese or finely grated Parmesan if you prefer. If making ahead, layer into a large lasagne dish and allow to cool before covering and chilling (or freezing). Reheat from chilled in a preheated oven at 200°C/Fan 180°C/Gas 6 for around 40 minutes or until piping hot before serving.

Lovely lamb curry

Makes 6 servings

Nothing matches a curry for hitting the spot after a tiring day and most home-made curries freeze and reheat brilliantly as long as you follow the proper steps. I've developed this curry specifically for freezing and reheating in the microwave. It uses lamb neck fillet simmered in a rich tasting medium spiced sauce, fresh garlic, ginger and chilli for flavour and a good curry paste for convenience. All you need to do is top with a spoonful of natural yogurt and serve with hot rice. Follow the instructions on page 206 for how to cook and freeze the rice.

1.2kg lamb neck fillets
3 tbsp sunflower oil
3 medium-large onions, roughly chopped
4 large garlic cloves, roughly chopped
25g chunk fresh root ginger, peeled and roughly chopped
1 plump fresh red chilli, roughly chopped (deseed first if you like your curry a little milder)
4 tbsp medium curry paste

2 tbsp plain flour
400g can chopped tomatoes
450ml water
2 bay leaves
2 tsp flaked sea salt, plus extra to season
2 tsp caster sugar
bag young spinach leaves (roughly 100g, optional)
freshly ground black pepper

To FREEZE (up to 3 months)
Divide the curry between 6 freezer-proof containers. Cool. Cover, label and freeze.

To SERVE
Turn one portion of the frozen curry out of the packaging and into a wide microwave-proof bowl. Cover with cling film and microwave on HIGH for 5 minutes. Stand for 2 minutes. Stir well. Microwave on HIGH for a further 2 minutes or until piping hot throughout. Stand for 2–3 minutes before serving.

Trim the lamb of any hard fat and cut into roughly 3cm chunks. Heat one tablespoon of oil in a large non-stick frying pan and fry the lamb in 2–3 batches until lightly coloured on all sides. Transfer to a flameproof casserole or large non-stick saucepan as soon as each batch is browned.

Heat 2 tablespoons of oil in the same frying pan and add the onions. Cook over a medium heat for 5 minutes or until lightly browned, stirring constantly. Reduce the heat, add the garlic, ginger and chilli and cook for 5 minutes more, stirring. Don't allow the garlic to burn or it will make your curry sauce taste bitter.

Tip the vegetables into a food processor and leave to cool for 10 minutes. Add the curry paste and blend until it is as smooth as you can make it. You may need to remove the lid and push the mixture down a couple of times with a rubber spatula until the right consistency is reached.

Add the spiced onion mixture to the lamb. Place the casserole over a medium heat and stir together for 2–3 minutes. Stir in the flour then add the tomatoes, water, bay leaves, salt and sugar.

Bring to a gentle simmer then reduce the heat. Cover the pan loosely with a lid and simmer gently for 50–60 minutes or until the lamb is very tender, stirring occasionally. Adjust the seasoning to taste and stir in the spinach if using.

To eat now, cook for another minute or so until the spinach wilts, stirring constantly. Serve with rice or naan bread for mopping up the delicious sauce.

Roast butternut squash with goat's cheese and pine nuts

Makes 6 servings

You need to choose small squashes for this recipe as each person is served half a squash stuffed with roasted vegetables, goat's cheese, pine nuts and sun-dried tomatoes. Perfect for supper or lunch for one, but also ideal to have as a veggie choice at a bigger gathering. It also works well with Stilton or Cheddar instead of the goat's cheese. For a non-veggie version, fried bacon or some chorizo make a nice addition.

3 small butternut squashes
(each around 1kg)
2 tbsp olive oil
2 tsp dried chilli flakes
3 medium courgettes, halved
lengthways and cut into thick slices
2 red peppers, deseeded
2 yellow or orange peppers, deseeded
2 small red onions, cut into thin
wedges

10 sun-dried tomato pieces in oil,
drained and roughly chopped
75g pine nuts, preferably Italian
1 tbsp fresh thyme leaves or 1 tsp
dried thyme
200g fairly firm goat's cheese,
chopped into small pieces
(with or without rind)
flaked sea salt
freshly ground black pepper

To FREEZE (up to 2 months)
Do not return the stuffed squash to the oven for the final 15 minutes but allow it to cool instead. Place each squash half in an individual foil dish, filled side up. Cool. Cover, label and freeze.

To SERVE
Take one of the frozen stuffed squash halves and transfer to a baking tray. Cook in a preheated oven at 190°C/Fan 170°C/Gas 5 for around 40 minutes or until the squash and vegetables are hot and lightly charred. If reheating more than 2 squash at a time, add an extra 5–10 minutes to the time.

Preheat the oven to 200°C/Fan 180°C/Gas 6. Cut the squash in half and scrape out the seeds with a teaspoon. Set the squash halves on a large baking tray, cut side up and score in a criss-cross pattern across the top, going about 5mm down into each squash.

Drizzle with one tablespoon of the oil and season with a little salt, plenty of freshly ground black pepper and a sprinkling of dried chilli flakes. Bake for 30 minutes or until the squash begins to soften.

While the squash are baking, put the courgettes, peppers and onions in a large mixing bowl and toss with the remaining oil. Stir-fry in 2 batches in a large non-stick frying pan or wok over a high heat for 4–5 minutes until softened and lightly browned. Cooking the vegetables slightly before freezing will help maintain their colour and taste. As soon as each batch is ready, tip into a large mixing bowl and toss with the sun-dried tomato pieces, pine nuts and thyme.

Take the butternut squash out of the oven and fill the hollows with the stir-fried vegetables. Dot with the goat's cheese. To eat now, return to the oven for a further 15 minutes or until the vegetables are lightly charred and the goat's cheese has melted.

If you have a spare afternoon or evening to spend on a little cooking, it's well worth preparing a few family-sized meals for the freezer. You have the benefit of knowing exactly what is in each dish and can adjust the ingredients to suit your family's tastes. I don't tend to cook in bulk but I'll often put a stew on the hob while I'm busy in the kitchen cooking something else. It's a great way of using your time effectively and if two dishes can cook in the oven at the same time, so much the better.

I have kept the preparation down to a minimum and all the ingredients for these recipes are easy to buy and relatively inexpensive. For the sake of convenience, most of my family meals all cook from frozen, giving you the flexibility to cook what you want, when you want it.

Cooking from frozen takes longer than thawing the food first but it does mean that you can put a casserole in the oven before heading out for a long walk or a trip to the shops and know that it will be bubbling hot when you return. Some of the family meals in this chapter can also be heated from frozen on the hob, which saves time. This way, my chicken curry can be ready to serve in less than half an hour.

There are obviously a few safety rules that you should observe. The meals should be prepared as hygienically as possible, cooked properly and cooled quickly before freezing. Always freeze family-sized meals in fairly shallow containers so they reheat quickly too. Don't forget to use a digital food thermometer (probe) to check temperatures if you aren't quite sure (see page 223).

If you are able to plan ahead, all the meals can also be cooked once thawed. I recommend that you thaw them for 18–24 hours or overnight in the fridge and then cook according to the general method, adding an extra 10 minutes or so to compensate for the chill factor.

FAMILY MEALS

Proper beef stew with dumplings

Serves 8 (Makes 2 stews serving 4)

A proper beef stew and dumplings makes a great weekend lunch or dinner but takes some time to prepare. My version can be made and frozen when you have time on your hands, then reheated in less than an hour just when you need it. I've found that using Oxo cubes and a good tablespoon of Marmite adds a toasty, caramelised flavour. If using good braising (chuck) steak instead of stewing steak, you can cut the initial cooking time by 30 minutes.

To FREEZE (up to 3 months)
Spoon the stew into 2 large, shallow freezer-proof containers. Cool. If you use 2 containers the stew will freeze and reheat more quickly and it will give you more flexibility on serving size. Cover, label and freeze. The uncooked dumplings should be open frozen before transferring to a freezer bag or rigid container (see page 224).

To SERVE
Take one or both stews out of the freezer and uncover. Transfer to a large flameproof casserole dish or saucepan. Add an extra 100ml of just-boiled water for 4 servings and an extra 200ml for 8 servings, pouring around the sides. Reheat over a low heat for about 30 minutes until thawed, stirring very occasionally so the meat doesn't begin to fall apart. Bring to a simmer, add the frozen dumplings, allowing 2 per person. Cover tightly and simmer for 20 minutes or until the dumplings are light and fluffy and the stew is hot throughout.

Alternatively, thaw the stew in the fridge overnight and transfer to a large saucepan. Bring to a gentle simmer, stirring regularly. Add the frozen dumplings and cook as shown.

2 tbsp sunflower oil
2 large onions, sliced
4 tbsp plain flour
1 ½ tsp flaked sea salt
2 heaped tsp dried mixed herbs
1.6kg well trimmed stewing steak, such as shin
2 bay leaves
1.5 litres beef stock (fresh or made with 2 beef stock cubes)
2 tbsp tomato purée
2 tbsp Marmite
2 tsp caster sugar

3 large parsnips (roughly 450g), peeled and cut into chunks
5 medium carrots, peeled and thickly sliced
freshly ground black pepper

Dumplings
200g self-raising flour, plus extra for rolling
100g shredded suet
good pinch of flaked sea salt
2 tbsp finely chopped fresh parsley (optional)
150ml cold water
freshly ground black pepper

Preheat the oven to 180°C/Fan 160°C/Gas 4. Heat the oil in a large flameproof casserole. Fry the onions over a medium-high heat for about 6–8 minutes until lightly browned, stirring regularly.

Put the flour, salt and dried herbs in a large bowl. Season with lots of freshly ground black pepper. Trim the beef of any hard fat or sinew and cut into roughly 3cm cubes. Toss the meat in the flour until evenly coated all over.

Tip the beef into the pan with the onions and cook together for 5 minutes or until the beef is lightly coloured all over. Add the bay leaves, stock, tomato purée, Marmite and sugar. Stir well and bring to the boil. Cover with a lid and carefully transfer to the oven. Cook for 2 hours or until the beef is almost tender. Take the stew out of the oven, and stir in the parsnips and carrots. Cover and return to the oven for a further 45 minutes or until the beef and vegetables are just tender.

To prepare the dumplings, mix together the flour, suet, salt and the parsley, if using, in a large bowl. Slowly add the cold water, stirring constantly until the mixture comes together and forms a soft dough. Roll the dough into 16 small balls, with lightly floured hands, and place on a plate or tray.

To eat now, take the casserole out of the oven once more and place gently on the hob. Season with more salt and pepper to taste. Return to a gentle simmer. Gently lower the dumplings on top of the bubbling stew in a single layer. Cover tightly with the lid and cook for 15–20 minutes or until the dumplings are well risen, light and fluffy.

Fabulous freezer fish pie

Serves 6

This is my youngest daughter's favourite weekday supper but it's also special enough to serve at a weekend lunch. You can vary the type of fish according to what you can buy. Place thinner fish fillets on top of thicker ones so there is less chance they will overcook. If you can't get hold of fresh dill, use a couple of teaspoons of freeze-dried dill or freshly chopped parsley instead.

500g thick white fish fillets, such as
　　cod or haddock
300g smoked haddock fillet
300g thick salmon fillet
750ml full-fat or semi-skimmed milk
1 medium onion, cut into wedges
2 bay leaves
75g butter
75g plain flour
small bunch of fresh dill (roughly 15g)
　　or 2 tsp freeze-dried dill

flaked sea salt
freshly ground black pepper

Cheesy potato topping
1.25kg medium potatoes, preferably
　　Maris Piper
300ml tub half-fat crème fraîche
50g mature Cheddar cheese,
　　finely grated

To FREEZE (up to 3 months)
Cool the assembled pie completely without baking. Cover with a lid or a double layer of foil. Label and freeze.

To SERVE
To reheat from frozen, uncover and cook on a baking tray in a preheated oven at 210°C/Fan 190°C/Gas 6½ for 1¼ –1½ hours or until piping hot throughout. Cover with foil if the potato begins to over brown.

Alternatively, thaw in the fridge overnight then cook the pie as if freshly made, adding an extra 5–10 minutes to allow for the chill factor.

To make the filling, place the fish fillets in a large saucepan and pour the milk over. Add the onion wedges and bay leaves, tucking them in around the fish. Bring to a very gentle simmer. Cover with a lid and remove from the heat immediately. Leave to stand and infuse for 10 minutes until the fish is just cooked. Drain the liquid from the fish through a colander into a bowl over a large jug.

While the fish is infusing, make the cheesy mash. Peel the potatoes and cut into roughly 4cm even chunks. Put the potatoes in a large saucepan and cover with cold water. Bring to the boil, then reduce the heat and simmer for 15 minutes or until the potatoes are very soft but not falling apart. Test with the tip of a knife. Drain well in a colander then return to the pan and mash with the crème fraîche until smooth. Season to taste and set aside.

To finish the filling, melt the butter in a medium saucepan and stir in the flour. Stir for a few seconds over a medium heat, then gradually add the infused milk, stirring for 5 minutes until the sauce is smooth and thick. Remove from the heat and snip the dill into the sauce with scissors. Discard the stalks. Stir well and season with salt and pepper.

Spoon a third of the sauce into the base of a 2-litre shallow freezer and ovenproof dish – remember that the pie will cook more quickly from frozen if the dish is fairly shallow. Scatter half the fish fillets over the sauce, breaking them into chunky pieces and discarding the skin, any stray bones, onion and bay leaves as you go. Pour over another third of the sauce then top with more fish. Continue the layers once more, finishing with the sauce.

Spoon the potato over the fish mixture, starting at the edges before making your way into the centre. Swirl the potato with the back of a spoon and sprinkle with the cheese. To cook now, place the dish on a baking tray and bake in the centre of a preheated oven at 200°C/Fan 180°C/Gas 6 oven for 40–45 minutes or until the potato topping is golden and the filling is bubbling and hot throughout.

Really good chicken curry

Serves 8 (Makes 2 curries serving 4)

*Everyone loves a good chicken curry and this is a really good one.
I freeze the cooked curry in two separate containers so I either use both
at once for a large gathering or each on a different occasion to serve
four. Once frozen, the curry can be thawed overnight and reheated
or reheated from frozen. This recipe makes a medium spiced, creamy
curry, but you can deseed the chilli before chopping if you like your
curry a little milder.*

To FREEZE (up to 2 months)
Spoon the cooked curry sauce into
2 large, shallow freezer and ovenproof containers, such as lidded foil
trays. Cool completely. (If you use 2
containers the curry will freeze and
reheat more quickly and it will give
you more flexibility on serving size.)
Sprinkle with the coriander and
cover tightly. Label and freeze.

To SERVE
Take one or both curries out of the
freezer and uncover. Cover loosely
with foil and cook from frozen in
a preheated oven at 190°C/Fan
170°C/Gas 5 for 55–65 minutes.
Take out of the oven and stir well
halfway through the cooking time.
Return to the oven until the chicken
is thoroughly cooked and piping
hot throughout.

Alternatively, thaw overnight in
the fridge and reheat in a large
non-stick saucepan stirring
regularly over a medium heat for
15–20 minutes or until piping hot
throughout, add water if necessary.

small pinch of saffron strands
500ml hot chicken stock
   (fresh or made with 1 chicken
   stock cube)
50g butter
4 tbsp sunflower oil
5 medium onions, sliced
6 garlic cloves, sliced
40g chunk fresh root ginger,
   peeled and roughly chopped
1 plump red chilli, roughly chopped
1 tbsp garam masala
2 tsp ground cumin
2 tsp ground coriander

1 tsp ground turmeric
1 tbsp caster sugar
1 tbsp cornflour
150ml double cream
8 boneless, skinless chicken breasts
   (1kg total weight)
4 tbsp roughly chopped fresh
   or frozen coriander (optional)
flaked sea salt
freshly ground black pepper

Garnish
25g flaked almonds, lightly toasted
   in a dry pan (optional)

Stir the saffron into the hot chicken stock and leave to stand. Melt
the butter with 2 tablespoons of the oil in a large, wide based non-
stick saucepan, sauté pan or flameproof casserole. Add the onions,
garlic, ginger and chilli. Cook over a low heat for 15 minutes, stirring
occasionally until soft.

Increase the heat. Cook the onion mixture for a further 5 minutes,
stirring constantly until lightly browned. Add the garam masala,
cumin, coriander and turmeric to the pan and cook with the onions
for one minute, stirring constantly. Add the stock and simmer for a
further 10 minutes, sitrring regularly. Remove from the heat and leave
to cool for a few minutes.

Transfer the spiced onions to a food processor and blend until as
smooth as possible. Remove the lid of the food processor a couple of
times and push the mixture down with a rubber spatula until the right
consistency is reached. Add the sugar, cornflour and cream. Blend once
more. Alternatively, blitz the ingredients together with a stick blender.

Put the chicken on a board and cut each breast into 7–8 even chunks. Place the pan used to cook the onion mixture back over a medium heat and add the remaining 2 tablespoons of oil and chicken pieces. Cook for 4 minutes, turning often until very lightly coloured all over. Add all the creamy curried sauce to the pan.

Bring to a gentle simmer and cook for 4–5 minutes, stirring occasionally. Make sure the chicken is cooked through and no pinkness remains, but be careful not to overcook it. Season with salt and ground black pepper to taste and stir in the chopped coriander, if using. Spoon the curry into a serving dish, sprinkle with toasted almonds and serve.

Creamy chicken, ham and leek pie

Serves 6 (Makes 1 pie serving 6)

This classic pie and family favourite is best made in a fairly shallow pie dish so the filling has a good chance to fully reheat while the pastry is baking. If the dish is too deep, the crust will be ready before the centre of the pie. Ideally, use a chunk of thick-cut ham for the filling but if you can't get hold of this, cut thin slices of the ham into centimetre-wide long strips instead and make what I call a tangle filling.

500ml just-boiled water
1 chicken stock cube
4 boneless, skinless chicken breasts
75g butter
3 medium leeks, trimmed and cut into
  1cm slices
1 garlic clove, crushed
50g plain flour
250ml full-fat or semi-skimmed milk,
  plus 2–3 tbsp
3 tbsp white wine or vermouth
  (optional)

150ml double cream
150g thickly carved ham
  (preferably smoked)
flaked sea salt
freshly ground black pepper

Pastry
beaten egg, to glaze
500g block of chilled puff pastry
  (thawed if frozen)
plain flour, for rolling

To FREEZE (up to 2 months)
Open freeze the glazed, unbaked pie for one hour, then wrap tightly with a double layer of foil. Label and freeze.

To SERVE
Thaw overnight in the fridge and cook as page 55 for 35–40 minutes or until golden brown and piping hot throughout.

Pour the water into a medium saucepan over a low heat and crumble over the stock cube. Stir until dissolved. Place the chicken breasts gently into the water and bring to a low simmer. Cover with a lid and cook for 10 minutes. Take the chicken breasts out of the stock and place on to a plate to cool. Pour the stock into a large jug. As soon as the chicken is cooled, cover and chill until needed.

Melt 25g of the butter in a large non-stick saucepan over a medium heat. Stir in the leeks and fry for 2 minutes, stirring regularly until softened but not coloured. Add the garlic and cook for one minute more. Tip into a bowl. Return the pan to the heat and add the remaining butter. Stir in the flour as soon as the butter has melted. Cook for 30 seconds, stirring constantly.

Slowly pour the milk into the pan, just a little at a time, stirring well in between each addition. Gradually add 250ml of the reserved stock and wine, if using, stirring until the sauce is smooth and thick. Bring to a gentle simmer and cook for 3 minutes, stirring constantly. Season to taste with salt and pepper. Remove the sauce from the heat and stir in the cream. Pour into a large bowl. Cover the surface of the sauce with cling film to prevent a skin forming and leave to cool.

Tear or cut the chicken breasts into roughly 3cm chunks. Cut the ham into roughly 2cm chunks or into long strips if using thinly sliced ham. Stir the chicken, ham and leeks into the cooled sauce. If the sauce is a bit too thick to smoothly coat the chicken, loosen with a little more milk. Spoon the chicken filling into a 1.75-litre fairly shallow pie dish. Brush the rim of the dish lightly with beaten egg.

Roll out the pastry on a lightly floured surface until just 5mm thick and roughly 4cm larger than the top of the pie dish. Cut 2 or 3 x 2cm wide strips from around the edge of the pastry and press onto the edge of the pie dish, overlapping where necessary and securing with a little more egg.

Brush the pastry edge lightly with beaten egg. Cover the dish with the rolled pastry and press the edges together firmly to seal. Trim the pastry carefully and knock up the edges with a sharp, horizontally held knife. Make a hole in the centre of the pie with the tip of a knife. Glaze the top of the pie with more egg and chill for at least an hour if possible.

To cook now, place on a baking tray and bake in the centre of a preheated oven at 220°C/Fan 200°C/Gas 7 for about 30 minutes or until the pastry is puffed up and golden brown and the filling is piping hot.

The best sticky chicken

Serves 6 (Makes 12 chicken portions)

Succulent chicken thighs and drumsticks with a delicious sticky ginger, garlic and chilli glaze. Serve hot with jacket potatoes and a salad or cold for picnics and packed lunches. I usually make the full recipe quantity and bake half immediately and freeze the rest marinated but uncooked for another day. The sauce is also great for wings and skinless thighs and breasts but you'll need to adjust the cooking time.

To FREEZE (up to 3 months)
Divide the uncooked chicken and sticky sauce between two large, labelled zip-seal bags. Lay flat and press out as much air as possible. Seal and flat freeze.

To SERVE
Rinse one or both bags of chicken under the hot tap for a few seconds. Unseal and slide the frozen chicken and marinade onto a baking tray lined with baking parchment. Cover loosely with foil and bake in a preheated oven at 200°C/Fan 180°C/Gas 6 for 30 minutes. Remove the foil and brush the chicken pieces with the sauce. Return to the oven for 15 minutes. Remove and brush with the sauce once more then return to the oven for a further 5 minutes or until piping hot throughout.

Alternatively, thaw the chicken in the fridge overnight then cook as fresh, adding 5–10 minutes to the cooking time to compensate for the chill factor.

6 bone-in chicken thighs, with skin
6 chicken drumsticks, with skin

Sticky sauce
50g chunk fresh root ginger,
   peeled and roughly chopped
4 large garlic cloves, halved
2 plump red chillies, trimmed and cut
   into 3–4 pieces or 1½ tsp dried
   chilli flakes

6 tbsp tomato ketchup
6 tbsp runny honey
2 tbsp Worcestershire sauce
1 tbsp sunflower oil
1 heaped tsp flaked sea salt
freshly ground black pepper

Preheat the oven to 220°C/Fan 200°C/Gas 7. To make the sauce, put the ginger, garlic, chilli, ketchup, honey, Worcestershire sauce, oil, salt and a good grinding of black pepper in a food processor. Blitz on the pulse setting for about 30 seconds or until the ingredients form a thick purée. You may need to remove the lid and push the mixture down once or twice with a rubber spatula.

Put the chicken thighs and drumsticks on a board and slash the thickest part of each one twice with a knife. Place them in a large bowl and pour the sticky sauce over them. Turn until well coated.

To cook now, put a large sheet of baking parchment on your biggest baking tray and scrunch the sides up roughly 5cm all the way round. This will help prevent the sticky juices burning on the tray.

Tip the chicken and sauce into the tray and turn the chicken pieces until the slashed side is facing up. Brush generously with the sauce. Bake for 20 minutes. Remove the tray from the oven and brush the sauce and any juices back over the chicken. Return to the oven for a further 10–15 minutes or until the chicken is cooked through, glossy and gloriously sticky. Serve hot or cold.

Deep-filled lasagne

Serves 12 (Makes 2 lasagnes serving 6)

Bought lasagnes never seem large or deep enough, so if you have a big family or a few to feed, it's always best to make your own. Making lasagne can take a while but it's easy to double up the ingredients, so I always make two; bake one now and freeze the other. This recipe has layers of rich Bolognese and a creamy sauce with cheddar and Parmesan cheeses. You could try freezing in a square silicone cake pan and flipping out when solid. Unwrap and pop into a ceramic dish for baking – you can find out how on page 218.

To FREEZE (up to 3 months)
Allow the unbaked lasagnes to cool completely. Cover with foil, label and freeze. If using silicone pans, open freeze then flip out of the containers once solid and double wrap in foil. Label and freeze.

To SERVE
To cook from thawed, thaw overnight in the fridge, uncover and bake as page 59 for 40–45 minutes until hot throughout.

To cook from frozen, uncover and place the lasagne into a suitable baking dish if necessary. Place on a baking tray and cover loosley with foil. Bake in a preheated oven at 200°C/Fan 180°C Gas 6 for 30 minutes, remove the foil and continue to bake for a further 45 –55 minutes or until nicely browned and hot throughout. Add an extra 10–15 minutes to the cooking time if cooking both lasagnes at the same time.

2 tbsp olive oil
2 medium onions, chopped
2 garlic cloves, finely chopped
2 bay leaves
800g lean minced beef
200ml red wine, or extra stock
2 x 400g cans chopped tomatoes
2 tbsp tomato purée
500ml beef stock (fresh or made with 1 beef stock cube)
1 tsp caster sugar
2 tsp dried oregano
2 tbsp cornflour
2 tbsp cold water

18–24 dried egg lasagne sheets (roughly 450g)
flaked sea salt
freshly ground black pepper

Cheese sauce
100g butter
100g plain flour
1 litre semi-skimmed or whole milk
200g mature Cheddar cheese, coarsely grated
50g Parmesan cheese, finely grated
flaked sea salt
freshly ground black pepper

Heat the oil in a large non-stick saucepan or flame-proof casserole and fry the onions and garlic with the bay leaves over a low heat for about 5 minutes until well softened, stirring regularly. Increase the heat a little, add the mince and cook for a further 10 minutes, using 2 wooden spoons to break up the meat.

Stir in the wine followed by the tomatoes, tomato purée, beef stock, sugar and oregano. Season well with salt and plenty of freshly ground black pepper. Bring the sauce to the boil, then reduce the heat and simmer gently for 30 minutes, stirring occasionally until the mince is tender and the sauce has reduced to a similar consistency to Bolognese.

In a small bowl, mix together the cornflour and water to form a smooth paste and stir into the Bolognese. Cook for 4–5 minutes more until the sauce thickens further, stirring constantly. Remove from the heat and pick out and discard the bay leaves. Cover loosely and leave to stand.

To make the cheese sauce, melt the butter in a large non-stick saucepan and stir in the flour. Cook over a low heat for about 30 seconds, while stirring. Gradually add the milk to the pan, stirring constantly between each addition. Increase the heat a little and bring to a gentle simmer. Cook for 5 minutes, stirring constantly. Stir in 150g of the Cheddar cheese and simmer for a further 1–2 minutes, while stirring until the cheese melts. Season to taste with salt and pepper.

Divide around a third of the mince mixture between 2 lasagne dishes. They will need to be around 24cm square or hold roughly 2 litres of liquid. Cover with a layer of lasagne, snapping off the bits that don't fit snugly. Repeat the layers twice more, using up all the mince and ending with the pasta. Divide the cheese sauce between the lasagnes and spread gently to the corners. Mix the remaining Cheddar and Parmesan together and sprinkle over the top.

To cook now, bake in a preheated oven at 200°C/Fan 180°C/Gas 6 for 35–40 minutes until nicely browned and bubbling.

Cottage pie with cheesy mash

Serves 6

A really good cottage pie is the perfect freezer standby. A single serving can be cooked from frozen in just 30 minutes or less when thawed.

2 tbsp sunflower oil
1 medium onion, chopped
2 slender celery sticks, thinly sliced
2 carrots, peeled and cut into 1cm dice
2 garlic cloves, crushed
500g lean minced beef or lamb
2 tbsp plain flour
400g can chopped tomatoes
300ml beef or lamb stock (fresh or
    made with 1 stock cube)
100ml red wine, or extra stock

2 tbsp tomato purée
1 bay leaf
flaked sea salt
freshly ground black pepper

Cheesy mash
1.25kg floury potatoes, such as
    King Edwards or Maris Piper
50g butter, cubed
100g mature Cheddar cheese,
    coarsely grated

To FREEZE (up to 3 months)
Cool the unbaked pie then cover with a double layer of foil. Label and freeze. If using a silicone pan, open freeze then flip out of the container once solid and double wrap in foil. Label and freeze.

To SERVE
To reheat from frozen, uncover and place the cottage pie in a suitable baking dish if necessary. Cook the pie on a baking tray in a preheated oven at 190°C/Fan 170°C/Gas 5 for about 1½ hours or until piping hot throughout. Cover with a piece of foil for the first 30 minutes.

Heat the oil in a large non-stick saucepan over a medium heat and gently fry the onion, celery and carrots for 8–10 minutes or until the onion has softened and lightly coloured. Add the garlic and cook for 2 minutes more.

Add the mince to the pan and cook for 4–5 minutes, stirring frequently, until the meat is well coloured. Squish the mince against the pan to help break it up. Sprinkle over the flour and stir well to help prevent lumps.

Add the tomatoes, stock, red wine, tomato purée and bay leaf to the pan. Bring to a gentle simmer and cook over a low heat for 25 minutes, stirring regularly, until the mince is tender and the sauce has thickened. Season with salt and black pepper. Remove from the heat and spoon the mince into a 2-litre ovenproof dish or 25cm silicone cake pan.

While the mince is cooking, peel the potatoes and cut into roughly 4cm even chunks. Put the potatoes into a large saucepan and cover with cold water. Bring to the boil, then reduce the heat to a simmer and cook for about 15 minutes, or until the potatoes are very soft.

Drain the potatoes well in a colander then return to the pan. Add the butter and cheese. Mash until smooth and creamy. Season with salt and pepper. Spoon the mash over the mince, starting at the sides of the dish before working your way into the middle.

To cook now, place the dish on a baking tray and bake in the centre of a preheated oven at 200°C/Fan 180°C/Gas 6 for 30–35 minutes or until the mash is golden brown and the filling is bubbling.

Chilli and garlic pork ribs

Serves 4

My kids and their friends really love these ribs. They are perfect summer food and reheat brilliantly on the barbecue. Serve with jacket potatoes, salad and coleslaw for lots of happy, smiling… and sticky faces!

1kg pork spare ribs (roughly 12 ribs)
3 star anise (optional)

Sticky sauce
50g chunk of fresh root ginger,
    peeled and roughly chopped
5 large garlic cloves, halved

2–3 tsp dried chilli flakes,
    depending on taste
2 tsp Chinese five-spice powder
150ml tomato ketchup
8 tbsp runny honey
5 tbsp teriyaki sauce
1 tsp flaked sea salt
150ml cold water
freshly ground black pepper

To FREEZE (up to 1 month)
Cool the baked ribs and sauce thoroughly. Divide between 2 labelled zip-seal bags and flatten. Seal and freeze.

To SERVE
Remove from the freezer and leave to thaw for 10 minutes to separate the ribs. Transfer the ribs and sauce to a large baking tray lined with foil as above. Cook from frozen on 200°C/Fan 180°C/Gas 6 for 20 minutes or until the ribs are piping hot throughout.

Put the ribs in a large saucepan and cover with cold water. Add the star anise, if using, and bring to a fast simmer. Cook for 50–60 minutes or until the pork is very tender and beginning to fall off the bone. Drain in a colander. Discard the star anise.

While the pork is cooking, make the sauce. Put the ginger, garlic, chilli, five-spice powder, ketchup, honey, teriyaki sauce, salt and a good grinding of black pepper in a food processor. Blitz on the pulse setting for about 30 seconds or until the ingredients form a thick purée. You may need to remove the lid and push the mixture down once or twice with a spatula.

Transfer the sauce to a small saucepan and add the water. Bring to a gentle simmer and cook for 5 minutes, stirring occasionally. Remove from the heat.

Preheat the oven to 200°C/Fan 180°C/Gas 6. Line a baking tray with a large sheet of foil and fold up the sides so that it creates a shallow bowl to hold the sauce. Tip the ribs onto the foil in an even layer. Pour over the sauce and bake for 30 minutes, turning twice until hot and sticky. Brush generously with the sauce each time the ribs are turned and when they're out of the oven. Serve immediately..

Mum's mole in the hole

Serves 3–4

Mole in the hole is what my mum used to call toad in the hole when we were kids. It's a simple recipe to knock together next time you have a few spare sausages handy and will sit happily in the freezer for a couple of months. Use a metal tin to freeze the toad if possible as the heat will conduct more quickly into the frozen batter. You can always add extra sausages if you have them or double the recipe when feeding a crowd. There's definitely enough batter here to serve four and whether it's mole or toad, it's always nice served with a rich gravy (page 174).

2 tbsp sunflower oil
6-8 thick, good-quality pork sausages

Batter
2 large eggs
115g plain flour
250ml semi-skimmed milk
½ tsp flaked sea salt

To FREEZE (up to 2 months)
Cool the sausages completely before pouring over the batter. Do not bake. Cover the tin or dish tightly with foil. Label and freeze.

Alternatively, freeze in a silicone cake pan and transfer to a metal tin when you are ready to bake.

To SERVE
Place a baking tray in the oven and preheat to 220°C/Fan 200°C/Gas 8. Uncover the frozen mole in the hole. Place the tin on the preheated tray in the oven and cook for 35–40 minutes or until the batter is well-risen and the sausages are hot. If the batter begins to over-brown, cover the dish with foil.

Heat 2 tablespoons of the oil in a large non-stick frying pan and fry the sausages for 10 minutes over a medium-high heat, turning often until nicely browned on all sides. Transfer the sausages and any fat to a medium-sized roasting tin or ovenproof dish. They should fit fairly snugly but not so close that the batter isn't able to puff up around them.

To make the batter, break the eggs into a food processor and add the flour, milk and salt. Blitz until smooth. Alternatively, beat the eggs together in a bowl and add the flour, salt and half the milk. Beat until smooth then whisk in the remaining milk with a large metal whisk. Pour the batter around the sausages. It should rise around 2.5cm up the sides of the dish.

To cook now, bake in the centre of a preheated oven at 220°C/Fan 200°C/Gas 7 for 22–25 minutes or until the batter is well-risen and golden brown.

Lamb Provençal

Serves 6

This is my take on a simple one-pot dish, made from slowly simmered lamb in a rich tomato sauce with peppers, courgettes, red wine and herbs – and it freezes incredibly well. Unusually, the vegetables and meat aren't browned before simmering, but doing it this way will save you around 20 minutes prep time and no one has ever noticed a difference. Serve with dauphinoise potatoes (page 165), rice or mash and perhaps a few green beans.

1kg boneless lamb leg meat
  or leg steaks
3 tbsp plain flour
2 medium onions, sliced
2 garlic cloves, crushed
400g can chopped tomatoes
2 tbsp tomato purée
1 tsp caster sugar

450ml lamb stock
  (fresh or made with 1 stock cube)
200ml red wine, or extra stock
2 tsp dried mixed herbs
1 large red pepper
1 large yellow pepper
3 medium courgettes
flaked sea salt
freshly ground black pepper

Preheat the oven to 180°C/Fan 160°C/Gas 4. Trim the lamb of any hard fat or sinew and cut into roughly 3cm chunks. Put in a large flameproof casserole and toss with the flour and plenty of salt and freshly ground black pepper. Add the onions, garlic, tomatoes, tomato purée, sugar, stock and wine.

Sprinkle over the herbs and stir well. Cover and bring to a simmer. Transfer to the oven and cook for 1½ hours or until the lamb is tender.

Halve and deseed the peppers then cut into roughly 3cm chunky pieces. Trim and thickly slice the courgettes into 2cm pieces. Remove the lamb from the oven and stir in the vegetables.

Cover and cook the vegetables with the lamb in the oven for 15 minutes. To cook now, stir the lamb and vegetables and return the dish to the oven for a further 30 minutes until the vegetables are just cooked. Adjust the seasoning to taste.

To FREEZE (up to 3 months)
Spoon the part-cooked casserole into a large freezer-proof container. If you plan to reheat the casserole from frozen make sure you freeze the casserole in a fairly shallow dish. Cover, label and freeze.

To SERVE
Transfer the frozen casserole to a suitable dish if necessary. Cover loosely with foil and cook from frozen in a preheated oven at 190°C/Fan 170°C/Gas 5 for around 1½ hours or until piping hot throughout. Stir halfway through the cooking time. Alternatively, thaw overnight in the fridge and reheat it in a covered microwave-proof dish in the microwave on HIGH for about 10–15 minutes, stirring every 5 minutes.

Chicken goujons with lemony garlic mayo

Serves 5

Delicious strips of crisp chicken breast served with a lemon and garlic mayonnaise dip. Great for a quick meal or snack and very popular with kids. Straight from the freezer they don't need frying and only take 15 minutes in the oven before being ready to serve. Add paprika to the breadcrumbs to make them a little more golden if you like.

4 boneless, skinless chicken breasts
40g plain flour
good pinch fine sea salt
2 medium eggs
150g fresh white breadcrumbs
    or 125g panko breadcrumbs
1 tsp paprika (optional)

5 tbsp sunflower oil
freshly ground black pepper

Lemony garlic mayo
150g mayonnaise
1 garlic clove, crushed to a paste
finely grated zest ½ lemon

To FREEZE (up to 3 months)
Instead of frying the coated chicken strips, open freeze for 1–2 hours until solid. Take the tray out of the freezer and, working quickly, dab each frozen chicken piece generously with sunflower oil on both sides. You'll need around 5 tbsp oil in total. Pack into freezer-proof containers. Cover, label and freeze.

To SERVE
Place as many frozen chicken pieces as you need on a baking tray. Cook in a preheated oven at 220°C/Fan 200°C/Gas 7 for 15 minutes, turning halfway through the cooking time, until the chicken is crisp, pale golden brown and cooked through. Serve with the freshly made dip.

Put the chicken breasts on a board and cut each one into 8–10 slices at a slight diagonal angle from one end to the other. Line a large baking tray with baking parchment or easy-leave sheets (see page 223).

Sift the flour onto a large plate and season with salt and pepper. Beat the eggs in a medium bowl with a whisk until smooth. Sprinkle half the breadcrumbs into a large bowl and toss with half the paprika if using.

Take the chicken breast pieces one at a time and dust first in the flour. Shake off any excess and dip straight into the beaten eggs and then coat in the breadcrumbs until evenly covered. Place on the lined tray while the rest are prepared, adding the reserved breadcrumbs and paprika to the large bowl after coating roughly half the chicken pieces. This will stop the crumbs getting too sticky.

To eat now, pour the sunflower oil into a large non-stick frying pan and set over a medium heat. Do not allow the oil to overheat or leave hot oil unattended. Using tongs, gently lower half the chicken pieces into the hot pan.

Cook for 3–4 minutes on each side until the chicken is crisp, golden brown and cooked through. There should be no pinkness remaining in the centre. Keep warm while the rest is cooked in the same way, adding a little extra oil between batches if necessary.

While the chicken is frying, make the lemony garlic mayo. Put the mayonnaise, garlic and lemon zest in a small serving bowl and mix well. Cover and set aside.

I love sharing home-cooked meals with good friends or extended family but I know that entertaining can be incredibly stressful for many people. This is where the freezer can really help – giving you the chance to cook a delicious meal at a convenient time, then stash it away in the freezer until it is needed. You will be left with more time to spend with your guests and a lot less hassle on the night.

My entertaining style has become more relaxed as time has passed. Now, I like sitting down and enjoying a range of dishes, informally served. Nothing needs to take too long to prepare and a scattering of fresh herbs and a dribble of olive oil is often all it takes to turn the ordinary into something very good indeed.

I never aim to provide the whole meal from the freezer and so more often I pick a few pieces to prepare ahead that I know my friends will appreciate. A rich, wine-drenched beef casserole or a fragrant pork curry will please most guests. Even freezing a few dishes of pâté or a flavour-packed soup a few days ahead will make the event run more smoothly. Bread rolls, flat breads and flavoured butters can sit in the freezer for months and all your vegetables can be frozen ahead too; although sometimes a large, fresh salad with a good dressing is all that's needed.

A selection of simple canapés made for the freezer will save you a fortune over the ready-prepared kind – many of which have been previously frozen anyway – and can be ready to heat with very little notice if necessary. Little rounds of toasted bread can be topped with a huge assortment of ingredients for the freezer. I generally freeze my crostini ready topped to save time later on, but you can also freeze the toasts on their own and top with fresh ingredients when you are ready. Making crostini is also a good way to use up a baguette that might not otherwise get eaten.

I've had great success freezing all sorts of shop-bought dips. Sometimes they separate a little on thawing but a quick stir usually brings the mixture back together again. Cream- or mayonnaise-based dips are less successful as they can become a little grainy once frozen. Try instead with bean or guacamole and not freezing for more than a month for the best results. Serve with breadsticks, fresh vegetable sticks, or cheese twists (see page 189) for dipping.

ENTERTAINING

Mini quiche Lorraine

Makes 24

These mini quiches taste so much better than the ones you can buy. Freeze them uncooked and then bake from frozen and they will taste every bit as fresh as the day you assembled them. For vegetarian quiches, use fried chestnut mushrooms and chopped chargrilled peppers in place of the bacon and pick a veggie-friendly cheese. My pastry takes less than five minutes to make but you can use a 500g block of ready-made shortcrust pastry instead if you like.

Pastry
250g plain flour, plus extra for rolling
150g cold butter, cut into cubes
1 large egg, beaten

Filling
1 tbsp sunflower oil
100g smoked rindless streaky bacon
    rashers, cut into 1cm slices

½ small onion, finely chopped
2 large eggs
200ml half-fat crème fraîche
50g Gruyère or mature Cheddar
    cheese, finely grated
flaked sea salt
freshly ground black pepper

To FREEZE (up to 3 months)
Freeze the uncooked quiches in the tins until solid. Remove from the tins by flipping out with a teaspoon and transfer to a rigid container, interleaving with easy-leave or baking parchment. Cover, label and freeze.

To SERVE
Place the frozen quiches back into the bun tins and bake in a preheated oven at 200°C/Fan 180°C/Gas 6 for 20–22 minutes or until the pastry is nicely browned and the filling is cooked.

To make the pastry, put the flour and butter in a food processor and blitz on the pulse setting until the mixture resembles fine breadcrumbs. With the motor running, slowly add the beaten egg and blend until the mixture begins to come together.

Gather the pastry into a ball and flatten slightly. Roll out on a lightly floured surface, until about the thickness of a 50 pence piece. Cut out into 6cm rounds using a biscuit cutter. Use the pastry rounds to line 2 shallow 12-hole bun tins. The sort you would use for fairy cakes but not a muffin or Yorkshire pudding tin as they will be too deep. Press well into the base and sides and chill in the fridge. If you only have one tin, make the quiches in 2 batches instead.

To make the filling, heat the oil in a small non-stick frying pan and fry the bacon until it begins to crisp, stirring occasionally. Add the onion and cook for a couple of minutes more until softened, stirring regularly. Leave to cool.

Whisk the eggs in a bowl until just combined – try not to incorporate too much air. Stir in the crème fraîche and cheese. Add a good pinch of salt and plenty of ground black pepper.

Divide the bacon and onion mixture between the pastry cases and spoon a little of the egg mixture into each one, filling each pastry case to the top.

To cook now, bake in a preheated oven at 200°C/Fan 180°C/Gas 6 for 18–20 minutes or until the pastry is nicely browned and the filling has cooked. Serve warm or cold.

Broad bean, feta and mint crostini

Makes 20–24 (depending on size of loaf)

Packed with fresh, summery flavours, these colourful canapés are a real treat. Serve without freezing or heat from frozen for the best results. Just take out what you need and don't worry if the mint has darkened a little once frozen, it will still taste good and you can always garnish with a few fresh mint leaves if you like.

½ fresh baguette, cut into 5mm slices
100g frozen broad beans
100g feta cheese, drained
2 tsp fresh lemon juice

1 tbsp extra virgin olive oil,
   plus a little extra to drizzle
2 tbsp roughly chopped fresh mint
   leaves
freshly ground black pepper

To FREEZE (up to 2 months)
Follow all the steps as above but instead of placing the finished crostini on a platter, arrange on a baking tray and open freeze for 1–2 hours until solid. Transfer to a rigid container, interleaving with easy-leave or baking parchment. Cover, label and freeze.

To SERVE
Preheat the oven to 180°C/Fan 160°C/Gas 4. Arrange the frozen crostini on a baking tray and cook for 4–5 minutes until the toast is hot and the cheese softened. Transfer to a platter, drizzle with a little olive oil and serve. Add a few fresh mint leaves if you have some.

Preheat the oven to 200°C/Fan 180°C/Gas 6. Place the baguette slices in a single layer on a large baking tray. Bake for 12 minutes or until dry and very lightly browned. Be careful not to let them burn or become too hard and brittle. Remove from the oven and leave to cool.

Half-fill a medium saucepan with water and bring to the boil. Add the frozen beans and return to the boil. Cook for 3 minutes. Drain the beans in a sieve and rinse well under running water until cold then drain again.

Pop each broad bean out of its skin and into a small mixing bowl. This takes a little time but is very easy and makes all the difference to the texture of the finished topping. Discard the skins.

Crumble the feta cheese into the bowl with the skinned beans and add the lemon juice, olive oil and mint leaves. Season with plenty of ground black pepper and mash roughly with a fork. Spread the bean mixture generously over each crostini.

To eat now, arrange the crostini on a platter or board, drizzle with a little more olive oil and serve.

Tomato and prosciutto crostini

Makes 20–24 (depending on size of loaf)

I've given you a recipe for my own sun-dried tomato pesto, but you could use ready-made pesto or a good, thick pasta sauce to top these little toasts. Add some strips of Parma ham or salami and you'll have some simple but gutsy canapés. Simply reheat what you need and garnish with tiny fresh basil leaves just before serving if you like.

½ fresh baguette, cut into 5mm slices
5 slices of Parma ham or other
   prosciutto
freshly ground black pepper
fresh basil leaves, to garnish (optional)

Sun-dried tomato pesto
50g Parmesan cheese

10 sun-dried tomato pieces in oil,
   drained, reserve 1 tbsp of oil
1 garlic clove, halved
2 tbsp extra virgin olive oil, plus a little
   extra to drizzle
½ tsp flaked sea salt
25g pine nuts, preferably Italian

To FREEZE (up to 1 month)
Follow all the steps as fresh but instead of placing the finished crostini on a platter, arrange on a baking tray and open freeze for 1–2 hours until solid. Transfer to a rigid container, interleaving with easy-leave or baking parchment. Cover, label and freeze.

To SERVE
Preheat the oven to 180°C/Fan 160°C/Gas 4. Arrange the frozen crostini on a baking tray and cook for 4–5 minutes or until the toast is hot and the Parma ham is beginning to frazzle. Transfer to a platter, drizzle with a little olive oil and serve.

To make the pesto, cut the Parmesan cheese into chunky pieces and put in a food processor with the tomatoes. Add the garlic and olive oil, plus a tablespoon of oil from the sun-dried tomatoes. Season with salt and lots of ground black pepper. Blitz until as fine as possible. Add the pine nuts and blend until finely chopped but not completely smooth. Set aside.

Preheat the oven to 200°C/Fan 180°C/Gas 6. Place the baguette slices in a single layer on a large baking tray. Bake for 12 minutes or until dry and very lightly browned. Do not allow them to burn or become too hard and brittle. Remove from the oven and drizzle with the olive oil.

Spread a little of the pesto on to each warm crostini. You will only need to use half the pesto sauce for 20–24 slices of baguette but you can easily freeze the rest for another time. It will keep well in the freezer for 3 months. Cut each slice of Parma ham into 4–5 pieces and arrange on top, curling them over the sauce rather than placing them flat.

To eat now, arrange the crostini on a platter or board, drizzle with a little more olive oil and serve garnished with fresh basil leaves if you have some handy.

Smoked mackerel pâté

Serves 6

Some people think that smoked mackerel pâté is a bit old-fashioned but I love it – and it works in so many ways. These creamy pots are perfect for a light meal, served with crusty bread and a salad garnish. They also make a great starter and can easily stretch to serve eight if necessary. I also serve the pâté as a dip with crunchy vegetable sticks or hot, toasted pita bread.

300g smoked mackerel fillets, skinned
½ small onion
200ml full-fat crème fraîche
1 tbsp creamed horseradish sauce
finely grated zest and juice ½ lemon
flaked sea salt

freshly ground black pepper
3-4 fresh chives
½ lemon, to garnish
warm, crusty Granary bread or hot melba toast, to serve

To FREEZE (up to 1 month)
Cover each ramekin dish tightly with foil. Label and freeze.

To SERVE
Uncover and thaw as many pâtés as you need at room temperature for 30-40 minutes or in the fridge for 3-4 hours before serving.

Flake the mackerel into a food processor. Peel the onion and coarsely grate onto a board. Put the grated onion in one hand and squeeze hard over the mackerel to release the juice as this will add flavour to the pâté. Discard the onion flesh.

Add the crème fraîche, horseradish sauce, lemon zest and one tablespoon of the juice to the mackerel and season well with a good pinch of salt and plenty of ground black pepper.

Blend all the ingredients together until smooth. You may need to remove the lid and push the mixture down with a rubber spatula a couple of times. Adjust the seasoning to taste and add a little more lemon juice if needed. Spoon the pâté into 6 x 125ml ramekin dishes and smooth the surface with the back of a teaspoon.

Snip the chives into 1cm lengths. Cut 3 thin slices from the lemon half. Cut each lemon slice into 4 quarter triangles and place 2 triangles, overlapping slightly, on each pâté. Sprinkle with the chives and add a couple of twists of black pepper.

To eat now, place the ramekin dishes on small plates and serve with warm, crusty bread or toast.

Harissa marinated olives

Serves 6–8

You can freeze drained olives just as they are, in a tub with a tight-fitting lid, but mixing them with a gutsy marinade makes them much more interesting and delicious. As well as making harissa by hand, you can also use an electric spice grinder or mini processor. Ready made harissa won't taste quite as good as the fresh variety but is a decent compromise when you are short of time.

1 large red pepper
1 tsp cumin seeds
1 tsp coriander seeds
½ tsp fennel or caraway seeds
1 heaped tsp dried chilli flakes
2 garlic cloves

finely grated zest of ½ small lemon
½ tsp flaked sea salt
1 tbsp extra virgin olive oil
400g drained green or black olives, pitted if preferred

To FREEZE (up to 1 month)
Divide the marinated olives between 4 labelled zip-seal freezer bags. Remove as much air as possible, seal and flat freeze (see page 216).

To SERVE
Take a bag of olives from the freezer. Tip into a bowl and thaw at room temperature for 1–2 hours. Stir well and transfer to a serving dish with a handful of cocktail sticks to spear them.

Place the red pepper on a foil-lined baking tray and place under a very hot grill for roughly 10 minutes, turning the pepper each time the skin becomes blackened and blistered. You can also blacken the skin by carefully holding the pepper with tongs over a gas ring. Put the hot pepper into a heatproof bowl, cover with cling film and leave until cool enough to handle.

To make the harissa paste, place the cumin, coriander and fennel or caraway seeds in a pestle and mortar. Add the chilli, garlic, lemon zest and salt. Pound hard until the spices are crushed.

Carefully strip all the blackened skin off the pepper and discard. Put the pepper on a plate and cut into quarters, collecting as much juice from inside it as you can. Throw away the seeds and place the pepper in the pestle with the spices and garlic. Pound together until the mixture forms a thick paste – this may take up to 5 minutes, so you will need to be patient – and strong.

Add any reserved pepper juices and the oil to the paste. Pound together for a minute or so more then tip the mixture into a serving dish. Add the olives and toss them well in the harrissa.

To eat now, cover and chill for at least an hour before serving to allow the flavours to blend.

To FREEZE (up to 3 months)
Spoon the cooled caponata into
3 labelled zip-seal freezer bags.
Remove as much air as possible,
seal and flat freeze.

To SERVE
Take as many bags of caponata
from the freezer as you need. Thaw
at room temperature for 3–4 hours
or in the fridge overnight. Transfer
to a serving dish and drizzle with a
little olive oil before serving.

Caponata

Serves 10–12

A chunky Italian dish of fried aubergines and onions stewed with tomatoes in a tangy sweet and sour sauce, served at room temperature. It makes a large amount but you can freeze in three separate bags and simply thaw what you need each time. As well as serving with traditional Italian cold meats, it is wonderful spread on fresh bread and topped with thick wedges of mature Cheddar.

4 tbsp mild olive oil
1 medium-large aubergine (roughly 300g), cut into 2cm chunks
2 medium red onions, finely sliced
2 celery sticks, trimmed and finely sliced
3 garlic cloves, finely sliced

400g can chopped tomatoes
75g soft light brown sugar
4 tbsp red wine vinegar
2 tbsp pine nuts, preferably Italian
flaked sea salt
freshly ground black pepper
extra virgin olive oil, to serve

Heat the oil in a large, deep non-stick frying pan or wide-based saucepan over a medium heat and fry the aubergine for 8–10 minutes until lightly browned, stirring regularly. Add the onions and fry with the aubergine for 5 minutes, stirring regularly until the onions are softened. Add the celery and garlic and cook for a further 5 minutes, stirring constantly. Make sure not to let the vegetables burn and reduce the heat if necessary.

Tip the chopped tomatoes into the pan with the vegetables. Half-fill the can with cold water and add to the tomatoes. Stir in the sugar and vinegar and bring to a gentle simmer. Cook for 35–45 minutes or until very thick, stirring every now and then and more regularly towards the end of the cooking time as it thickens.

Stir in the pine nuts and season with a good pinch of salt and plenty of ground black pepper. Cook for 1–2 minutes more then remove from the heat and tip into a heatproof serving bowl. Leave to cool then cover. You can keep the caponata in the fridge for up to 5 days if necessary. Drizzle with a little extra virgin olive oil each time you serve it.

Garlicky smashed bean dip

Serves 8–12

To FREEZE (up to 2 months)
Divide the beans between 2 freezer-proof containers. Cover, label and freeze.

To SERVE
Thaw either one or both of the bean dips at room temperature for 3–5 hours or in the fridge overnight. Stir well and drizzle with a little olive oil before serving.

This homemade dip is incredibly quick and simple to make. Blitz the ingredients and pop in the freezer when you have a few spare minutes.

2 x 400g cans cannellini beans
2 garlic cloves, crushed
3 tbsp roughly chopped fresh parsley
4 tbsp extra virgin olive oil, plus extra for drizzling
1 tbsp fresh lemon juice
½ tsp flaked sea salt
freshly ground black pepper

Put the beans into a sieve and rinse under lots of cold running water. Drain thoroughly and tip into a food processor. Add the garlic, parsley, oil, lemon juice and salt. Season well with ground black pepper. If you don't have a food processor, put all the ingredients in a saucepan and smash with a potato masher.

Blitz on the pulse setting until coarsely blended. Adjust the seasoning to taste, adding a little extra salt, pepper and lemon juice if needed. To eat now, spoon into a serving dish, drizzle with a little extra oil and serve.

Guacamole

Serves 8–12

To FREEZE (up to 1 month)
Divide the guacamole between
2 or 3 small lidded freezer-proof
containers. Cover, label and freeze.

To SERVE
Take as many tubs as you need
from the freezer and thaw at room
temperature for up to 2 hours or in
the fridge for 4–6 hours. Stir well
and spoon into a serving dish.

*Surprisingly, avocados freeze rather well when mashed, so this quick
dip is great to make when you are able to buy them cheaply. Fresh
coriander freezes well and seems to retain its colour better than some
other herbs, so it's a good recipe for using up a large bunch. Serve with
tortilla chips that you have gently warmed on a baking tray in the oven.*

3 ripe avocados
2 garlic cloves, crushed
½ small red onion, finely grated
1 plump red chilli, deseeded
   and finely diced
freshly squeezed juice of 1 lime

pinch of cayenne pepper
3 tbsp finely chopped fresh coriander
   (optional)
flaked sea salt
freshly ground black pepper

Cut the avocados in half and remove the stones. Scoop the flesh
into a bowl and add the garlic, onion, chilli, lime juice, cayenne and
coriander, if using. Mash with a large fork or a potato masher until the
ingredients form a thick paste. Season well with salt and freshly ground
black pepper.

To eat now, spoon into a serving bowl and cover the surface of the
guacamole with cling film to prevent it turning brown. If possible, chill
for about an hour before serving to allow the flavours to develop. It will
keep in the fridge for 24 hours if well covered.

Soured cream and chive dip

Serves 6

To FREEZE (up to 1 month)
Mix the ingredients in a small
freezer-proof container. Cover,
label and freeze.

To SERVE
Thaw at room temperature for up
to an hour or in the fridge for 4–6
hours. Stir well and spoon into a
serving dish.

*This dip is actually made with half-fat crème fraîche rather than
traditional soured cream as it freezes better. Serve with crunchy
vegetable sticks.*

200ml half-fat crème fraîche
½ garlic clove, crushed
2 tbsp finely chopped fresh chives

flaked sea salt
freshly ground black pepper

Mix the crème fraîche, garlic and chives in a small bowl. Season with
salt and pepper to taste. Cover and chill for about an hour if possible to
allow the flavours to blend. Serve the same day if not freezing.

Smoked salmon blinis

Makes 30

The perfect vehicle for any smoked fish, these canapés freeze very well and will always get wolfed down at a party. They are simple to make – I've stuck with wheat flour and baking powder rather than going down the buckwheat/yeast route. For a smoked salmon pâté, blitz the salmon topping ingredients roughly and serve with pickles and toast.

15g butter	**Salmon topping**
140g self-raising flour	150g half-fat crème fraîche
½ tsp baking powder	2 tbsp finely chopped dill
1 medium egg	150g smoked salmon slices
1 tbsp caster sugar	flaked sea salt
200ml full-fat milk	freshly ground black pepper
2 tbsp sunflower oil, for greasing	

Melt the butter in a small pan over a low heat and leave to cool for 5 minutes. Put the flour, baking powder, egg, sugar, milk and butter in a food processor and blend until smooth. If you don't have a food processor, beat with an electric whisk instead. Pour into a large bowl.

Pour a little of the oil into a large non-stick frying pan and set over a medium-high heat. Wipe around the base of the pan with a thick wad of kitchen paper to lightly grease. Take care as it will be extremely hot.

Using a dessertspoon, drop 7–8 spoonfuls of the pancake mixture into the frying pan, spacing them well apart. Cook for 40 seconds or until the pancakes rise, bubbles appear and their surface appears almost dry. Flip them over with a palette knife and cook on the other side for a further 40–50 seconds until pale-golden brown. Transfer to a couple of serving platters or boards.

Cook the remaining pancakes in exactly the same way, greasing the pan with oil between each batch. If the pancake mixture begins to get too thick to spread, simply whisk in a little extra milk.

Mix the crème fraîche with dill and seasoning to taste. Cut the smoked salmon into 30 fairly wide strips. Top each blini with a small dab of the dill sauce until it is all used up. Arrange a piece of smoked salmon on top of each blini, curling it on top of the sauce rather than placing flat.

To eat now, season with a little freshly ground black pepper and garnish with fresh dill and serve. You can also cover the blinis with cling film and keep in the fridge for a couple of hours before serving.

To FREEZE (up to 1 month)
Follow all the steps as fresh but instead of placing the finished blinis on a platter, arrange on a baking tray and open freeze for 1–2 hours until solid. Transfer to a rigid container, interleaving with easy-leave or baking parchment. Cover, label and freeze.

To SERVE
Place the frozen blinis on a board or tray and leave to thaw at room temperature for 30 minutes. Cover and place in the fridge if leaving any longer. Preheat the oven to 200°C/ Fan 180°C/Gas 6. Place a baking sheet in the oven and leave to heat for about 5 minutes. Just before serving, remove the baking tray from the oven and top quickly with the thawed blinis. Leave for 2 minutes then transfer the blinis to a serving platter, while the pancakes remain hot. Sprinkle with freshly ground black pepper or fresh dill if you have some and serve.

Caramelised onion and goat's cheese tarts

Serves 8

This is definitely one of those starters that people seem to love. It may seem like a lot of onions for just eight tarts but this recipe does need all of them to create just the right amount of unctuous topping. I think the caramelised onions marry perfectly with the mild but tangy goat's cheese but you can always use Brie or Camembert instead.

50g butter
4 medium red onions, finely sliced
50g soft light brown sugar
3 tbsp red wine vinegar
500g chilled puff pastry
1–2 tbsp plain flour, for rolling

150g rindless soft fresh goat's cheese
logs (if it does have a rind, allow an
extra 50g)
freshly ground black pepper
extra virgin olive oil, for drizzling
lightly dressed young salad leaves,
to serve
young growing thyme or basil leaves

To FREEZE (up to 2 months)
Cool the part-baked pastries then top with the onion and goat's cheese. Open freeze on a baking tray until solid then transfer to a rigid container, interleaving with easy-leave or baking parchment. Cover, label and freeze.

To SERVE
Place the frozen tarts on a baking tray and cook in a preheated oven at 220°C/Fan 200°C/Gas 7 for 12 minutes until the pastry is golden and the topping is hot.

Melt the butter in a large non-stick saucepan and gently fry the onions for 15 minutes or until very soft but not coloured, stirring occasionally. Increase the heat and fry for 4–5 minutes more, stirring constantly until they are beginning to brown.

Stir the sugar and vinegar into the onions and simmer for 5 minutes, stirring until the liquid has almost completely reduced. Remove from the heat and leave to cool. Preheat the oven to 220°C/Fan 200°C/Gas 7.

Roll the pastry on a lightly floured surface until around 3mm thick. Cut into 8 x 12cm circles using cookie cutters or an upturned bowl. Place the circles on two baking trays and prick lightly with a fork. Bake for 12 minutes until well risen and beginning to brown.

Take the circles out of the oven and flatten gently with a spatula. Spoon a little of the onion mixture into the centre of each of the circles. Cut the cheese into roughly 2cm and scatter on top. Season with freshly ground black pepper.

To cook now, return to the oven and bake for 6–8 minutes or until the pastry is golden brown, the topping is hot and the cheese has melted. Transfer to plates and drizzle with olive oil. Serve warm with a simple, dressed salad. Scatter with a few thyme or basil leaves if you like.

Pan-fried scallops and bacon with minted pea purée

Serves 4

You're probably used to finding this combination in a restaurant but there's no reason why you can't make it at home too. Nearly everything comes out of the freezer and cooks straight from frozen, so this starter could be ready to serve in under 20 minutes.

1 tbsp sunflower oil
8 rindless rashers smoked streaky
  bacon (fresh or frozen)
200g frozen scallops (roeless)
a couple of handfuls of mixed salad
  leaves or rocket
1 tsp fresh lemon juice
1 tsp good quality balsamic vinegar
freshly ground black pepper

Minted pea purée
25g butter
½ small onion, finely chopped
1 garlic clove, crushed
250g frozen peas
1 heaped tsp freeze-dried
  or frozen mint
125ml chicken stock (made with
  ½ chicken stock cube)
flaked sea salt
freshly ground black pepper

To make the pea purée, melt the butter in a small saucepan over a low heat. Add the onion and garlic and cook over a low heat for 5 minutes until softened, stirring often. Add the peas, mint and stock. Bring to a simmer and cook for 5 minutes.

Remove from the heat and blitz with a stick blender or in a food processor until smooth. Press through a fine sieve to make a smooth purée. Return the purée to the pan and adjust seasoning to taste. Keep warm over a low heat, stirring occasionally.

Meanwhile, heat the oil in a large non-stick frying pan over a high heat. Add the bacon rashers and cook for 1½ minutes on each side until lightly browned and beginning to crisp at the edges.

Move the bacon to one side of the pan and add the scallops in a single layer. Cook the scallops for 6–7 minutes, turning occasionally until golden. They need to be lightly but fully cooked throughout. If the scallops are thawed, cook them for around 1 minute on each side.

Toss the salad leaves or rocket with the lemon juice, vinegar and some ground black pepper. Divide between 4 plates. Spoon the warm purée onto each plate and top with the hot scallops. Place the bacon on top of the salad, season with a little more pepper and serve.

Sun-dried tomato and basil stuffed sea bass

Serves 6

This is a very simple but stunning dish that never fails to impress. And as cook and host, what you will especially love is that it can be cooked from frozen in 25 minutes. To get the flavour just right use basil leaves taken from a growing plant as they have a more subtle taste. If using older, larger basil leaves, cut the quantity by half. Serve with sautéed or boiled potatoes and a colourful mixed salad or some sliced courgettes.

2 tbsp olive oil
12 sea bass fillets, each around 100g
  (make sure the fish match up in 6
  pairs, so they look their best)
6 fresh bay leaves (optional)
lemon wedges, to serve
black pepper

Tomato and basil stuffing
1 tbsp olive oil
½ medium onion, finely chopped
50g dried white breadcrumbs
  (see page 184)
50g pine nuts, preferably Italian
7 sun-dried tomato pieces (roughly
  50g), drained and chopped
20 medium basil leaves, shredded
finely grated zest of ½ small lemon
flaked sea salt
freshly ground black pepper

To make the stuffing, heat the oil in a large non-stick frying pan and fry the onion gently for 3 minutes until softened, stirring occasionally. Stir in the breadcrumbs and pine nuts and cook for 3–4 minutes more until the pine nuts are lightly toasted.

Add the sun-dried tomatoes, basil leaves, lemon zest, a good pinch of flaked sea salt and plenty of ground black pepper. Fry for a further 2 minutes, stirring constantly. Remove from the heat, tip onto a plate and leave to cool completely.

Drizzle a large baking tray with a tablespoon of olive oil. Place one of the fish fillets on a board, skin-side down, top with a sixth of the stuffing mixture and sandwich with the other fillet. Tie kitchen string 3 times down the length of the fish to secure the filling. Tuck a bay leaf under the middle piece of string if you like. Trim off the excess string. Repeat with the remaining fish fillets and stuffing. Drizzle the fish with another tablespoon of oil and season with black pepper.

To cook now, bake in a preheated oven at 200°C/Fan 180°C/Gas 6 for 15–18 minutes or until the fish is cooked and the filling is hot.

To FREEZE (up to 1 month)
Open freeze the raw stuffed fish on a baking tray lined with easy-leave or baking parchment for 2 hours. Take the fish off the tray and put it in a large rigid container, interleaving with easy-leave or parchment. Cover, label and freeze.

To SERVE
Put the frozen fish on a lightly oiled baking tray and cook in a preheated oven at 200°C/Fan 180°C/Gas 6 for 25 minutes or until the fish is cooked and the filling is piping hot. The fish is cooked when the flesh feels soft when pressed with your finger towards the head end where the fillet is thickest part.

Clever idea
If you don't want to stuff the sea bass you can serve just one fillet per person instead. Look out for larger fillets if you can — up to about 175g should be right. Open freeze with the stuffing pressed gently on top, then wrap each fillet in foil and freeze in a rigid container. Unwrap, place on an oiled and lined baking tray. Drizzle with a little olive oil and roast from frozen in a preheated oven at 200°C/Fan 180°C/Gas 6 for 15–20 minutes. You can use the same method for any fillets of fish.

Garlic and chilli prawns

Serves 6

These are a favourite in our house. I use any frozen raw prawns for this dish, but tiger or king prawns work particularly well. Most frozen prawns can be cooked straight from the freezer but it is worth checking the instructions on your pack. Make sure you choose ones that have been cleaned or deveined. I use a combination of fresh and dried chillies for the best colour and flavour. Start by adding half a teaspoon of dried chilli flakes to the oil and then increase it if you need a little more heat.

To FREEZE (up to 1 month)
Cool the infused oil then stir in the parsley and pour, with the garlic and chilli, into 3 round foil pie plates or silicone cake pans. Open freeze for 45 minutes or until the oil is solid. Quickly divide the frozen prawns between the 3 dishes. Cover tightly with foil, label and freeze.

To SERVE
Turn the frozen prawns and flavoured oil out of one of the containers and transfer straight into a large non-stick frying pan, oil side down. Reheat gently until the oil is hot. Do not allow the oil to overheat or it will begin to spit. Stir occasionally and cook the prawns in the oil from frozen until they are pink throughout and thoroughly cooked. If cooking more than one batch of prawns at a time, allow them to stand at room temperature for around 15 minutes before adding to the pan.

6 garlic cloves
2 plump red chillies
250ml olive oil
½ tsp flaked sea salt
½ -1 tsp dried chilli flakes (optional)

500g frozen peeled raw king prawns
small bunch (about 15g) flat-leaf
    parsley, leaves roughly chopped
freshly ground black pepper
lemon wedges, to serve

Peel the garlic and cut it into very fine slices from top to bottom. Put the garlic in a large non-stick frying pan. Finely chop the red chillies, deseeding before chopping if you like a little less heat, and add to the saucepan. Pour over the oil, season with the salt and lots of ground black pepper.

Set over a very low heat. Infuse the garlic and chilli into the oil for 10 minutes without allowing it to colour. Remove from the heat, stir in the dried chilli flakes if using.

To cook now, reheat the oil over a medium heat for about a minute. Do not allow it to overheat and do not leave hot oil unattended. Add the frozen prawns gently to the oil and cook for 4–5 minutes or until they turn completely pink, stirring occasionally. Don't let the oil get too hot or it may start to spit. The prawns will start to curl as they cook but should remain in juicy loose Cs rather than tight pink circles.

When you are sure the prawns are thoroughly cooked, remove from the heat, stir in the parsley and season with a little more ground black pepper. Serve hot with warm crusty bread to mop up all of the delicious juices and lemon wedges for squeezing.

Chicken in creamy tarragon sauce

Serves 8

The perfect dinner party dish that can be cooked from frozen in just over an hour. Chicken breasts are stuffed with sautéed leeks and sun-dried tomatoes then gently baked in white wine and stock, enriched with crème fraîche and infused with fresh tarragon. If you are freezing this dish, it is important to make sure the sauce and stuffed chicken breasts are completely cooled before you combine them. I use shallow foil trays to freeze this recipe but you can use ovenproof dishes or silicone cake pans instead.

To FREEZE (up to 2 months)
Leave the sauce to cool completely in the dishes. Place the stuffed chicken breasts, skin-side up and spaced well apart, in the trays or dishes, nestled into the completely cold sauce. Roughly chop the tarragon leaves and scatter over the top. Cover, label and freeze.

To SERVE
Uncover the frozen chicken and sauce and then cover loosely with foil. Place on a baking tray in a preheated oven at 190°C/Fan 170°C/Gas 5 for 45 minutes. Take off the foil and continue baking for a further 20–25 minutes or until piping hot throughout. Rest the chicken and cook the sauce as page 91, adding water if necessary.

Alternatively, thaw overnight in the fridge and reheat in a suitable dish as for fresh, adding an extra 5–10 minutes to compensate for the chill factor.

8 boneless chicken breasts (with skin)

Leek and tomato stuffing
1 tbsp sunflower oil
2 medium leeks (roughly 300g), trimmed and finely sliced
10 sun-dried tomato pieces, drained

Tarragon sauce
25g butter
2 tbsp sunflower oil
2 medium onions, each cut into wedges

2 garlic cloves, finely sliced root to tip
300ml white wine
500ml chicken stock (fresh or made with 1 chicken stock cube)
small bunch of fresh tarragon (roughly 10g)
3 tbsp cornflour
3 tbsp water
200ml crème fraiche
flaked sea salt
ground black pepper

To make the stuffing, heat the oil in a large, deep non-stick frying pan or wide-based saucepan and gently fry the leeks for 3–4 minutes until softened but not coloured, stirring regularly. Remove from the heat and tip into a medium mixing bowl. Put the sun-dried tomatoes on a board and roughly chop. Tip into the bowl with the leeks and mix well. Cool completely.

Put the chicken breasts on a board with the thickest end facing you. Using a sharp knife, carefully cut a 8cm pocket in each one, starting on one long side and working your way through the chicken almost through to the other side. Open the pockets and divide the leek and tomato stuffing between each breast. Close the pockets and season the chicken with freshly ground black pepper. Cover and place in the fridge until the sauce is ready.

To make the sauce, melt the butter with the oil in the same pan used to make the stuffing. Add the onions to the pan and fry over a medium heat for 6–8 minutes until softened and well-coloured, stirring regularly. Reduce the heat to low, add the garlic to the pan and cook for one minute more.

Pour the wine into the pan, stirring constantly and bring to a simmer. Stir in the stock and 3 sprigs of tarragon. Return to a simmer and cook for 5 minutes. Mix the cornflour with the cold water in a small bowl until smooth. Pour into the pan with the stock and simmer for 2–3 minutes, stirring until the sauce thickens. Remove the tarragon sprigs, stir in the crème fraîche and remove the pan from the heat. Pour the liquid into one large or two smaller shallow ovenproof dishes or trays.

To eat now, place the stuffed chicken breasts, skin-side up and spaced well apart, in the trays or dishes, nestling into the sauce. Bake in a preheated oven at 200°C/Fan 180°C/Gas 6 for 25–30 minutes or until the chicken is lightly browned and cooked throughout. (There should be no pinkness remaining in the chicken.)

Transfer the chicken breasts to a warmed serving dish, cover and leave to rest for 8–10 minutes. Carefully pour the sauce and onions into a saucepan and bring to a simmer. Cook for about 5 minutes, stirring regularly until slightly thickened.

While the sauce is simmering, strip the leaves from the remaining tarragon sprigs and cut or tear into short lengths. Remove the sauce from the heat and pour around the chicken in the dish. Scatter with the tarragon and serve.

Forget-about-it beef in Burgundy

Serves 6–8

A rich beef casserole recipe that actually improves on freezing and is very forgiving if dinner is later than planned. There's no need to brown the vegetables at the start, because adding a little Marmite will provide a lovely caramelised flavour to the casserole. I freeze this casserole in silicone cake pans, rewrap in foil, and then flop into one or two large casserole dishes straight from the freezer.

1.6kg well-trimmed chuck steak, or any
   good braising steak
3 tbsp sunflower oil
50g plain flour
200g rindless smoked streaky bacon,
   cut into 2cm wide strips
2 large onions, finely sliced
4 garlic cloves, crushed
1 bottle (75cl) of Burgandy or any red
   wine
450ml cold water
3 tbsp tomato purée

2 tbsp Marmite
1 beef stock cube
2 large bay leaves
3 bushy sprigs of thyme or
   2 tsp dried thyme
400g button chestnut mushrooms,
   sliced
flaked sea salt
freshly ground black pepper
flat-leaf parsley, roughly chopped,
   to serve (optional)

Preheat the oven to 180°C/Fan 160°C/Gas 4. Cut the steak into chunky pieces, each around 4cm large. Trim off any remaining hard fat or sinew. Season well with salt and pepper. Heat the oil in a large non-stick frying pan and fry the steak in 2 or 3 batches until nicely browned on all sides, adding a little extra oil between batches if necessary. Put in a large flameproof casserole. Add the flour and toss until it lightly coats the meat.

Add the bacon, onions and garlic to the pan with the meat. Pour over the wine and water. Stir in the tomato purée and Marmite. Crumble over the stock cube, add the herbs and bring to a simmer. Stir well. Cover the surface of the casserole with a large piece of baking parchment, pop a lid on top and transfer to the oven.

Cook for about 2½ hours or until the beef is very tender. Remove the lid and check the beef after 1½ hours and every 30 minutes thereafter. The meat will break easily with a fork when tender.

To cook now, a few minutes before the beef is ready, heat the remaining 1 tbsp of oil in a large non-stick frying pan and fry the mushrooms for 2–3 minutes over a fairly high heat until golden, turning often. Remove the casserole from the oven. Take out the thyme stalks and bay leaves. Stir in the mushrooms. Sprinkle with the parsley if you like and serve.

To FREEZE (up to 3 months)
Follow the recipe up until the mushrooms are cooked but do not add them to the beef. Spoon the beef, vegetables and sauce into 2 shallow freezer-proof containers or silicone cake pans and leave to cool. Scatter the mushrooms and parsley over the top. Cover, label and freeze.

To SERVE
To cook from frozen, place the frozen beef in Burgundy in one or two large flameproof casseroles or saucepans. Pour 100ml of just-boiled water into each one. Reheat slowly for around 20 minutes until thawed. Bring to a simmer and cook for a further 10 minutes until piping hot throughout. Don't stir too often or the meat could break up.

Alternatively, thaw in the fridge overnight. Lightly stir in the mushrooms. Transfer to a large flameproof casserole and reheat gently on the hob, stirring occasionally until piping hot.

Asian lemongrass pork curry

Serves 6

A fabulous curry that always has people coming back for another helping. Similar to a Thai or Malaysian style dish, this curry is rich, fragrant and medium hot. The pork adds its own sweetness to the dish but you could also make it with beef chuck steak, lamb shoulder or even chicken pieces. A garnish of fresh coriander and sliced spring onions looks great.

To FREEZE (up to 3 months)
Cook the curry for 45 minutes rather than 60. Follow the rest of the method as described then spoon the curry into a shallow freezer-proof container and leave to cool. Sprinkle with the reserved fresh coriander. Cover, label and freeze.

To SERVE
Thaw the curry overnight in the fridge and put in a large non-stick saucepan or casserole. Add 150ml of just-boiled water. Heat gently on the hob for about 10 minutes or until piping hot throughout, stirring occasionally so as not to break up the meat. Add a bit of water if the curry seems dry while reheating.

2 lemongrass stalks
1 medium onion, quartered
4 garlic cloves, halved
6 bird's eye chillies, trimmed and roughly chopped
25g chunk fresh root ginger, peeled and roughly chopped
small bunch fresh coriander (roughly 15g)
1.5kg boneless rindless pork shoulder (use thickly cut steaks if you like)
3 tbsp sunflower oil
1 heaped tbsp garam masala

1 heaped tbsp ground cumin
1 tsp ground turmeric
400ml can coconut milk
400ml water
5 kaffir lime leaves (ideally fresh or frozen)
2 tbsp nam pla (Thai fish sauce)
1 tbsp soft light brown sugar
4 tsp cornflour
2 tbsp cold water
flaked sea salt
freshly ground black pepper

Trim the lemongrass at each end and remove the papery outer layer. Chop the lemongrass into thin slices – you need around 20g. Put the sliced lemongrass in a food processor and add the onion, garlic, chillies and ginger. Save a few sprigs of coriander for garnishing and put the rest in the food processor along with its stalks (but not any roots).

Blitz all the aromatic ingredients to a fine curry paste. You will need to remove the lid and push the mixture down 2–3 times with a rubber spatula until the right texture is reached. Cut the pork into roughly 3cm chunks and season with salt and ground black pepper.

Preheat the oven to 190°C/Fan 170°C/Gas 5. Heat one tablespoon of the oil in a large non-stick frying pan and cook the pork in 2 batches over a fairly high heat until nicely browned, adding a little extra oil if necessary. Transfer to a large flameproof casserole.

Add the remaining oil, the curry paste, garam masala, cumin and turmeric to the frying pan. Fry over a medium heat for 3–4 minutes, stirring constantly until the mixture smells very fragrant and begins to colour. Pour the coconut milk into the frying pan and stir well.

Tip the curried coconut milk over the browned pork in the casserole, add the water and stir in the kaffir lime leaves, fish sauce and sugar. Bring to the boil. Remove the pan from the heat, cover with a lid and place in the centre of the oven. Cook for 1 hour.

Take the curry out of the oven. Stir well and return to the oven for a further hour or until the pork is very tender. Place on the hob and mix the cornflour with the water and stir into the curry. Cover over a medium heat for 1–2 minutes, stirring until thickened.

Remove all the lime leaves and skim off any excess fat that might be floating on the surface of the curry. Season with salt and pepper to taste. Garnish with chopped coriander or sliced spring onions and serve with freshly cooked rice or steamed vegetables.

Chicken with bacon and mushrooms in a Madeira sauce

Serves 8

Perfect for freeze-ahead entertaining, it looks very impressive and is equally good served to a crowd or saved for a special night in (see photo on page 218). Freeze and reheat in shallow foil trays then transfer to a warmed serving dish before taking to the table. Dauphinoise or mashed potatoes and some green beans make ideal accompaniments.

To FREEZE (up to 1 month)
Cool the sauce and stuffing completely before stuffing the chicken. Place the stuffed chicken breasts, spaced well apart, in the trays or dishes, nestling into the chilled sauce. Cover, label and freeze.

To SERVE
Uncover the frozen chicken and sauce and then recover loosely with foil. Place on a baking tray in a preheated oven at 190°C/ Fan 170°C/Gas 5 for 30 minutes. Take off the foil and continue baking for a further 30–40 minutes or until piping hot throughout. Alternatively, thaw overnight in the fridge and reheat in a suitable dish as for fresh, adding an extra 5–10 minutes to compensate for the chill factor.

8 boneless, skinless chicken breasts
16 rashers rindless smoked streaky bacon
flaked sea salt
freshly ground black pepper

Madeira wine sauce
40g butter
2 long shallots or 1 medium onion, finely sliced
2 garlic cloves, crushed
3 rashers rindless smoked streaky bacon, chopped
3–4 bushy sprigs of fresh thyme
150ml Madeira
1.3 litres chicken stock (fresh or made with 2 stock cubes)
3 tbsp redcurrant jelly

4 heaped tsp Marmite
4 tbsp cornflour
4 tbsp cold water

Mushroom stuffing
15g butter
1 tbsp sunflower oil
100g chestnut mushrooms, sliced
1 long shallot or ½ medium onion, finely chopped
2 rashers rindless smoked streaky bacon, cut into 1cm slices
1 tbsp plain flour
100g mature Cheddar cheese, finely grated
2 tbsp finely chopped flat-leaf parsley, plus extra for garnish

To make the sauce, melt the butter in a large non-stick saucepan and gently fry the shallots or onion, garlic, bacon and thyme until the shallots are softened and the bacon is coloured, stirring often. Add the Madeira, stock, redcurrant jelly and Marmite. Bring to a gentle simmer and cook for 15 minutes, stirring occasionally.

While the sauce is simmering, prepare the stuffing for the chicken breasts. Melt the butter with the oil in a large non-stick frying pan and fry the sliced mushrooms over a high heat for 2–3 minutes until lightly browned, stirring regularly. Lower the heat and add the shallot or onion, and sliced bacon. Cook together for 5 minutes until the shallot is softened, stirring occasionally.

Remove the pan from the heat and transfer to a mixing bowl. Stir in the flour and leave to cool for 5 minutes then stir in the cheese and parsley. Season well with salt and pepper and mix to a stiff paste. Cover and place in the fridge until needed.

In a small bowl, mix the cornflour with the cold water. Stir into the simmered stock mixture. Return to a simmer and cook for 2–3 minutes, stirring constantly until thickened. Remove from the heat. Pour the liquid into 2 large or 4 smaller, shallow ovenproof dishes or trays. Set aside.

To stuff the chicken, put the chicken breasts on a board with the thickest end facing you. Using a sharp knife, carefully cut a 8cm pocket in each one, starting on one long side and working your way through the chicken almost through to the other side. Open the pockets and divide the mushroom stuffing between each breast. Close the pockets and season the chicken with salt and freshly ground black pepper.

Place the bacon rashers on a board and stretch each one with the back of a knife until around a third longer. Wrap the bacon around the chicken breasts, keeping the ends tucked underneath. Season well.

To cook now, place the chicken breasts in the sauce, spacing them well apart. Cover loosely with foil and bake in a preheated oven at 220°C/Fan 200°C/Gas 7 for 15 minutes. Remove the foil and bake for a further 10 minutes.

Take out of the oven and spoon a little of the sauce over the chicken and bake for 5–10 minutes or until the sauce is piping hot and the chicken is cooked throughout. (There should be no pinkness remaining.) Remove from the oven and scatter chopped parsley before serving.

It's always useful to have a few puddings in the freezer for those evenings when the family feels like something extra for supper or to have on hand for last-minute entertaining.

Fruit puddings, such as crumbles or my spiced plum slump, are quick to make and freeze brilliantly. Make a few when plums, gooseberries or rhubarb are cheap and plentiful and you can whip one out of the freezer to cheer up a gloomy winter evening. Puddings like these can be cooked from frozen and they taste just as good as when freshly made.

If you're planning a meal for a special occasion it can really help to make the dessert ahead of time. That way you can enjoy preparing something truly scrumptious and save time on the day. Would you believe you can make a beautiful pavlova and freeze it fully decorated and ready to serve? Believe me, you can. My scrunchy lemon and lime tart doesn't even need any cooking – just put it together and freeze – then all you have to do is remember to take it out a few hours before you want to eat.

Another idea is to make batches of pancakes – crepes and the American versions – to store in the freezer. They can be defrosted in minutes to make super-quick puds that all the family will enjoy – great for a special brunch too. Other basics I keep in my freezer for the sweet course are bags of cooked fruit, such as apples, some freshly picked berries, portions of crumble topping, pastry cases and of course plenty of ice cream for that final touch.

PUDDINGS

Super-quick and saucy toffee pudding

Serves 6–8

An extraordinary dessert with a luscious, sweet sponge sitting above a bubbling toffee lava. Much quicker to make than the usual sticky toffee pudding variations that I've tried before and perfect for a weekend family lunch. It's a great one to pre-freeze in a rectangle silicone cake mould as it can be transferred to a lasagne dish while frozen when it is time to bake.

2 large eggs
1 tsp vanilla extract
200g dried pitted dates
100g unsalted butter, plus extra
 for greasing
250g soft light brown sugar
100ml semi-skimmed milk

1 tsp bicarbonate of soda
150g self-raising flour, sifted
1 tsp baking powder
500ml just-boiled water
ice cream, chilled double cream
 or custard, to serve

To FREEZE (up to 3 months)
Sprinkle over the sugar and dot the pudding with butter but do not pour over the water. Instead, leave to cool for 10 minutes, cover the dish with a double layer of foil, label and freeze.

To SERVE
Unwrap the frozen pudding and place the dish on a baking tray or transfer to an ovenproof dish. Preheat the oven to 190°C/Fan 170°C/Gas 5. Pour the just-boiled water over the frozen pudding and bake on the tray for 45–50 minutes. Cover the dish with foil if the sponge begins to over-brown before risen in the centre of the pudding.

Butter a 2-litre ovenproof dish or silicone cake pan. Beat the eggs and vanilla extract together in a bowl. Roughly chop the dates and put in a large non-stick saucepan. Add 75g of the butter, 150g of the sugar and all of the milk.

Place over a low heat, bring to a very gentle simmer and cook for 2 minutes, stirring regularly with a wooden spoon. Remove from the heat and stir in the bicarbonate of soda. The liquid will rise in a mass of bubbles when the soda is added.

Working quickly, pour the beaten eggs and vanilla on to the date mixture, stirring constantly. Next, stir in the flour and baking powder until well combined. The batter will look fairly frothy at this point. Pour the batter into the prepared dish and place on a baking tray. Sprinkle with the remaining 100g of sugar and dot with the remaining 25g of butter.

To eat now, pour over the water as evenly as possible. The pudding will look very peculiar at this point but it's meant to, so don't worry.

Bake in the centre of a preheated oven 190°C/Fan 170°C/Gas 5 for 35–40 minutes until the sponge is risen and sits on a deep pool of toffee sauce. It will sway a little as you move it. Serve hot with ice cream, chilled double cream or custard.

To FREEZE (up to 2 months)

Let the pancakes cool as soon as they are made. Open freeze on a small baking tray for around an hour then transfer to a large labelled freezer bag. Seal and freeze.

To SERVE

Take as many pancakes as you need out of the bag and reheat from frozen in a very well-buttered non-stick frying pan over a medium heat for 2 minutes on each side.

Alternatively, arrange the pancakes in a single layer on a microwave-proof plate and reheat in the microwave on HIGH for 60–90 seconds until hot. Or put a couple of the pancakes in the toaster and heat for around 2 minutes until hot.

American-style maple and banana pancakes

Makes 20–22 pancakes

Serve these small fluffy American-style pancakes layered with thick slices of fresh banana, drizzled with maple syrup and topped with whipped cream for a quick and easy dessert that kids will love. They are also a great breakfast standby. I've given the basic mix here, but you can also add fresh fruit and nuts to the batter if you like.

25g butter, cubed
275g self-raising flour
1 tsp baking powder
2 medium eggs
2 tbsp caster sugar

400ml full-fat milk
1–2 tbsp sunflower oil
3 medium bananas, peeled and sliced
maple syrup, golden syrup or honey,
  to serve

Melt the butter in a small pan over a low heat and leave to cool for 5 minutes. Put the flour, baking powder, eggs, sugar, milk and melted butter in a food processor and blend until smooth. If you don't have a food processor, beat with an electric whisk instead. Pour into a large bowl.

Pour a little of the oil into a large non-stick frying pan and set over a medium-high heat. Wipe around the base of the pan with a thick wad of kitchen paper to lightly grease. Take care as it will be extremely hot.

Drop 3 serving spoons or small ladlefuls of the pancake mixture into the frying pan, spacing them well apart. Each pancake should spread slowly to be around 9cm in diameter. Cook for one minute or until the pancakes rise, bubbles appear and their surface appears not quite set. Flip over with a palette knife and cook on the other side for a further minute until pale-golden brown.

To eat now, transfer the 3 cooked pancakes to a warmed plate, cover with foil and a dry tea towel to help retain the heat. Cook the remaining pancakes in exactly the same way, greasing the pan with a little oil between each batch. If the pancake mixture begins to get too thick to pour, simply whisk in a little extra milk.

Divide the pancakes between warmed plates, layering with sliced bananas if you like. Serve with maple syrup, golden syrup or honey for pouring.

Spiced plum slump

Serves 6–8

With its bubbling, spiced fruit filling underneath a soft, scone-like topping, this scrumptious pudding tastes like Christmas in a bowl. If you see plums on offer, why not knock this together and freeze until needed. Use gooseberries or rhubarb instead of plums if you like.

Topping
75g granulated or golden caster sugar, plus 2 tbsp
75g well-softened butter
1 large egg
150ml semi-skimmed milk
finely grated zest of ½ large orange
200g self-raising flour, sifted
1 tsp baking powder

Filling
800g firm but ripe fresh plums (around 12)
50g granulated or golden caster sugar
1 tbsp cornflour
½ tsp ground mixed spice
freshly squeezed juice 1 large orange (roughly 125ml)
double cream or ice cream, to serve

To FREEZE (up to 3 months)
Make the plum slump in a silicone cake pan or oven and freezer-proof dish. Open freeze for 2–3 hours until solid. Remove from the silicone cake pan if using. Cover with a double layer of foil. Label and freeze.

To SERVE
Remove the slump from the freezer and transfer to an ovenproof dish if necessary. Cover loosely and thaw at room temperature for 3–4 hours or in the fridge overnight. Preheat the oven to 190°C/Fan 170°C/Gas 5. Place the pudding on a baking tray and cook for 40–45 minutes.

To make the topping, put the 75g sugar in a large bowl and add the butter, egg, milk, orange zest, flour and baking powder. Beat well with a wooden spoon or electric whisk. The batter should be thick and smooth and drop easily from the spoon. Don't worry if there are a few small lumps of butter in the mix.

Cut the plums into quarters, discarding the stones. Put the plums in a 2-litre shallow ovenproof dish and toss with the sugar, cornflour and mixed spice. Pour over the orange juice.

Put large spoonfuls of the batter on top of the fruit. There will be a few big gaps but the mixture will soften to fill them. Sprinkle with the remaining 2 tablespoons of sugar.

To cook now, place the dish on a baking tray and bake in a preheated oven at 190°C/Fan 170°C/Gas 5 for 35–40 minutes until the fruit has softened, the juice is bubbling and the topping is well risen and golden brown. Serve with cream or ice cream.

Luscious raspberry and lemon pavlova

Serves 8–10

Light billowing clouds of crisp meringue topped with a lemony cream filling and juicy raspberries make this the perfect summer dessert. The pavlova can be taken fully filled and decorated from the freezer in the morning and will be ready to serve at lunchtime. All it needs is a quick shake of icing sugar to frost the berries, leaving you more time to enjoy the sunshine and your guests. It's worth warning the rest of the family that the meringue is in the freezer to avoid it getting bashed.

Meringue	Filling
sunflower oil, for greasing	300ml double cream
6 large egg whites	200ml half-fat crème fraiche
325g caster sugar	4 tbsp good-quality lemon curd
2 tsp cornflour	400g raspberries
½ tsp pure vanilla extract	1 tsp icing sugar, sifted, to decorate

To FREEZE (up to 1 month)
Fill the cooled meringue while on the lined baking sheet and open freeze for 2 hours. Carefully take the meringue off the baking sheet and double wrap in foil. Put in a small cardboard or plastic box to protect the sides of the meringue. Label and freeze.

To SERVE
Unwrap the frozen meringue and transfer to a serving plate or cake stand. Leave to thaw at room temperature for 3–4 hours. Sprinkle with sifted icing sugar and serve. If leaving the pavlova longer than 5 hours, pop it in the fridge.

Preheat the oven to 150°C/Fan 130°C/Gas 2. Lightly grease your largest baking sheet with a little oil and line with baking parchment. If you don't have a really large baking sheet, use an upturned roasting tin instead.

Put the egg whites in a large bowl and whisk with an electric whisk until stiff but not dry. They are ready when you can turn the bowl upside down without the eggs sliding out.

Gradually whisk in the sugar a tablespoon at a time, whisking for a few seconds in between each addition. When you have just 3–4 tablespoons of sugar still to add, stir the cornflour into the remaining sugar and continue spooning the sugar gradually onto the meringue as before. Finally, whisk in the vanilla extract until well combined.

Place large spoonfuls of the meringue on the centre of the baking sheet and use the bottom of a serving spoon to create a deep nest shape with billowing sides. Place the meringue in the oven and immediately reduce the temperature to 120°C/Fan 100°C/Gas ½.

Bake the meringue for 3 hours until it appears completely dry. It needs to be dry to freeze without going soggy and should look a very pale creamy white. Reduce the oven temperature further if the meringue begins to colour. Turn off the oven and leave the meringue to cool inside the oven for several hours or overnight.

Whip the cream and crème fraîche together in a large bowl with an electric whisk until soft peaks form. Gently whisk in the lemon curd until lightly combined.

To eat now, transfer the meringue very carefully to a serving plate or cake stand. Spoon the lemon cream onto the meringue – don't worry if it sinks or cracks a little – and scatter the raspberries on top. Sift over the icing sugar and serve.

Scrunchy lemon and lime tart

Serves 8

This tangy no-bake dessert really couldn't be simpler. The acid in the citrus fruits reacts with the cream and condensed milk to thicken the filling naturally. It's one of those puddings that can be made in minutes and is best served still slightly frozen. In the summer I like to top it with lightly sugared berries and serve with lots of chilled cream.

275g oaty biscuits, such as Hobnobs
75g unsalted butter
2 medium lemons
2–3 limes

397g can sweetened condensed milk
200ml double cream
extra lime and lemon zest,
    to decorate (optional)

To make the biscuit base, break the biscuits into chunky pieces and blitz into crumbs in a food processor. Melt the butter in a small saucepan and add the crumbs with the motor running. Blend until evenly combined. If you don't have a food processor, crush the biscuits in a strong plastic food bag by bashing with a rolling pin. Tip the crumbs into a bowl and stir in the melted butter.

Press the biscuit crumbs onto the base and the sides of a 23cm loose-based fluted tart tin or ceramic quiche dish. It will need to be over 3.5cm deep. Make sure you push the crumbs right into the corners or you will be left with a wedge of biscuit instead of an even layer. Cover with cling film and freeze for 30 minutes.

Finely grate the lemons and limes and squeeze the juice. You'll need exactly 125ml of juice for the filling to set, so if you have any less, squeeze an extra lime or lemon. Take the biscuit base out of the freezer and remove the cling film.

Beat the condensed milk and cream together in a large bowl using an electric whisk for 3 minutes or until it begins to thicken. Reserve 1 teaspoon of citrus zest. Add the rest of the lemon and lime zest and all juice to the condensed milk and cream and whip for just a few seconds more. The mixture will thicken quickly.

Spoon immediately into the biscuit base. Swirl the surface with the back of a spoon. Sprinkle with the reserved lemon and lime zest. Cover the filled biscuit base loosely with cling film and chill for 1–2 hours before serving. Carefully remove from the tin and slide onto a serving plate. If the pudding is being stubborn, place the base on a teatowel soaked in hot water and then rung dry. The heat from the teatowel will begin to melt the butter and the pudding should be easier to release.

To FREEZE (up to 1 month)
Open freeze the filled biscuit base for 2 hours then double wrap in foil and return to the freezer. You can remove the tart from a metal tin and double wrap in foil as soon as it is solid.

To SERVE
Unwrap the tart and transfer it to a serving plate if necessary. Cover loosely and leave to thaw at room temperature for 1½–2 hours.

To **FREEZE** (up to 3 months)

Prepare the crumble mixture as described. Tip into a freezer bag, seal, label and freeze. The gooseberries can be frozen whole in bags or freezer-proof containers. To fully prepare the pudding for freezing, follow all the steps as fresh, but make the pudding in a freezer and ovenproof container. Instead of baking, double wrap the dish in foil. Label and freeze.

To SERVE

Scatter the frozen gooseberries into a 1.75-litre ovenproof dish and toss with the sugar and cornflour if necessary. Top with the frozen crumble mixture and bake as page 111 for about 40 minutes. If cooking the fully assembled pudding, place on a baking tray and bake for around 60 minutes, covering the dish with foil for the first 20 minutes of cooking time.

Gooseberry crumble

Serves 6–8

Who doesn't like gooseberry crumble? I think it is probably my favourite pudding of all time, so I always find space for a few bags or punnets of gooseberries in my freezer. Gooseberries cook really well from frozen and can be teamed up with a ready-frozen crumble mixture for a fantastically simple dessert. If using fresh gooseberries, you can cut the cooking time by 10 minutes or so. If you are using frozen gooseberries, you don't need to thaw them before top and tailing, just rub between your fingertips while they are still frozen.

700g fresh or frozen gooseberries,
    topped and tailed
75g caster sugar
1 tbsp cornflour

Crumble mix
175g plain flour
50g porridge oats
125g demerara sugar
125g cold butter, cubed

Preheat the oven to 200°C/Fan 180°C/Gas 6. To make the crumble mix, put the flour, oats and sugar in a large bowl and add the butter. Rub together with your fingertips until the mixture resembles coarse breadcrumbs.

Place the frozen gooseberries in a shallow 1.75-litre ovenproof dish and toss with the sugar and cornflour. Sprinkle the crumbs evenly over the top.

To eat now, bake in the centre of the oven for 35–45 minutes or until the topping is golden brown and the filling is bubbling.

Surprisingly simple profiteroles with hot chocolate sauce

Serves 8–12

To FREEZE (up to 1 month)
As soon as all the buns are filled with the cream, place them on a baking tray and open freeze for 1–2 hours to allow the cream to harden. Transfer to 2 large labelled freezer bags. Remove as much air as possible (see page 223). Seal and freeze. To freeze the chocolate sauce, cool then pour into 2 labelled zip-seal freezer bags. Seal and freeze.

To SERVE
Arrange a pile of the frozen profiteroles on a large serving platter and dust with sifted icing sugar. Leave to stand at room temperature for one hour to soften slightly. To heat the frozen chocolate sauce, rinse one or both bags under a hot tap and transfer to a large non-stick saucepan. Add 3 tbsp of just-boiled water and heat very gently, stirring regularly until smooth and glossy. Pour the hot chocolate sauce over the profiteroles and serve immediately.

Clever idea
Freeze the profiteroles unfilled then thaw for 30 minutes and fill with vanilla ice cream. Pour the hot chocolate sauce over the cold profiteroles.

These profiteroles are frozen filled with whipped vanilla cream and only need to thaw for an hour before serving. When a special occasion arrives, just pile as many of the profiteroles as you need, straight from the freezer, high on a platter.

250ml water
100g butter, cut into cubes
140g plain flour
4 medium eggs, beaten
1 tbsp icing sugar, to dust

Vanilla cream
450ml double cream

2 tbsp caster sugar
½ tsp vanilla extract

Hot chocolate sauce
200g plain, dark chocolate, broken into pieces
300ml double cream
2 tbsp just-boiled water

Preheat the oven to 200°C/Fan 180°C/Gas 6. Line 2 baking trays with baking parchment and set aside. To make the choux pastry, pour the water into a medium non-stick saucepan set over a low heat and add the butter. Sift the flour into a bowl. Melt the butter slowly in the water then increase the heat and bring it to the boil.

Immediately add the flour into the bubbling water and stir vigorously with a wooden spoon until the mixture forms a thick, smooth paste. Remove from the heat.

Continue to stir for 2–3 minutes until the paste has cooled a little. Add the beaten eggs, just a little at a time to the paste, beating well in between each addition. The paste will become softer as the eggs are added.

Spoon heaped dessertspoons of the choux paste onto the baking trays to make 12–14 mounds on each tray. Space them well apart to allow for rising. Bake one tray above the other in the oven for 30-35 minutes until the buns are well risen and golden brown. You may need to switch the shelves after 20 minutes if the buns are browning unevenly.

Remove the trays from the oven. Holding each bun with a clean teatowel, turn upside down on a wire rack and make a 1cm hole in the base with the tip of a knife to allow the steam to escape. Leave to cool.

While the profiteroles are cooling, make the chocolate sauce. Place the chocolate and cream in a non-stick saucepan over a low heat, stirring regularly. Remove from the heat and stir in the just-boiled water.

To eat now, whip the cream with the sugar and vanilla until soft peaks form. Spoon into a large piping bag fitted with a small plain nozzle. Pipe the cream into each choux bun through the base. Alternatively, split the buns and spoon the cream inside. Pile up on a serving plate and dust with icing sugar. Warm the sauce and pour over the profiteroles to serve.

Tutti-frutti ice cream pudding

Serves 8–10

A fruity, spicy, creamy ice cream dessert finished with a dark chocolate drizzle. Rich but refreshing, it makes a perfect alternative to a traditional Christmas pudding or a dazzling dessert any time of year. Either use a traditional metal ring-shaped cake tin or a 24cm silicone one for easy release once frozen.

100g raisins
100g sultanas
100g glacé cherries
100g ready to eat dried apricots,
    cut into sixths
75g cut mixed peel
4 balls of stem ginger in syrup, drained
    and diced
1 tsp ground mixed spice

75ml cherry brandy or brandy
freshly squeezed juice and finely
    grated zest of 1 orange
300ml double cream
500ml good-quality vanilla custard

Chocolate drizzle
50g plain dark chocolate, broken
    into pieces

To FREEZE (up to 1 month)
Once the chocolate has hardened on the ice cream, cover the ring tightly with foil. Label and return to the freezer.

To SERVE
Remove the ice cream from the freezer, transfer to a serving plate and stand at room temperature for 15–20 minutes before serving.

Put the raisins, sultanas, glacé cherries, apricots, mixed peel, stem ginger and mixed spice into a small saucepan and pour over the cherry brandy or brandy. Stir in the orange juice and zest. Bring to a gentle simmer and cook for 2 minutes, stirring constantly. Tip the mixture into a heatproof bowl and leave to cool.

Line a 1.2-litre ring-shaped cake tin with 2 layers of cling film, leaving plenty hanging over the edges or use a 24cm silicone ring mould instead. Place the ring on a baking tray.

Whisk the double cream in a large bowl until soft peaks form. Fold in the custard and cooled fruit mixture. Spoon immediately into the prepared ring, smooth the surface and cover with cling film. Freeze for several hours or overnight until solid.

Once the ice cream is solid, make the chocolate drizzle. Melt the chocolate in a heatproof bowl over a saucepan of gently simmering water – or in the microwave – until almost smooth. Remove from the heat and stir until smooth and runny. Leave to cool for 10 minutes.

Take the ice cream ring out of the freezer and leave to stand for 5 minutes. Turn out onto a freezer-proof serving plate, tray or board, using the cling film to help if necessary, before peeling it off. If your ice cream won't drop easily out of the container, dunk the base of the tin in a large bowl of very hot water for a few seconds.

Using a teaspoon, drizzle the chocolate sauce slowly over the ice cream, allowing it to dribble down the sides. Return at once to the freezer for at least 20–30 minutes to allow the chocolate to harden.

To eat now, remove the ice cream from the freezer and stand at room temperature for 10–15 minutes before slicing to serve.

Chocolate-fudge ice cream pie with hot toffee sauce

Serves 8–10

Perhaps not surprisingly, this goes down a treat with kids. I like to make it with a couple of varieties of ice cream – vanilla and chocolate are ideal – but you can stick to one flavour if you prefer. I love serving it with my hot, and very easy, toffee sauce, but you can always use a ready-made toffee sauce.

Biscuit base
275g chocolate Bourbon biscuits
75g butter

Ice Cream filling
1 litre ice cream; vanilla, chocolate or
  a mixture

2 x 27g chocolate flake bars
75g dairy fudge pieces, unwrapped
2 x 37g bags Maltesers

Toffee sauce topping
75g soft light brown sugar
150ml double cream

To FREEZE (up to 1 month)
Freeze the ice cream pie until solid then gently remove from the tin as described, double wrap in foil, label and return to the freezer. Cool the sauce, pour into a labelled freezer bag, seal and freeze. You can also top the pie with the cooled sauce and freeze them together.

To SERVE
Unwrap the pudding and transfer to a serving plate. Stand for 20 minutes to allow the ice cream to soften a little. Put the frozen sauce in a small saucepan and heat gently, stirring constantly until hot. Drizzle the sauce over the ice cream and serve.

To make the base, break the biscuits into chunky pieces and blitz into crumbs in a food processor. Melt the butter in a small saucepan and pour onto the crumbs with the motor running and blend until evenly combined. Alternatively, crush the biscuits in a strong plastic food bag by bashing them with a rolling pin. Tip the biscuits into a bowl and stir in the melted butter.

Line a 23cm metal pie dish (or a ceramic quiche dish) with a large sheet of foil. Press the biscuit crumbs onto the base and sides, keeping the layer as even as possible, especially where the base and sides meet. Cover loosely with cling film and freeze for 30 minutes.

Just 10 minutes before assembling the base, take the ice cream out of the freezer. Remove the cling film from the base and leave to stand for 5 minutes to soften a little. Roughly chop the flake bars on a board and cut the fudge into small chunks. Scoop the ice cream into the biscuit base, dotting with flaked chocolate, fudge pieces and Maltesers as you go. Return to the freezer for at least an hour until solid, covering with cling film after the first 30 minutes.

To make the toffee sauce, put the sugar and cream in a small saucepan and heat gently until the sugar dissolves. Bring to a gentle simmer and cook for one minute, stirring constantly. Remove from the heat and leave to stand.

When ready to serve, set the tin on a damp tea towel that has been dipped in hot water and then wrung well. The heat from the hot cloth will help loosen the frozen pudding. Gently ease the chocolate base away from the edge with the point of a knife. Peel off the foil and transfer the pudding to a serving plate. Leave to stand for 20 minutes.

While the pudding is standing, warm the sauce through gently until hot, stirring occasionally. Drizzle the sauce over the ice cream and serve immediately.

Silken chocolate pots with raspberries

Serves 6

An absolute classic with a white chocolate and raspberry decoration that can be frozen at the same time. My chocolate pots are rich without being heavy and will go down well with everyone.

200g plain, dark chocolate (around
   70% cocoa solids)
200ml double cream
50ml semi-skimmed milk

Decoration
50g white chocolate, broken into pieces
100ml double cream
1 tsp caster sugar
100g fresh raspberries

To FREEZE (up to 3 months)
Open freeze the raspberry and chocolate-topped puddings on a tray for 1–2 hours until solid then cover individually with foil, label and freeze.

To SERVE
Thaw the puddings at room temperature for about 1 hour, until soft. Place in the fridge to defrost if you are leaving them any longer than an hour but try to serve them within 3 hours as the raspberries are best when still a tiny bit icy in the middle.

Put the chocolate on a board and finely chop. You'll need to use a large knife and a sturdy board. Alternatively, break into chunks and blitz in a food processor on the pulse setting until chopped. Pour the cream and milk into a medium non-stick saucepan and bring slowly to the boil, stirring. Remove from the heat.

Tip the chocolate into the pan with the cream and milk and stir vigorously until the chocolate melts. Pour into 6 small espresso coffee cups, ramekins or heatproof glass tumblers and leave to cool.

To make the white chocolate topping, place the chocolate in a medium heatproof bowl. Set over a pan of gently simmering water until almost melted. Remove the bowl carefully from the pan and stir with a wooden spoon until the chocolate is smooth. Leave to cool, stirring occasionally. Do not allow it to set.

Whip the double cream for the decoration with the caster sugar until soft peaks form. Add a spoonful to each chocolate pot. Top with a few raspberries.

Using a teaspoon, drizzle the white chocolate over the raspberries and cream. Place the desserts on a small tray. Cover loosely with cling film and chill for at least an hour before serving. If leaving for longer, you may find the chocolate stiffens just a bit too much, so it is worth taking the puddings out of the fridge around 30 minutes before serving.

Bakewell pudding

Serves 8–10

Bakewell tart or pudding – this deep-filled dessert is perfect after Sunday lunch or served in slices with a cup of tea. The golden puff pastry makes a delicious flaky base topped with a moist almondy filling. You will need a roughly 3.5cm deep, 25cm loose-based fluted tart tin. If you don't have one the right size, a small roasting tin will work well but you will need to adjust the cooking times slightly.

500g block puff pastry,
   thawed if frozen
1–2 tbsp plain flour, for rolling

Filling
200g well-softened butter

200g ground almonds
200g caster sugar
50g self-raising flour
4 medium eggs
150g raspberry jam
15g flaked almonds

To FREEZE (up to 3 months)
Cool the cooked pudding completely then remove it carefully from the tin and double wrap in foil. Label and freeze.

To SERVE
To serve cold, unwrap the pudding and transfer to a serving plate. Cover loosely and thaw at room temperature for 2–3 hours. To serve hot, return the pudding to its tin. Put on a baking tray and cover loosely with foil. Bake from frozen in a preheated oven at 180°C/Fan 160°C/Gas 4 for about 30 minutes or until hot throughout.

Preheat the oven to 200°C/Fan 180°C/Gas 6. Place the pastry on a lightly floured surface and press the corners towards the middle to make a slightly more rounded shape without loosing the layers too much. Make three indentations down the length of the pastry with a rolling pin. They only need to be around 5mm deep but will help ensure you are able to roll the pastry evenly.

Roll the pastry out until around 3mm thick and as round as you can make it. Lift and turn the pastry every now and then. Lift the pastry over the rolling pin and gently lower into a fluted tart tin, there is no need to grease first. Press firmly into the base and sides. Prick the base lightly with a fork. Trim the edges with a sharp, horizontally held knife.

Put the butter, ground almonds, sugar, flour and eggs in a food processor and blend until smooth. Alternatively, put them in a large mixing bowl and beat well with a wooden spoon or an electric whisk.

Spoon the jam into the uncooked base and use the back of a spoon to spread it gently and evenly right up to the edges. Spoon all the almond mixture on top of the jam, spreading it around the outside before working towards the middle of the pastry case. Smooth the surface and sprinkle with the flaked almonds.

Bake for 30 minutes. Reduce the oven temperature to 180°C/Fan 160°C/Gas 4 and cook for a further 20–25 minutes or until the filling is firm and nicely risen and the pastry is golden brown. Test the filling is cooked by inserting a skewer into the centre of the pudding– it should come out clean. Cover the tart with a piece of foil if it begins to overbrown before the filling is ready.

There's no doubt about it, most cakes and cookies freeze brilliantly. I always keep at least one cake and maybe a few scones or muffins and some cookies in the freezer. This way there is always something sweet to offer friends if they drop round for a cuppa. What's more, making cakes for the freezer is a great way to occupy the kids at the weekend.

If you're baking a cake anyway, it's not much bother to make two cakes so you can serve one right away and pop the other in the freezer for another day. Using your freezer also means that you can make cakes for parties and self-catered holidays well ahead of time, leaving you more time to get ready and less time in the kitchen frantically baking.

Most large cakes take 2–3 hours to thaw and individual slices are usually ready to eat in less than an hour. All kinds of sponge freeze well – there's no real point in freezing rich fruitcakes as they keep well anyway. You can freeze sponge bases separately and decorate them later or sandwich them with butter icing so they are ready to serve as soon as they have thawed. I have read that whisked sponges aren't suitable for freezing but I've never had a problem with mine. Scones are simple to make and freeze and I find that they taste just as good as freshly baked once warmed through for a few seconds in the microwave.

Cakes don't just have to be served at teatime. Squidgy home-made brownies are a great pudding when teamed up with vanilla ice cream from the freezer, and my roll around lemon sponge makes a delicious summery dessert scattered with fresh or frozen raspberries. I can guarantee that no one will ever guess you only took it out of the freezer that morning.

Cookies and shortbread can be frozen after baking too, so you can just take out what you need and thaw for around 20–30 minutes before serving – perfect for kids' home-time snacks. I also freeze stacks of uncooked cookies ready to bake from frozen when I want them soft and chewy. It's almost no effort and the house is filled with the mouth-watering smell of warm baking biscuits.

CAKES &
COOKIES

Rainy day coconut and lime drizzle cake

Makes 9 squares

Baking is the perfect occupation for a cold or rainy weekend when you don't want to venture too far from home. This cake can be cut into squares so what's not eaten immediately can be wrapped up and tucked away in the freezer for another time. Cut your butter into cubes and leave it to soften at room temperature and you'll find it will blend much more easily.

Sponge
175g well-softened butter,
   plus extra for greasing
175g caster sugar
3 medium eggs
150g self-raising flour
65g desiccated coconut
finely grated zest of 2 limes

Topping
150g caster sugar
freshly squeezed juice of 2 limes
3 tbsp desiccated coconut

To FREEZE (up to 3 months)
Open freeze the completed cake on a small baking tray for one hour then wrap tightly in foil. Label and freeze. Alternatively, cut into 9 squares and wrap tightly in foil. Label and freeze.

To SERVE
Unwrap the whole cake as soon as it is taken from the freezer and transfer to a plate or cake stand. Leave to thaw at room temperature for 2–3 hours before serving. Individual pieces of cake will take under an hour to thaw.

To make the cake, preheat the oven to 190°C/Fan 170°C/Gas 5. Butter a 20cm square loose-based cake tin and line the base with baking parchment. If you don't have a square tin the right size, use a roughly 23cm round cake tin instead.

Put the butter, sugar, eggs, flour, coconut and lime zest in a food processor or food mixer and blend or beat until well combined, thick and creamy. Do not over blend or the cake will be heavy rather than light. If you don't have a food mixer, simply put all the ingredients in a bowl and beat hard with a wooden spoon until creamy and soft.

Spoon the mixture into the prepared tin and smooth the surface with the back of a spoon. Bake in the centre of the oven for 25–30 minutes or until well risen, pale golden brown and just beginning to shrink back from the sides of the tin.

Remove from the oven and leave to cool for 5 minutes before running a knife around the edge of the cake and turning it out onto a wire rack. Peel off the baking parchment and carefully tip the right way up again. Make around 30–40 holes in the cake with a skewer.

Mix the sugar and lime juice in a small bowl and spoon half of it over the cake while still warm. Allow the mixture to run into the holes made by the skewer and down the sides of the cake. Leave for 5 minutes then pour or spread the rest of the sugary lime juice very slowly over the top. Sprinkle with the coconut and leave to stand and set for 30–60 minutes before serving.

Quick mix carrot cake with creamy orange frosting

Serves 12

A good carrot cake with a cream cheese topping always goes down a treat. This one not only tastes fantastic but is also very quick and easy to make – you don't even need a mixer. I've found that the moistness of the cake really lends itself to freezing and once the soft cheese has been mixed with butter and icing sugar it's stable enough to freeze for several weeks. Break the pecan nuts with your fingers rather than a knife to get good chunky pieces.

4 medium carrots (about 250g
   unpeeled weight)
3 large eggs
200ml sunflower oil, plus extra
   for greasing
125g soft light brown sugar
200g self-raising flour
100g sultanas
100g pecan nuts, roughly broken
finely grated zest of 1 orange
1 tsp ground cinnamon

1 tsp finely grated nutmeg
1½ tsp baking powder

Creamy orange frosting
125g icing sugar, sifted
75g softened unsalted butter
200g full-fat soft cheese, such as
   Philadelphia
finely grated zest of ½ large orange
25g pecan nuts, roughly broken

To FREEZE (up to 1 month)
Open freeze the completed cake on a small baking tray for 2 hours then wrap tightly in foil. Label and freeze.

To SERVE
Unwrap the cake as soon as it is taken from the freezer and put it on a plate or cake stand. Leave to thaw for about 3 hours before serving and pop into the fridge after the first hour.

Preheat the oven to 190°C/Fan 170°C/Gas 5. Grease a 20cm square, loose-based cake tin with oil and line the base with baking parchment. If you don't have a square tin this size, use a 23cm round tin instead.

Peel the carrots and grate them until you have 200g of grated carrot. Use your grater on a medium-fine side rather than coarse for the best texture – the carrot should be in thin shreds.

Beat the eggs in a large bowl with a large whisk. Add the sunflower oil and sugar and whisk until well combined. Stir in the grated carrots. Add the flour, sultanas, pecan nuts, orange zest, spices and baking powder. Stir together until just combined. Pour the mixture into the prepared cake tin.

Bake in the centre of the oven for 28–30 minutes or until the cake is well risen and feels springy to the touch. It should be just beginning to shrink back from the sides of the tin. Leave to cool in the tin for 5 minutes then turn out and remove the baking parchment. Turn the right way up and leave to cool on a wire rack. Transfer to a serving plate.

To make the frosting, combine the icing sugar with the butter in a bowl. Beat together with a large wooden spoon until light and creamy. Add the cheese and orange zest and beat until smooth. Spread the frosting over the cake and sprinkle with the remaining pecan nuts.

Pecan coffee cake

Serves 12

This deliciously moist pecan nut and coffee cake pleases every time and despite its generous size needs only 3 hours to thaw. It's very similar to a traditional coffee and walnut cake but I often find walnuts taste bitter and prefer the caramel-like flavour and crunch of pecans.

2 tbsp instant coffee
1 tbsp just-boiled water
65g pecan nuts
225g well-softened butter,
    plus extra for greasing
225g caster sugar
4 medium eggs
225g self-raising flour

1 tsp baking powder

Icing
2 tsp instant coffee
2 tsp just-boiled water
150g softened butter, cubed
350g icing sugar, sifted
20 pecan nuts

To FREEZE (up to 3 months)
Open freeze the completed cake on a small baking tray for 2 hours then wrap tightly in foil. Label and freeze.

To SERVE
Unwrap the cake as soon as it is taken from the freezer and put it on a plate or cake stand. Leave to thaw for 2–3 hours before serving.

To make the cake, preheat the oven to 190°C/Fan 170°C/Gas 5. Grease 2 x 20cm loose-based sandwich tins (the shallow ones) and line the bases with baking parchment. Spoon the coffee for the cake into a mug and stir in the water until dissolved. Leave to cool.

Put the 65g pecan nuts in a food processor and blitz to form fairly fine crumbs. Tip the crumbs into a bowl. Put the butter, sugar, eggs, flour, baking powder and coffee mixture in the food processor and blend on the pulse setting until well combined, thick and creamy. Add the blitzed pecans to the batter and mix until just combined. If you don't have a food processor, finely chop the nuts, tip all the ingredients into a large mixing bowl and beat with an electric whisk or wooden spoon until thoroughly combined.

Spoon the mixture evenly into the tins and smooth the surface. Bake on the same shelf in the centre of the oven for 23–25 minutes or until well risen and just beginning to shrink back from the sides of the tin. Remove the tins from the oven and leave to cool for 5 minutes before carefully turning them out onto a wire rack. Peel off the baking parchment and leave to cool completely.

To make the icing, dissolve the coffee in the water and leave to cool. Put the butter in a food processor, or mixing bowl, add the icing sugar and add the coffee mixture. Beat until the icing is smooth and creamy.

Place one of the sponges on a plate or cake stand and spread with half the coffee icing. Top with the second sponge and spread with the remaining icing. Decorate with the pecan nuts. Leave to stand for at least an hour before serving to allow the icing to become a little firmer.

Rich chocolate truffle cake

Serves 10–12

A superb centrepiece and showstopper for any party or celebration. Amazingly, this rich, dark chocolatey cake can be frozen with all the decorations in place, so it makes a fantastic freezer standby. For a more casual appearance, try topping with chocolate curls or drizzle with melted white chocolate instead. Psst… without the truffles, it also makes a delicious hot chocolate fudge cake, sliced into wedges and heated for a few seconds in the microwave until soft and gooey.

50g cocoa powder
6 tbsp just-boiled water
225g well-softened butter, plus extra
   for greasing
225g caster sugar
4 large eggs
225g self-raising flour
1 tsp baking powder

Chocolate icing
400g plain dark chocolate (around
   70% cocoa solids), broken into pieces
450ml double cream

Decoration
12 chocolate truffles, dark, white,
   milk chocolate or a mixture

To FREEZE (up to 3 months)
Open freeze the decorated cake on a small baking tray for 3 hours then wrap tightly in foil. Label and freeze in a rigid container.

To **SERVE**
Unwrap the cake as soon as it is taken from the freezer and put on a plate or cake stand. Leave to thaw at room temperature for 3–4 hours before serving.

Preheat the oven to 190°C/Fan 170°C/Gas 5. Grease 2 x 20cm loose-based sandwich tins and line the bases with baking parchment. Put the cocoa powder into a bowl and stir in the water to make a smooth, fairly thick liquid.

Place the butter, sugar, eggs, flour, baking powder and cocoa paste in a food processor and blend until thick and creamy. Do not allow to over blend or the cake will be heavy rather than light. If you don't have a food processor, simply put all the ingredients in a bowl and beat hard with a wooden spoon until creamy and soft.

Spoon the mixture evenly into the prepared tins and smooth the surface. Bake on the same shelf in the centre of the oven for 23–25 minutes or until well risen and beginning to shrink away from the sides of the tins.

Remove the tins from the oven and leave to cool for 5 minutes before running a knife around the edge of the cakes and turning out onto a wire rack. Peel off the baking parchment and leave to cool completely. When the cakes are completely cold, horizontally cut through each one very carefully with a serrated bread knife to make 4 thin sponges.

To make the icing, place the chocolate in a heatproof bowl set over a pan of gently simmering water until almost fully melted. Remove the bowl from the water using an oven cloth and stir until smooth. Leave to cool for 5 minutes then gradually stir in the double cream until the mixture is smooth and glossy.

Place one of the sponges on a plate or cake stand, cut side up. Spread with roughly a fifth of the chocolate icing – just enough to cover the sponge. Use a paddling motion with a palette knife or rubber spatula for the best result, trying to prevent the sponge from lifting.

Cover with a second cake, cut side up. Spread with more chocolate icing and repeat the layers once more. Finish with the final cake, cut side down. By this stage you should have layered 4 cakes with chocolate icing between 3 of them. Spread the remaining icing to all over the top and sides of the cakes to cover the cake completely. Decorate with the chocolate truffles and leave to stand for one hour before serving.

Sticky ginger cake

Serves 12

Using ground spice and chopped stem ginger gives this cake the heat of ginger along with a sticky sweetness that makes it the perfect cake to go with a cup of tea. If you've always enjoyed a McVitie's Jamaica Ginger Cake, you'll love this home-made version and what's more, it doesn't require any special skills to make it. Heat slices in the microwave from frozen and serve with double cream or ice cream for an impromptu pudding.

250g self-raising flour
1 tsp bicarbonate of soda
5 tsp ground ginger
1 tsp ground cinnamon
5 stem ginger balls in syrup
  (roughly 100g), drained

125g butter, plus extra for greasing
125g dark muscovado sugar
100g black treacle
150g golden syrup
200ml semi-skimmed milk
2 large eggs, beaten

To FREEZE (up to 3 months)
Turn the cake out of the tin and remove the baking parchment. Wrap the cooled cake tightly in foil. Label and freeze in a freezer bag. If preferred, the cake can be cut into wedges and frozen in individual portions.

To SERVE
Unwrap the cake as soon as it is taken from the freezer and put on a plate or cake stand. Leave to thaw at room temperature for 3–4 hours before serving. Individual slices will take less than an hour to thaw.

Preheat the oven to 180°C/Fan 160°C/Gas 4. Grease a 24cm round loose-based cake tin and line the base with baking parchment. Put the flour, bicarbonate of soda and spices in a large heatproof mixing bowl. Finely chop the stem ginger and add to the bowl with the dry ingredients and toss lightly together. Make a well in the centre.

Put the butter, sugar, treacle and golden syrup in a medium saucepan. Melt together over a low heat, stirring regularly until the sugar dissolves. Increase the heat a little and simmer gently for a minute, while stirring.

Remove the pan from the heat and gradually stir in the milk and then the beaten eggs. Pour slowly into the flour mixture, stirring constantly with a wooden spoon to form a thick batter. If there are still a few floury lumps, give it a good whisk but don't forget that the grated ginger will stop the cake batter looking completely smooth.

Pour the mixture into the prepared tin. Bake in the centre of the oven for 45 minutes or until the cake is well risen and a skewer inserted into the centre comes out clean. Serve warm or leave to cool in the tin.

Paddington bear muffins

Makes 12

With these muffins in the freezer, even when time in the morning is short, you can still be sure of giving everyone a filling and delicious start to the day. Pop them in the microwave to warm up and eat them at home or grab one direct from the freezer to take to work or school and by mid-morning, it will have thawed and be ready to eat. The easy-to-mix basic muffin batter makes a good base for lots of different ingredients, so try adding chocolate drops, dried cranberries or any of your family's favourite flavourings.

100g butter
275g self-raising flour
1½ tsp bicarbonate of soda
125g golden caster sugar
100g sultanas

finely grated zest of 1 orange
150ml full-fat natural yogurt
2 large eggs
12 tsp orange marmalade

To FREEZE (up to 3 months)
Put the cooled muffins into 2–3 labelled freezer bags, remove as much air as possible, seal and freeze.

To SERVE
To serve cold, thaw at room temperature for 1–2 hours. To serve warm, take a frozen muffin and put it on a heatproof plate. Microwave the muffin on HIGH for 45–60 seconds or until hot. Leave to cool for a while before eating as the marmalade will be very hot. Reheat as many muffins as you need in the same way. Reseal the bag and return any unused muffins to the freezer.

Preheat the oven to 200°C/Fan 180°C/Gas 6. Line a 12-hole muffin tin with paper cases, or use a greased silicone muffin tray. Melt the butter in a small pan over a low heat, pour it into a mixing bowl then set it aside to cool for a few minutes.

Sift the flour and bicarbonate of soda into a large bowl and stir in the sugar, sultanas and orange zest. Make a well in the centre.

Add the yogurt and eggs to the cooled melted butter and mix with a metal whisk or electric beaters until well combined. Stir the wet mixture into the dry ingredients with a large metal spoon until mixed.

Divide the batter between the muffin holes. Top each uncooked muffin with a teaspoon of marmalade. Bake for 20 minutes or until well risen and golden brown.

Serve warm or turn out of the tin and leave to cool on a wire rack. Take care when you serve the muffins as the marmalade will remain hot for some time.

Fantastic freezer cookies

Makes 16

Take a handful of uncooked cookies from the freezer and place on a tray in a preheated oven and 15 minutes later you could be enjoying delicious, chewy, crunchy biscuits. When making the dough, you can leave it plain or knead in any of your favourite dried fruits, chocolate or nuts. I've given a few variaitons below to get you started.

To FREEZE (up to 4 months)
Stack the unbaked cookies in piles of 4 or 5, interleaving between each one with small squares of baking parchment or easy-leave. Wrap each stack tightly in foil, label and freeze. Alternatively, pack cooked biscuits in a freezer-proof container, seal, cover and freeze.

To SERVE
Take a stack of the frozen unbaked cookies out of the freezer and remove as many cookies as you need. Place on a baking tray and bake in a preheated oven at 180°C/Fan 160°C/Gas 4 for 14–16 minutes. Rewrap the unused dough tightly and return to the freezer.

Alternatively, thaw baked, frozen biscuits at room temperature for around 30 minutes before serving.

200g well-softened butter
300g golden caster sugar
2 large egg yolks, beaten
1 ½ tsp vanilla extract
350g plain flour
1 tsp baking powder

White chocolate and cranberry
Add 150g roughly chopped white chocolate, or white chocolate chips, and 100g sweetened dried cranberries.

Triple chocolate chip
Swap 25g of the flour with sifted cocoa powder and add 100g roughly chopped white chocolate and 100g roughly chopped plain dark chocolate.

Mint chocolate chip
Add 110g very roughly chopped bubbly mint chocolate, such as Aero.

Pecan and stem ginger chip
Add 100g roughly chopped pecan nuts and 3 balls of chopped stem ginger.

To make the cookie dough, put the butter and sugar in a large bowl and beat with an electric whisk or a wooden spoon until pale. Add the egg yolks a little at a time, beating well between each addition.

Beat in the vanilla followed by the flour and baking powder. Stir in any of the flavouring ingredients listed here, using your hands when the cookie dough gets too stiff to stir. If you prefer, divide the dough in 2 and then flavour each half differently.

Line a large baking tray with baking parchment. Divide the dough into 16 pieces and roll into small balls. Flatten until around 1.5cm thick and 8cm wide. Place 4–6 cookies on the baking tray, spacing them evenly apart as they will spread a little.

To cook now, preheat the oven to 180°C/Fan 160°C/Gas 4. Bake the cookies in the centre of the oven for 12–14 minutes until lightly browned around the edges. Allow them to cool for a couple of minutes then transfer to a wire rack. Continue cooking the remaining cookie dough in the same way. Serve just warm and chewy or cold and crisp. The biscuits can be stored in an airtight tin for up to 7 days.

Roll around lemon sponge

Serves 8

This is a lovely light and fluffy sponge, filled with a zesty, rich lemon cream. If you fancy a more traditional Swiss roll, flavour the sponge with half a teaspoon of vanilla extract and fill with raspberry jam and buttercream icing instead.

softened butter, for greasing
3 large eggs
115g caster sugar, plus 4 tbsp
finely grated zest of 1 lemon
115g plain flour

Lemon cream
250ml double cream
150g good-quality lemon curd

To FREEZE (up to 2 months)
Open freeze the cake on a small baking tray for 2 hours then wrap tightly in foil. Label and freeze in a freezer bag.

To SERVE
Unwrap the cake as soon as it is taken from the freezer and put it on a serving platter or cake stand. Leave to thaw for 2–3 hours before slicing and serving.

Grease the base and sides of a 33 x 23cm Swiss roll tin and line the base with a sheet of baking parchment. Butter the paper lightly too. Preheat the oven to 200°C/Fan 180°C/Gas 6.

Put the eggs, sugar and lemon zest in a heatproof bowl and place over a pan of gently simmering water. Using an electric whisk, mix until the mixture is pale, creamy and thick. Make sure you keep the wire of the whisk well away from the hob as they have been known to melt!

Carefully remove the bowl from the heat using an oven cloth and continue whisking for a further 5 minutes. Sift over half the flour and, using a large metal spoon, lightly fold into the egg mixture. It's important to use gentle, quick movements to retain as much air as possible in the batter.

Sift over the remaining flour and fold in very lightly. Take a large metal whisk and draw through the batter 3–4 times – this will help get rid of any floury lumps that might have formed. Pour the mixture into the prepared tin and gently spread into the corners with a rubber spatula. Bake for 10 minutes or until the cake is well risen and is just beginning to shrink away from the sides of the tin. Don't let it overcook or it will dry out and become difficult to roll.

While the cake is cooking, place a damp tea towel on the work surface and cover with a sheet of baking parchment. Dredge with the 4 tablespoons of sugar – this will help stop the outside of the sponge sticking. Working quickly, turn the cake out onto the sugared paper and carefully remove the lining paper. Using a sharp knife, cut off the crusty edges from the 2 long sides.

Make a cut a third of the way through the cake, about 2.5cm up from one short edge, working from one side to the other. Roll the Swiss roll from the cut end, starting with a tight turn to make a good round shape and keeping the sugared paper inside the roll. Set on a wire rack and leave to cool.

To make the filling, whip the cream until soft peaks form. Gently fold in the lemon curd. When the cake is completely cold, carefully unroll and remove the sugared paper. Do not flatten out or the cake could crack. Using a dessertspoon, spread the inside of the cake with the lemon cream to within 1cm of the edges. Slowly re-roll the cake to enclose the filling. Lift very gently onto a serving platter and cut into thick slices to serve.

The perfect jam and buttercream sponge

Serves 12

The classic home-made Victoria sandwich cake, the must-have of cake stalls and tea shops up and down the country. Made in advance, it will sit very happily in your freezer for up to two months – but no one will ever guess. You can also freeze the cake in slices for lunchboxes and picnics. It will be completely thawed in under an hour.

225g well-softened butter, plus extra
    for greasing
225g caster sugar
4 medium eggs
250g self-raising flour
1 tsp baking powder
½ tsp vanilla extract

Icing and filling
150g softened butter, cubed
½ tsp vanilla extract
300g icing sugar, plus extra
    for dusting
½ x 454g jar of strawberry, raspberry
    or blackberry jam

To FREEZE (up to 3 months)
Open freeze the cake on a small baking tray for one hour then wrap tightly in foil. Label and freeze in a freezer bag.

To SERVE
Unwrap the cake as soon as it is taken from the freezer and put on a plate or cake stand. Leave to thaw at room temperature for 2–3 hours before serving. Individual slices will take less than an hour to thaw.

To make the cake, preheat the oven to 190°C/Fan 170°C/Gas 5. Grease 2 x 20cm loose-based sandwich tins (the shallow ones) and line the bases with discs of baking parchment. Put the butter, sugar, eggs, flour, baking powder and vanilla in a food processor or food mixer and blend or beat until well combined, thick and creamy. Be careful not to over blend or the cake will be heavy.

Spoon the mixture evenly into the prepared tins and smooth the surface. Bake on the same shelf in the centre of the oven for 23–25 minutes or until well risen and just beginning to shrink back from the sides of the tin.

Remove the tins from the oven and leave to cool for 5 minutes before running a knife around the edge of the cakes and turning them out onto a wire rack. Peel off the baking parchment and leave to cool completely.

To make the filling, put the butter in a food processor or mixing bowl, add the vanilla extract and sift the icing sugar on top. Blend or beat until smooth and creamy. Place one of the sponges on a plate or cake stand, spread with the buttercream filling, using a palette knife or rubber spatula and taking care to keep contact with the cake so the sponge doesn't lift.

Stir the jam to loosen and spoon onto the base of the second cake. Spread almost all the way to the edges. Sandwich the cakes carefully together and dust with sifted icing sugar.

Doubly delicious scones

Makes 12

Doubly delicious because they rise beautifully and contain hidden dried fruit. Doubly useful because they work just as well as a modern-day rushing out-the-door, warmed-in-the microwave breakfast, as they do split. Serve with clotted cream and jam for a traditional all-the-time-in-the-world cream tea.

100g butter, plus extra for greasing
500g self-raising flour, plus extra
   for rolling
50g mixed dried fruit (optional)
40g caster sugar

300ml full-fat or semi-skimmed milk,
   plus extra for brushing

To serve
butter, clotted cream and strawberry jam

To FREEZE (up to 3 months)
Transfer the cooled scones to a freezer bag. Squeeze out as much air as possible, seal, label and freeze. Alternatively, wrap individual scones tightly in foil, place in a freezer bag, label and freeze.

To SERVE
Take out the number of scones that are required and return the rest to the freezer immediately. Place the frozen scones on a baking tray and reheat in a preheated oven at 190°C/Fan 170°C/Gas 5 for 6–8 minutes. Alternatively, thaw the scones at room temperature for 20–30 minutes then warm in a microwave on HIGH for 20–30 seconds.

Preheat the oven to 220°C/Fan 200°C/Gas 7. Grease a large baking tray with butter. In a large mixing bowl, rub the butter and flour together, using your fingertips, until the mixture resembles fine breadcrumbs. Stir in the dried fruit, if using, and the sugar.

Make a well in the centre of the flour and slowly add the milk, stirring continuously until the mixture comes together and forms a light, spongy dough. Turn out onto a well-floured surface and knead lightly until smooth and soft. Press the dough with the palms of your hands or a rolling pin until it is no less than 2.5cm thick.

Using a 6cm plain biscuit cutter, cut rounds from the dough and place them on the prepared baking tray, spacing them well apart. Cut the dough cleanly and avoid squidging or dragging for the best rise. Re-knead and roll the trimmings and cut 2 more rounds from the dough.

Brush the tops of the scones with a little milk or beaten egg and bake in the centre of the oven for 13–15 minutes or until well-risen and golden brown. Remove from the oven and set aside to cool for a few minutes.

To serve, cut the scones in half, spread with butter and clotted cream and top with strawberry jam. Eat warm or cold.

Party cupcakes

Makes 24

These useful little cakes can be frozen with their decoration in place, saving you a load of hassle on the day of a party. I think the balance of icing to sponge is just right as they are not at all sickly like most bought cupcakes. Decorate with jelly sweets to freeze complete or wait until thawed and adorn with Smarties, chocolate buttons or fresh raspberries. Needing only an hour to thaw, they can soon be piled high on a tiered cake stand and the party can begin.

175g well-softened butter,
    plus extra for greasing
225g caster sugar
3 large eggs
1 tsp vanilla extract or finely
    grated zest of 1 lemon
300g self-raising flour, sifted
½ tsp baking powder

200ml semi-skimmed milk
sweets or fresh berries, for decorating

Lemon butter icing
250g well softened butter
finely grated zest of 1 lemon
2 tsp fresh lemon juice
500g icing sugar, plus extra
    for dusting

To FREEZE (up to 3 months)
Open freeze the iced cakes, without the decoration, on a baking tray for 2 hours. Transfer to a large lidded freezer-proof container, interleaving with easy-leave or baking parchment. Label and freeze.

To SERVE
Take as many cakes as you need from the freezer and put them on a plate or cake stand. Leave to thaw at room temperature for about an hour before decorating, if necessary, and serve.

Preheat the oven to 190°C/Fan 170°C/Gas 5. Line 2 x 12-hole muffin tins with paper cup cases. Put the butter in a saucepan and melt very gently. Remove from the heat and leave to cool for 10 minutes.

Put the sugar and eggs in a large bowl and beat with an electric whisk until very pale and thick. Add the vanilla or lemon zest, flour, baking powder, cooled melted butter and a dash of the milk. Whisk until just combined.

Gradually add the rest of the milk, whisking constantly until the batter is smooth – about the texture of custard. Leave to stand for about 10 minutes. Spoon a heaped dessertpoon of the mixture evenly into each cake case.

Bake the cakes one tray at a time in the centre of the oven for 16–18 minutes or until well risen and springy to the touch. Take out of the oven and leave to cool for 5 minutes before transferring to a wire rack. Leave to cool completely. You can cook both trays of cakes at the same time, but the lower tray will need to be left in the oven for a few minutes longer.

To make the icing, put the softened butter into a food processor, or mixing bowl, add the lemon zest and juice; sift the icing sugar on top. Blend or beat until smooth and creamy. Spoon into a large piping bag fitted with a star nozzle.

Pipe the butter icing onto each of the cakes. If you don't have a piping bag, spread the icing onto the cakes with a dessertspoon or rubber spatula instead. Decorate with sweets or fresh berries and serve.

Squidgy chocolate brownies

Makes 16–20 squares

Rich and gooey, the perfect chocolatey hit. Fantastic served warm and melted with vanilla ice cream or broken into chunks and muddled through ice cream for a sundae. For a crunchier treat, add some pecan nuts. My daughter Jess, who also loves to make these brownies, leaves out the plain chocolate. Her version is less rich but just as delicious.

250g butter, plus extra
    for greasing
400g golden caster sugar
4 large eggs
75g plain flour

50g cocoa powder
150g plain dark chocolate (around
    70% cocoa solids) or milk chocolate
100g pecan nuts, roughly broken
    (optional)

Preheat the oven to 190°C/Fan 170°C/Gas 5. Lightly grease a 20 x 30cm rectangular tin and line the base and sides with a large sheet of baking parchment. If you don't have a tin of exactly the right dimensions, don't worry, any tin will do, even a smallish roasting tin. As long as the mixture is about 2cm deep in the tin, the cooking time will stay the same.

Put the butter in a large saucepan and place over a low heat until just melted. Remove the butter from the heat and stir in the sugar until well combined. Whisk the eggs together in a large bowl. Gradually add the eggs to the butter and sugar, beating well with a wooden spoon in between each addition.

Place the flour and cocoa powder in a sieve and sift into the egg mixture. Beat hard with a wooden spoon until thoroughly combined. Leave to cool for 10 minutes. This will prevent the chocolate chunks melting too quickly when they are added to the batter.

Put the chocolate on a board and cut into chunky pieces with a knife. You want the chunks to be roughly 1.5cm. Pour the cooled cake batter into the prepared tin and spread into all the corners. Scatter the chocolate pieces and pecan nuts if using, over the batter and place the tin in the oven straight away before the chocolate and nuts have a chance to sink.

Bake the brownie in the centre of the oven for 30–35 minutes until it appears crusty on the surface and lightly cooked inside. Try not to overcook as the cake will become spongy rather than gooey.

Remove from the oven and leave to cool for 5 minutes. To serve warm, cut into squares or rectangles or leave to cool completely if serving cold or freezing.

To FREEZE (up to 3 months)
Cut the cooled brownie into squares or rectangles and wrap each one tightly in foil. Label and freeze.

Alternatively, transfer a batch to a large lidded freezer-proof container, interleaving with easy-leave or baking parchment. Label and freeze in a large freezer bag.

To SERVE
Unwrap individual brownies and thaw at room temperature for about 30 minutes. Reheat individually from frozen on a suitable plate in the microwave on HIGH for around 30 seconds.

When my children were younger I used to make all the sandwiches for the week's packed lunches on Sunday night and put them in the freezer. **Every day I took a** couple out of the freezer and by lunchtime they were perfectly defrosted. Maybe they weren't quite as good as freshly made and I wouldn't want to freeze them for more than a week or two, but they were very helpful at the time.

Now I am more likely like to freeze a selection of fillings so there's always something on hand for a sandwich. I also keep a selection of fruity lunchbox bars to nibble on that are more nutritious than chocolate and much more sustaining.

For times when you want something other than a lunchbox sandwich, I've provided recipes that are brilliant for those of us who are always on the move.

Home-made soup makes an ideal take-to-work meal and can be transported hot in a thermos or heated up later if you have a microwave in your office.

A portion of stew is a wonderful treat on a cold winter day and can be microwaved or reheated at work. In the summer, try taking little pots of frozen dips that you can enjoy with some crisp bread or vegetables at your desk.

Don't forget that leftovers can also make excellent lunches. If you have extra casserole or chilli con carne one night but don't fancy eating it again the next day, pop it in the freezer for a few days and enjoy it later in the week.

FOOD ON THE MOVE

To FREEZE (up to 3 months)
Cool the soup completely then ladle
into 4 rigid containers or labelled
freezer bags. Cover or seal, label
and freeze.

To SERVE
Thaw the soup in the fridge
overnight. Reheat in a saucepan or
transfer portions into a microwavable container and cook for
about 3 minutes on HIGH or until
piping hot throughout.

Warming chicken stoup

Makes 4 servings

A stoup is a combination of stew and soup – and that's just what you get from this eclectic mix of ingredients. Warming and fragrant, it's perfect for reheating at work or served as a filling lunch at home. I wouldn't advise keeping it in a flask as it contains chicken.

4 large, ripe tomatoes (around 400g)
2 tbsp olive oil
1 medium onion, finely chopped
2 celery sticks, very finely chopped
25g chunk fresh root ginger, peeled and finely grated
1 tsp ground cumin
3 tbsp tomato purée
small pinch saffron strands

1 tsp flaked sea salt
1.5 litres chicken stock (fresh or made with 1 cube)
400g can chickpeas, drained and rinsed
2 boneless, skinless chicken breasts
140g vermicelli pasta nests or fine egg noodles
1 small bunch coriander (roughly 20g), leaves roughly chopped
freshly ground black pepper

Make a small cross incision at the base of each tomato and put together in a large heatproof bowl. Cover with just-boiled water and leave to stand for one minute. Drain the tomatoes and put on a chopping board to cool.

Heat the oil in a large non-stick saucepan and fry the onion, celery and ginger very gently for 10 minutes, stirring regularly and adding the cumin for the last minute of cooking time. While the vegetables are cooking, slip the skins off the tomatoes and discard along with the green stem end. Chop the tomato flesh fairly finely, discarding the cores.

Tip the chopped tomatoes and seeds into the saucepan with the onions and add the tomato purée, saffron, salt and stock. Bring to a simmer and stir in the chickpeas and plenty of ground black pepper. Nestle the chicken breasts into the soup mixture and return to a simmer. Partially cover with a lid and cook gently for 10 minutes.

Take the chicken out of the pan and allow it to cool for a short while. Loosely cover the soup again with a lid and cook for a further 20 minutes, stirring occasionally. Add the vermicelli pasta or noodles to the pan and cook for 5 minutes more, stirring regularly until softened. Add a little extra water if the pasta absorbs too much of the liquid.

As soon as the chicken is cool enough to handle, tear into shreds. Add the chicken to the soup, scatter over the chopped coriander and stir well. Simmer gently for a couple of minutes, stirring regularly. Adjust seasoning to taste. Serve hot.

Spiced red lentil soup

Makes 8 servings

Comforting and warming, this spicy soup is perfect for taking with you on a cold day. Heat and pour into a flask for an instant filling and nourishing meal. Alternatively take to work in a lidded plastic container, uncover and warm through in the microwave. If you prefer a milder soup, use mild curry powder instead of medium.

25g butter
1 tbsp olive oil
2 medium onions, roughly chopped
3 medium carrots, peeled and diced
2 garlic cloves, crushed
1 tbsp medium curry powder

275g dried split red lentils
1.75 litres vegetable stock
   (made from 2 vegetable stock cubes)
flaked sea salt
freshly ground black pepper

To FREEZE (up to 4 months)
Cool the soup thoroughly then divide it between labelled zip-seal bags (see page 222) or soup 'n' sauce bags. Squeeze out as much air as possible. Seal and freeze.

Alternatively, freeze in lidded freezer-proof containers.

To SERVE
Cook from frozen by rinsing the soup bag under warm water for a few seconds then opening and transferring the contents to a large saucepan. Warm through gently until thawed, stirring regularly. Add a little extra water if the soup is a little thick. Bring to a simmer and cook for 5 minutes, while stirring.

Alternatively, thaw in the fridge overnight and either reheat in the morning to fill a flask or put in a lidded container and take it with you to reheat in a microwave.

Melt the butter with the oil in a large non-stick saucepan and fry the onions and carrots over a medium low heat for 15 minutes, stirring occasionally until softened and lightly browned (the long cooking time will help bring sweetness to the soup). Add the garlic and curry powder and cook for one minute more, stirring constantly.

Rinse the lentils well in a sieve under cold running water then drain and tip them into the pan. Add the stock and season with a pinch of salt and plenty of freshly ground black pepper.

Bring to the boil then reduce the heat to a gentle simmer and cook for 30–40 minutes, stirring regularly until the lentils are very tender and the soup is thick. Add a little extra water towards the end of the cooking time if the soup looks like it needs it. Either serve the soup fairly chunky or blitz with a stick blender until smooth.

Simple mushroom soup

Makes 8 servings

This is a great everyday soup for taking with you but can be also jazzed up with herby croutons, fried bacon pieces, a swirl of cream and a sprinkling of herbs or even a drizzle of truffle oil for a special occasion.

50g butter
2 tbsp olive oil
2 medium onions, roughly chopped
750g chestnut mushrooms
   (or portobello mushrooms for
   a darker soup)

2 large garlic cloves, crushed
1.25 litres chicken or vegetable stock
   (made with 2 stock cubes)
200ml full-fat or semi-skimmed milk
freshly ground black pepper
flaked sea salt

To FREEZE (up to 4 months)
Cool the soup thoroughly then divide it between labelled zip-seal bags (see page 222) or soup 'n' sauce bags. Squeeze out as much air as possible. Seal and freeze.

Alternatively, freeze in lidded freezer-proof containers.

To SERVE
Cook from frozen by rinsing the soup bag under warm water for a few seconds then opening and transferring the contents to a large saucepan. Warm through gently until thawed, stirring regularly. Add a little extra water if the soup is a little thick. Bring to a simmer and cook for 2 minutes, while stirring.

Alternatively, thaw in the fridge overnight and either reheat in the morning to fill a flask or put in a lidded container and take it with you and reheat in a microwave.

Melt the butter with the oil in a large non-stick saucepan. Add the onion and cook over a low heat for 10 minutes, stirring occasionally until very soft but not coloured.

Slice the mushrooms fairly thinly and add them to the pan. Cook over a high heat for 5 minutes, stirring regularly. Add the garlic and cook for a few seconds more. Season with lots of ground black pepper and a good sprinkling of flaked sea salt.

Pour over the water and add the stock cube. Bring to the boil then reduce the heat slightly and leave to simmer uncovered for 15 minutes.

Remove the pan from the heat and blitz the soup with a stick blender until very smooth. Stir in the milk, adding a little extra if required, until the perfect consistency is reached. Adjust the seasoning to taste. If you don't have a stick blender, stir in the milk then blend in a food processor or blender instead.

If eating now, reheat gently just before serving, stirring constantly until piping hot.

Roasted tomato soup

Makes 4 servings

This will be one of the simplest soups you'll ever make. It's perfect for using up tomatoes and is easy to double. Serve either hot or chilled.

1kg large, ripe tomatoes
2 medium onions
3 tbsp olive oil
1 tsp caster sugar, plus extra to taste
3 garlic cloves, very finely sliced

700ml chicken or vegetable stock
(made with 1 stock cube)
flaked sea salt
freshly ground black pepper
1–2 tbsp basil or chilli oil, or soured
    cream and a sprinkling of chives,
    to serve (optional)

Preheat the oven to 200°C/Fan 180°C/Gas 6. Cut the tomatoes in half and place them, cut side up, on a large baking tray. Peel the onions and cut each one into 6 wedges. Scatter the onion wedges over the tomatoes on a tray.

Drizzle with the oil, sprinkle with sugar, a little flaked sea salt and plenty of ground black pepper. Roast in the oven for 30 minutes or until the tomatoes are softened and juicy.

Take the tray out of the oven and scatter the garlic around the base of the tomatoes. Return to the oven for a further 10 minutes until the garlic is softened and just beginning to colour in places. Do not let the garlic burn or it will add a bitter flavour to the soup. Remove from the oven and leave to cool for 10 minutes.

Tip the contents of the baking tray into a food processer, scraping up any caramelised bits from the bottom of the tray as they will add lots of flavour. Blend until as smooth as possible. Pour the tomato and onion mixture in 3–4 batches into a fine sieve set above a medium saucepan and press with the bottom of a ladle to make a smooth purée. Discard the seeds and skins in between batches.

Stir the stock into the fresh tomato purée and season the soup with more salt and pepper if necessary. You may need to add a pinch more sugar if your tomatoes aren't particularly sweet. Cover and leave to cool.

To eat now, warm the soup over a low heat, stirring regularly until hot. Pour into bowls and top with a drizzle of basil or chilli oil, or soured cream and a scattering of snipped chives or fresh basil. If serving chilled, sieve into a serving bowl instead of a saucepan.

To FREEZE (up to 4 months)
Cool the soup thoroughly then divide between zip-seal or soup 'n' sauce bags. Squeeze out as much air as possible. Seal, label and freeze.

Alternatively, freeze in lidded freezer-proof containers.

To SERVE
Cook from frozen by transferring the contents of the bags to a large saucepan. Warm through gently until thawed, stirring regularly. Add a little extra water or milk if the soup is a little thick. Bring to a simmer and cook for 5 minutes, while stirring.

Carrot and coriander soup

Makes 6–8 servings

*A delicious blend of vibrant carrot and aromatic coriander. And so
very easy to make and freeze. I like using the combination of ground
and fresh coriander for the very best flavour.*

25g butter
1 tbsp sunflower oil
2 medium onions, roughly chopped
1kg carrots (about 9 medium ones),
    peeled and coarsely grated
2 garlic cloves, crushed
1 tbsp ground coriander

1.25 litre chicken or vegetable stock
    (made with 1 stock cube)
200ml whole or semi-skimmed milk
small bunch fresh coriander (roughly
    20g), leaves finely chopped
flaked sea salt
freshly ground black pepper

To FREEZE (up to 4 months)
Cool the soup thoroughly then
divide it between zip-seal or soup
'n' sauce bags. Squeeze out as
much air as possible. Seal, label
and freeze. Alternatively, freeze in
lidded freezer-proof containers.

To SERVE
Cook from frozen by rinsing the
soup bag under warm water for
a few seconds then opening and
transferring the contents to a large
saucepan. Warm through gently
until thawed, stirring regularly.
Add a little extra water or milk if
the soup is a little thick. Bring to
a simmer and cook for 5 minutes,
while stirring.

Alternatively, thaw in the fridge
overnight and either reheat in the
morning to fill a flask or put in a
lidded container to take with you
and reheat in a microwave.

Melt the butter with the oil in a large non-stick saucepan and gently
fry the onions for 10 minutes until softened and very lightly coloured,
stirring occasionally. Add the carrots, garlic and ground coriander and
cook for 5 minutes more, while stirring.

Pour over the stock and bring to the boil. Reduce the heat to a simmer
and cook for about 20 minutes until the carrots are very soft, stirring
occasionally. Remove from the heat.

Blitz with a stick blender until very smooth. If you don't have a stick
blender, allow the soup to cool for a few minutes then blend in a food
processor.

Stir in the milk and coriander, adding a little extra milk if required
until the perfect consistency is reached. Add salt and pepper to taste.

To eat now, reheat gently just before serving, stirring constantly.

Clever idea
If your chopping skills aren't brilliant, give the soup another whizz with the stick blender once
you've added the fresh coriander. For an even more velvety soup, pass through a fine sieve
after blending.

Extra special macaroni cheese

Makes 5 servings

The addition of chorizo, spinach and peas with a hint of spice takes this macaroni cheese from zero to hero in seconds. Perfect for weekday lunches or an easy supper, I haven't found anyone who doesn't love it.

250g dried macaroni or other short pasta shapes
100g chorizo sausage, preferably picante
65g butter, plus extra for greasing
½ medium onion, finely chopped
¼ tsp cayenne pepper
½ tsp paprika
good grating of nutmeg (about ¼ tsp)
50g plain flour

750ml milk
50g mature Cheddar cheese, coarsely grated
50g Gruyere cheese, coarsely grated
50g baby spinach leaves
100g frozen peas
18 sun-blushed tomatoes, drained (around 50g)
flaked sea salt
freshly ground black pepper

To FREEZE (up to 1 month)
Spoon the cooked but unbaked macaroni cheese from the saucepan into 5 freezer-proof containers and cool. Top with the tomato pieces and a good grinding or two of black pepper. Cover, label and freeze.

To SERVE
Thaw overnight in the fridge and pack with an ice block to take to work. Transfer to a microwaveable dish, cover with cling film and cook in the microwave on HIGH for 2 minutes. Stand for one minute then cook for a further minute until piping hot throughout.

Alternatively microwave from frozen for 5 minutes on HIGH. Stir and let stand for 2 minutes. Cook for a further 1–2 minutes on HIGH until hot.

Half-fill a large pan with water and bring to the boil. Add the pasta to the boiling water and stir well. Return to the boil and cook for 8–10 minutes or according to packet instructions, until almost tender, stirring occasionally. Drain in a colander under running water until cold.

Remove the skin from the chorizo and cut the meat into small pieces, each around 1cm. Melt the butter in a large non-stick saucepan over a low heat and fry the chopped onion for 4–5 minutes, stirring occasionally until well-softened. Add the chorizo and cook for 30–60 seconds more until it begins to release its oils.

Stir the cayenne pepper, paprika, nutmeg and flour into the onion mixture until well combined with the butter. Slowly add 600ml of the milk, stirring well between each addition. Bring the sauce to a gentle simmer and cook for 4–5 minutes, stirring regularly. Stir the grated cheeses into the sauce and cook over a low heat until melted.

Remove the pan from the heat and add the spinach leaves. Stir for a minute or so then add the remaining milk, pasta and frozen peas. Stir well and adjust the seasoning to taste. As the chorizo has lots of flavour, you may not need any additional seasoning.

To eat now, tip into a greased 1.75ml ovenproof dish, top with the tomato pieces and freshly ground black pepper. Bake in a preheated oven at 220°C/Fan oven 200°C/Gas 7 for 20–25 minutes or until bubbling and piping hot throughout.

Sandwiches, rolls and wraps

Sandwiches and rolls can freeze surprisingly well depending on the filling. I can't say they are exactly like freshly made sandwiches but if you have packed lunches for the family to prepare every day, a few standby sandwiches in the freezer will make a real difference to your life. Even freezing an assortment of sandwich fillings is worthwhile as you can always team them up with fresh bread when you are ready.

Some sandwich fillings to try

Flaked tuna in spring water or brine, drained and mixed with a little reduced-fat mayonnaise and some frozen sweetcorn.

Smoked ham and thick slices of cheese with a thin spreading of mustard, some chunky pickle or chutney.

Sliced cold roast pork used to fill thick slices of crusty granary style bread with generous spoonfuls of apple sauce.

Cold carved roast chicken or turkey with stuffing and a little cranberry sauce in crusty white bread.

Chicken tikka strips in pita bread with mango chutney and reduced fat mayonnaise with salad on the side.

Smoked salmon trimmings blitzed in a blender with lemon juice and half fat crème fraîche makes a great pâté to spread onto thin slice slices of brown bread.

I think bread rolls and thickly cut fresh granary or rustic breads work well, but you can also freeze pita bread, flat breads and wraps. I don't freeze sandwiches for too long – a week or two is enough to keep them in good condition – but sandwich fillings can be stored for a little longer. Avoid using any salad ingredients in your sandwiches as the high water content will make tomatoes, cucumbers and leafy greens soggy on thawing. Pack them into a small container to have on the side instead.

Pickles, chutneys and jam can be used in frozen sandwiches. They will taste fine once thawed but may stain the bread a little. You can always take them to work in small containers instead. I like to save those tiny jam jars that hotels use at breakfast as they are also good for small quantities of dressing.

Full-fat mayonnaise will freeze but does have a tendency to separate and become oily on thawing. However, most of the time you wouldn't really notice – not once it has been mixed into a sandwich filling – but I've discovered that reduced-fat mayonnaise freezes more successfully, so you can always try that as an alternative.

Spread the bread or wrap with a thin layer of butter first to stop fillings making the bread soggy. Fill the sandwich or rolls and wrap tightly in cling film or foil. Label and freeze. Pack into a lunchbox chilled with an ice block to thaw slowly. At room temperature, most sandwiches will only take around an hour to thaw.

Prepare toasties and paninis with sliced salamis or ham with cheese and a dribble of fresh pesto sauce if you have the facilities to heat them up at work. Or if you are grabbing a quick lunch at home, you can pop them into a sandwich toaster or cook them under the grill or in a griddle pan on the hob.

Take frozen dips such as smoked salmon blini topping (see page 82), smoked mackerel pâté (page 75) or guacamole (page 81) in small freezer-proof containers and serve with bought melba toast or crisp breads that you can keep at work, or thin slices of crisp bread or bruschetta that you can have ready in the freezer.

Falafel with minted yogurt sauce

Makes 20

These falafel make a really good addition to any picnic or packed lunch and can be eaten hot or cold. The yogurt dip is very easy to whip up on the day itself, so all you need is some pita or other flat bread, sliced tomatoes and cucumber. For some extra heat, add a dribble of chilli sauce.

1½ tsp cumin seeds
1 tsp coriander seeds
3 garlic cloves, peeled
1 tsp fine sea salt
400g chickpeas, drained and rinsed
½ medium onion, coarsely grated
bunch fresh coriander (roughly 20g),
    leaves roughly chopped
bunch fresh flat-leaf parsley (roughly
    20g), leaves roughly chopped

50g plain flour
1 medium egg, beaten
sunflower oil, for frying
freshly ground black pepper

Minted yogurt sauce
150ml plain bio yogurt
1 tsp mint sauce from a jar
1 tsp caster sugar

Put the cumin and coriander seeds in a pestle and mortar and pound until crushed to a powder. Add the garlic and salt and pound to a paste. Scrape into a food processor and then add half of the chickpeas and process to a purée. Add the rest of the chickpeas, onion and lots of freshly ground black pepper and blitz to a thick, slightly crunchy purée. It shouldn't be too smooth – you are looking for some texture to give the falafel some bite.

Transfer to a mixing bowl and stir in the chopped herbs, flour and beaten egg. Mix with clean hands until thoroughly combined. Form the mixture into 20 walnut-sized balls and flatten slightly. Place on a tray lined with baking parchment.

Pour the oil in a large, deep non-stick frying pan until around 1cm deep. Place over a medium heat and when the oil is hot, fry the falafel in 2–3 batches for 2–3 minutes on each side until nicely browned and hot throughout. Do not allow the oil to overheat and do not leave hot oil unattended.

Drain the falafel on kitchen paper as soon as each batch is ready. To eat now, cover with foil and a dry tea towel to keep them warm between batches. Mix the yogurt, mint sauce and sugar in a small bowl until thoroughly combined. Serve the hot falafel in warmed pita breads with salad and yogurt sauce.

500ml Cooks' Ingredients Chicken Stock

8 free range chicken thighs, skinned

150g baby topped carrots

500g miniature new potatoes

4 Little Gem lettuce hearts, halved

155g pack Popped Fresh Garden Peas

2 salad onions, thinly sliced

2 tbsp half-fat crème fraîche

4 tbsp chopped flat-leaf parsley

Have you heard?

Eating more fruit and vegetables is one of the most important things we can do to improve our health.

1 Place the stock and chicken in a large saucepan and bring to the boil. Cover and simmer for 10 minutes then add the carrots and potatoes. Simmer for a further 10 minutes until the vegetables are almost cooked through.

2 Add the lettuce, peas and salad onions. Cover and cook for a further 4-5 minutes until the peas are tender and the chicken is cooked through with no pink meat. Stir through the crème fraîche and parsley. Ladle into large soup bowls and serve.

Cook's tip

Prepare this up to the end of step 1 the day before or freeze. Defrost fully before continuing with step 2.

And to drink...

Try this lovely, bright New Zealand Sauvignon that has only 9% alcohol: **The Doctor's** Sauvignon Blanc, Marlborough, New Zealand. **drinkaware.co.uk** for the facts

We'd love to see how you got on with this recipe. Tweet us your pictures using @waitrose

By choosing LOVE Life recipes you are improving the nutritional balance of your daily diet. A varied balanced diet together with frequent activity supports a healthy lifestyle. For more information, visit waitrose.com/lovelife

Nutrition 517kcals/56.2g protein/29.3g carbohydrate/6.6g sugars/19.4g fat/6g saturated fat/4.8g fibre/0.6g salt per serving

PEFC Certified

This product is from sustainably managed forests and controlled sources

PEFC

PEFC/16-33-365   www.pefc.org

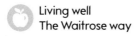

Living well
The Waitrose way

June 2013

Spring chicken casserole

1 of your 5 a day
low saturated fat

• Great for preparing ahead • Packed with British spring vegetables

To FREEZE (up to 3 months)
Cook the falafel as described then drain and return to the tray. Leave to cool. Transfer to a freezer-proof container. Cover, label and freeze.

To SERVE
Take as many falafel as you need from the freezer and thaw at room temperature for 2–3 hours. Eat cold or reheat on a suitable plate in a microwave oven. Six falafel will take around one minute to reheat on HIGH. Make the yogurt sauce fresh.

To FREEZE (up to 1 month)
Cool the burritos fully then wrap
individually tightly in foil.

Alternatively, place in labelled
freezer bags.

Cook one burrito at a time. Remove
the foil or bag and put the burrito
on a piece of kitchen roll in the
centre of a microwavable plate.
Cook from frozen for 2 minutes on
HIGH. Leave to stand for 1 minute
then cook for a further 1 minute
and 15 seconds more on HIGH
until hot throughout.

Alternatively, thaw for one hour at
room temperature and cook as if
freshly made.

Brilliant burritos

Makes 8

The new sandwich! Perfect for popping into the microwave at work for a filling lunch. Or for those days when you need something fast and tasty to keep everyone going, simply wrap in foil and warm through in a hot oven.

2 tbsp sunflower oil
1 medium onion, roughly
    chopped
1 yellow pepper, deseeded
    and thinly sliced
1 red pepper, deseeded and
    thinly sliced
1 tsp hot chilli powder
2 tsp plain flour
200ml cold water
400g can chopped tomatoes

400g can red kidney beans,
    drained and rinsed
1 tsp caster sugar
freshly squeezed juice of ½ lime
2 tbsp freshly chopped coriander
    (or 2 tbsp frozen coriander)
8 flour wraps or tortillas
200g mature Cheddar cheese,
    coarsely grated
flaked sea salt
freshly ground black pepper

Pour the oil into a large non-stick frying pan and place over a medium-high heat. Fry the onion and peppers for 10 minutes until well softened and the onion is beginning to brown, stirring regularly. Stir in the chilli powder and cook for one minute. Sprinkle over the flour and stir well.

Gradually add the water, stirring constantly, then add the tomatoes, kidney beans and sugar. Bring to a gentle simmer and cook for 15 minutes over a medium-low heat, until the sauce is thick and glossy. Remove from the heat, stir in the lime juice and coriander. Season with salt and plenty of freshly ground black pepper. Leave to cool.

Place one of the flour tortillas on a chopping board. Spoon an eighth of the bean mixture onto one side of the tortilla in a large pile. Scatter with an eighth of the cheese. Fold up the bottom of the tortilla almost over the filling and then the top over that. Roll up from the filled side. Turn over to prevent the burrito from unwrapping.

If eating now, put on heatproof plates and cook one at a time in the microwave on HIGH for 45–60 seconds until the beans are hot and the cheese melts. Serve warm. Alternatively, put the burritos on a baking tray, cover loosely with foil and place in a preheated oven at 190°C/Fan 170°C/Gas 5 for 15–20 minutes until hot throughout.

Lunchbox bars

Makes 16–20

These bars are jam-packed with dried fruit, nuts and oats. Quick to make and cook, you can cut the baked mix into bars or squares and freeze them individually. Full of flavour and texture, they give a chewy, crunchy lift to any lunchbox. Use your favourite dried fruit or even chocolate drops for these bars – just as long as you keep the weights roughly the same.

50g flaked almonds
50g ready-to-eat dried apricots
50g dried sour cherries or dried
    cranberries
50g sultanas
75g puffed rice cereal, such as
    Rice Krispies

50g desiccated coconut
75g porridge oats
125g soft light brown sugar
125g golden syrup
125g butter

To FREEZE (up to 4 months)
Cool the bars completely then wrap each one tightly in foil or pop into a small freezer bag. Label and place in a large freezer bag so they are all together and easier to find in the freezer. Seal and freeze.

To SERVE
Take as many bars as you need out of the freezer and thaw at room temperature for at least one hour before unwrapping and serving.

Clever idea
Add sunflower or pumpkin seeds or extra nuts instead of the fruit or leave the nuts out all together and increase the fruit.

Preheat the oven to 190°C/Fan 170°C/Gas 5. Scatter the almonds over a baking tray and bake in the oven for 6–8 minutes until lightly toasted.

Tip the toasted almonds into a large mixing bowl. Cut the apricots into quarters and add to the bowl along with the sour cherries or cranberries, sultanas, rice cereal, coconut and oats. Mix well until thoroughly combined. Line a 20 x 30cm rectangular tin with baking parchment.

Put the sugar, golden syrup and butter in a medium saucepan and melt them together over a low heat. Bring to a simmer and cook for one minute, stirring constantly. Pour the mixture into the bowl with the dry ingredients and mix well with a wooden spoon until the sugary liquid coats everything evenly. Take great care as the syrupy liquid will be very hot. Don't be tempted to touch or taste it.

Spoon the mixture into a rectangular tin and flatten the surface with a spatula to compress all the ingredients. Pop the tin into the oven and bake for 12–14 minutes or until lightly browned. Take the tin out of the oven and press once more with the spatula – this will make the bars easier to cut. Leave to cool in the tin.

Transfer the cooked mixture to a board and peel off the baking parchment. Cut it into 16 bars or 20 squares with a sharp knife. Store in an airtight container, interleaved with baking parchment for up to 5 days.

Fresh fruit compote with granola

Makes 8

A glut of summer fruit freezes brilliantly and can be turned into a light and healthy breakfast to take with you, saving you a fortune on buying ready-made pots. Serve the fruit topped with crunchy granola and spoonfuls of natural yogurt. Vanilla flavoured yogurt or other fruity yogurts freeze well if they have added stablisers. Use any of your favourite berry fruits for the compote. You'll need to hull the fruit and halve large strawberries. This fruity mix also makes a great crumble and pie filling.

2–3 Bramley apples (roughly 450g apples)
6 fresh plums or apricots,
500g mixed berries, such as blackberries, raspberries and strawberries
150–200g caster sugar

Granola
4 tbsp golden syrup or runny honey
3 tbsp sunflower oil
150g jumbo oats
25g flaked almonds

To serve
Yogurt or half-fat crème fraiche

To FREEZE (up to 6 months)
Cool the fruit and granola completely. Spoon into separate small freezer-proof containers. Cover, label and freeze.

To SERVE
Thaw the fruit pots and granola overnight in the fridge. Stir well before serving.

Preheat the oven to 190°C/Fan 170°C/Gas 5. Peel, quarter, core and thinly slice the apples. Stone the plums or apricots and cut into quarters. Toss the apples, plums or apricots, berries and 150g of the sugar together in a large, shallow ovenproof dish – a lasagne dish is ideal.

Cover loosely with a sheet of foil and bake for 30–40 minutes or until the fruit is soft and juicy but still holding its shape (it will continue to cook once removed from the oven). Adjust the sweetness to taste, adding more sugar if necessary, and leave to cool.

While the fruit is cooking, prepare the granola. Put the oil and golden syrup in a large non-stick saucepan and heat gently until runny, stirring. Add the oats and almonds and stir well. Spread the mixture over a baking tray. As soon as the fruit is out of the oven, bake the oat mixture for 15 minutes, turning once until golden. Leave to cool. Store in an airtight container if eating within a week.

To eat now, serve the fruit in deep bowls, topped with spoonfuls of the yogurt and sprinkled with granola.

Unless you grow loads of your own, I'm not sure that it's worth freezing vegetables just as they are. Naturally, if you're a gardener and have a glut of something such as green beans it makes sense to blanch and freeze some to enjoy in the depths of winter, but generally I prefer to turn the veg into something of a meal before freezing.

If you do blanch and freeze vegetables, it's best to cook them from frozen. They will retain their flavour and be ready in half the time as fresh, since they are already partly cooked. My preferred technique, though, is to make vegetable soups, sauces and other dishes – particularly when the ingredients are cheap and plentiful. In the summer, when tomatoes are at their best for instance, cook up a big batch of tasty pasta sauce and flat freeze for quick suppers.

I also like to freeze more elaborate vegetables dishes to use as accompaniments or as suppers on their own. I make batches of ratatouille and braised red cabbage with apple, which freeze well and are perfect for livening up cold roast meat or other leftovers.

I also freeze potato dishes such as mash and dauphinoise and I've discovered that the secret of freezing mash is using plenty of butter to help stabilise the potato and it tastes good too!

VEGETABLES

Chilli glazed parsnips and carrots

Serves 6–8

A traditional vegetable given a sweet, chilli twist. Scatter onto a baking tray and cook from frozen for an extra easy Sunday roast. Open freezing before packing into a bag means you can use what you need and then return the rest to the freezer for another time.

4 medium parsnips
4 medium carrots
2 tbsp sunflower oil
4 tbsp clear runny honey

1 tsp dried chilli flakes
½ tsp flaked sea salt
freshly ground black pepper

To FREEZE (up to 6 months)
Tip the oiled parsnips and carrots onto a foil-lined baking tray. Open freeze for 1–2 hours until solid then transfer to a labelled freezer bag. Remove as much air as possible, seal and freeze.

To SERVE
Preheat the oven to 200°C/Fan 180°C/Gas 6. Scatter the frozen vegetables in a single layer over a large oiled baking tray. Cook for 30 minutes or until the vegetables are golden and tender. Drizzle over the honey, sprinkle with chilli, season and toss well together. Return to the oven for a further 10 minutes.

Peel the parsnips and carrots and cut them into thick batons. Put the parsnips and carrots in a large saucepan and cover with water. Place over a high heat and bring the water to the boil.

Reduce the heat slightly and simmer for 4 minutes. Drain the vegetables in a large colander and return them to the saucepan. Pour in the oil and toss everything together well.

To cook now, scatter the vegetables over a large baking tray in a single layer. Roast in a preheated oven at 200°C/Fan 180°C/Gas 6 for 25 minutes or until the parsnips are golden and the carrots are tender.

Drizzle the honey over, sprinkle with the chilli and season with the salt and plenty of ground black pepper. Toss together well and return to the oven for a further 10 minutes or until the vegetables are glossy and lightly browned in places.

Ratatouille

Serves 6

This gorgeous ratatouille is made with chunky vegetables in a rich, garlicky tomato sauce. It makes great use of a summer glut of courgettes, aubergines and peppers. I like to serve mine at room temperature, tossed with some fresh basil. Perfect with grilled or barbecued meats and fish.

2 medium aubergines
3 medium courgettes, halved
   lengthways and cut into 2cm slices
2 tsp fine sea salt
8 tbsp olive oil (not extra virgin)
2 red peppers, deseeded
2 small onions, halved and finely sliced

4 garlic cloves, finely sliced
1 tsp coriander seeds, lightly crushed
400g can chopped tomatoes
handful fresh basil leaves, roughly torn
   (optional)
freshly ground black pepper

To FREEZE (up to 4 months)
Transfer the ratatouille to one or two shallow freezer-proof containers without adding the basil leaves. Cover, label and freeze.

To SERVE
Thaw overnight in the fridge. Tip into a large saucepan and reheat gently until warm. Throw in some fresh basil leaves and toss before serving.

Put the aubergines and courgettes in a colander, sprinkling with a little sea salt between layers. Leave to stand for 30 minutes then rinse thoroughly with cold water and drain. Tip into a bowl and toss with 4 tablespoons of the oil until well coated. Season with lots of ground black pepper.

Place a large non-stick frying pan over a high heat and fry the aubergines, courgettes and peppers in 3 batches until lightly browned but not cooked through, turning often. Each batch should only take 2–3 minutes if the pan is hot enough. Tip into a large mixing bowl as soon as each batch has fried.

Heat the remaining oil in a large non-stick saucepan or flame-proof casserole. Gently fry the onions for 5 minutes, stirring regularly. Add the garlic and coriander seeds and cook for 2 minutes more. Stir in the tomatoes and bring to a simmer.

Tip the other vegetables into the pan with the onions and tomatoes, cover with a lid and cook gently for 35–40 minutes or until all the vegetables are tender, stirring occasionally. Season with a little salt if needed and plenty of ground black pepper. Eat warm or cold, tossed with a few torn basil leaves if you like.

Make-ahead roast potatoes

Serves 8

I think the first secret of great roast potatoes is to choose a good floury variety; waxy potatoes are hopeless. Parboil the potatoes for a few minutes and drain. The second secret is to rough up the par-boiled potatoes on all sides, then toss liberally in oil while still in the saucepan. That way, you get a nice even coating of fat rather than potatoes swimming in oil as they roast. The recipe makes enough for eight, but you can always cook some to use straight away and freeze the rest, or adjust the recipe to suit the number you are cooking for.

2.25kg potatoes, preferably King
    Edward or Maris Piper
5 tbsp sunflower oil

1 tsp flaked sea salt
freshly ground black pepper

Peel the potatoes and cut them into even-sized chunks. (Medium potatoes can be cut into half.) Put the potatoes into a very large saucepan and cover with cold water. Bring to the boil over a high heat, then reduce the heat to a simmer and cook for 3 minutes.

Drain the potatoes in a large colander and return them to the saucepan. Shake vigorously to knock the potatoes about and scuff up their surfaces, as this will make them much crisper when they roast.

Pour the oil over the potatoes and season with the salt and plenty of freshly ground black pepper. Toss together well. Scatter the potatoes in a single layer over a large baking tray.

To cook now, place the tray in a preheated oven at 210°C/Fan 190°C/Gas 6½ . Cook for 45–55 or until the potatoes are golden, crisp and tender in the centre, turning them halfway through the cooking time to get an even colour.

To FREEZE (up to 3 months)
Cool the oiled and seasoned potatoes on the baking tray. Open freeze until solid then transfer them to a labelled freezer bag. Seal and freeze.

To SERVE
Preheat the oven to 210°C/Fan 190°C/Gas 6½. Scatter the frozen potatoes in a single layer over a large baking tray. Cook for 50–60 minutes or until the potatoes are golden, crisp and tender in the centre.

Clever idea
Freeze roast potatoes leftover from a roast dinner. Reheat from frozen in a preheated oven at 200°C/Fan 180°C/Gas 6 for 25–30 minutes.

Cheesy mashed potato

Serves 6

Mashed potatoes are another good freezer standby. I don't add any milk to mine as it can leak out when the potatoes are thawed. Lots of butter and cheese help stabilise the spuds and make them extra delicious too.

1.25kg floury potatoes, such as King Edward or Maris Piper
50g butter, cubed
150ml double cream

100g mature Cheddar cheese, coarsely grated
flaked sea salt
ground black pepper

To FREEZE (up to 3 months)
Cool the mashed potatoes completely. Divide between labelled zip-seal bags, in the most convenient serving size for your needs. Press to flatten and squeeze out as much air as possible. Seal and freeze.

To SERVE
Thaw the potatoes at room temperature or in the fridge overnight and tip them into a bowl. Beat them with a wooden spoon and use them as a topping for pies or reheat them in a microwave on HIGH for 1–2 minutes until hot.

Alternatively, to cook from frozen, run the bag or bags under a hot tap then squeeze the potato into a large non-stick saucepan and cook over a medium heat until hot, stirring with a wooden spoon. Add a little milk if necessary.

Peel the potatoes and cut them into even-sized chunks, each about 4cm. Put the potatoes into a large saucepan and cover them with cold water. Bring to the boil over a high heat, then reduce the heat to a simmer and cook for about 15 minutes, or until the potatoes are very soft but not breaking apart.

Drain the potatoes well and return them to the pan. Add the butter, cream and cheese. Mash with a potato masher until smooth and creamy. Season with salt and pepper to taste. For extra fluffy potatoes, beat with an electric whisk for a couple of minutes instead. Don't blend them in a food processor or the texture will become glue-like✳

Clever idea
Spoon the mashed potatoes into a piping bag and pipe into large rosettes on a baking tray. Open freeze, then transfer the rosettes to a freezer bag. Seal, label and freeze for up to 3 months. Take as many as you need from the freezer, put them on a suitable plate, cover loosely with cling film and microwave on HIGH until hot.

Fuss-free dauphinoise potatoes

Serves 8 (Makes 2, serving 4 each)

Sophisticated but comforting; luxurious but homely. Dauphinoise, with its layers of tender potatoes, baked with cream and garlic, elevates the humble spud to another level. These work brilliantly when frozen in silicone cake pans and then popped out, wrapped in foil and returned to the freezer. Cook from frozen in an ovenproof dish and you'll be able to take the dauphinoise straight to the table.

400ml semi-skimmed milk
3 tbsp cornflour
300ml double cream
3 large garlic cloves, crushed
2 tsp flaked sea salt

knob of butter, for greasing
1.25kg floury potatoes, such as King
Edward or Maris Piper
freshly ground black pepper

To FREEZE (up to 2 months)
Open freeze the cooled potatoes for 2–3 hours until solid. If you don't want to lose your ovenproof dishes to the freezer, prepare the potatoes in the foil dishes. You can also line your ovenproof dishes with foil or use silicone cake pans and then remove the potatoes when frozen. Cover, label and freeze.

To SERVE
Cover the frozen potatoes loosely with foil and place on a baking tray or ovenproof dish if necessary in a preheated oven at 180°C/Fan 160°C/Gas 4 for one hour. Uncover and bake for a further 30–40 minutes or until the potatoes are lightly browned and hot throughout.

Mix 4 tablespoons of the milk with the cornflour in a jug until smooth. Add the remaining milk, cream, garlic, salt and plenty of freshly ground black pepper. Whisk lightly until combined.

Grease 2 shallow foil dishes, around 24cm square or 2 x 1.5 litre ovenproof dishes with butter. Peel the potatoes and cut them into very thin slices, no more than 3mm thick. Arrange a layer of potatoes in the base of the dishes. Stir the cream mixture and pour a little over the potatoes.

Cover with another layer of potatoes and then add some more of the cream mixture. Repeat the layers until all the potatoes and cream are used. Season with a little more pepper.

To cook now, cover the dishes loosely with foil and bake in a preheated oven at 180°C/Fan 160°C/Gas 4 for 20 minutes. Remove the foil and cook for a further 30–40 minutes or until the potatoes are soft and lightly browned. You can test the potatoes are ready by sliding a knife into the centre. If you are cooking one dish of potatoes above the other, you may need to cook the potatoes on the lower shelf for 10 minutes longer.

To FREEZE (up to 4 months)
Cool the cabbage completely then spoon into 2 labelled zip-seal freezer bags. Press out as much air as possible, seal and freeze.

To SERVE
Thaw at room temperature for 3–4 hours or in the fridge overnight. Transfer to a large non-stick saucepan, add a splash of water and reheat for 8–10 minutes over a medium heat, stirring regularly until piping hot.

Braised red cabbage with apple

Serves 6–8

*This is a lovely dish of tangy red cabbage with fluffy apple pieces.
It works perfectly with roast turkey or chicken and is beautiful with
gammon or ham.*

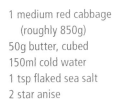

1 medium red cabbage (roughly 850g)	½ cinnamon stick
50g butter, cubed	3 medium eating apples (around 450g)
150ml cold water	75g soft light brown sugar
1 tsp flaked sea salt	4 tbsp red wine vinegar
2 star anise	freshly ground black pepper

Remove any damaged outer leaves from the cabbage and discard. Cut
the cabbage in half and cut out the tough white core. Halve the cabbage
again and slice into roughly 1.5cm pieces.

Put the cabbage in a large saucepan and add the butter, water, salt and
spices. Season with plenty of freshly ground black pepper. Bring to a
gentle simmer, cover with a lid and cook over a low heat for 15 minutes,
stirring occasionally.

Peel, quarter, core and cut the apples into roughly 2cm pieces. Add the
apple to the cabbage and stir in the sugar and vinegar. Return to a simmer.

Cook over a medium-high heat uncovered for 5 minutes or until the
liquid has evaporated, stirring constantly. Adjust the seasoning to taste.
Remove the star anise and cinnamon stick.

Simple stuffed courgettes

Serves 6–8 as an accompaniment or 3–4 as a main meal

Simple but packed with summer flavours. Make and freeze this dish when courgettes are plentiful. It can be served as a vegetable accompaniment to grilled or roasted meats and fish or as a light lunch just as it is.

6 medium courgettes
3 tbsp extra virgin olive oil
50g dried white breadcrumbs
50g pine nuts, preferably Italian
8 spring onions, trimmed and
   finely sliced
1 garlic clove, crushed

7 sun-dried tomatoes, drained
   (roughly 50g)
finely grated zest ½ lemon
1 tbsp fresh thyme leaves, chopped
40g Parmesan, finely grated
freshly ground black pepper
flaked sea salt

To FREEZE (up to 3 months)
Part cook the courgettes as described then allow to cool before sprinkling with the topping and drizzling with the oil. Cover with foil. Label and freeze.

To SERVE
Remove the foil and cook the courgettes from frozen in a preheated oven at 220°C/Fan 200°C /Gas 7 for 20–25 minutes or until the topping is golden and the courgettes are piping hot.

Preheat the oven to 220°C/Fan 200°C /Gas 7. Cut the courgettes in half lengthways and place fairly tightly together in a single layer in a shallow ovenproof dish or foil baking tray; cut side up. Brush with one tablespoon of the oil and bake for 20 minutes.

To make the stuffing, mix the breadcrumbs, pine nuts, spring onions, garlic, sun-dried tomatoes, lemon zest, thyme and Parmesan in a bowl. Season with lots of freshly ground black pepper and a little salt.

To cook now, take the courgettes out of the oven and sprinkle the stuffing on top. Drizzle with the remaining oil, bake for a further 10–15 minutes or until the courgettes are softened and the topping is golden and crisp. Serve hot.

My cauliflower cheese

Serves 6 as an accompaniment or 4 as a main meal

A brilliant freezer-standby, this cauliflower cheese has a crunchy gratin topping and a smooth cheese sauce. It cooks very well from frozen but remember to use a fairly shallow dish so it bakes quickly and evenly. I like to use a combination of Gruyère and Cheddar for my sauce but you could use all Cheddar if you prefer. Serve with grilled and roasted meats, sausages or chops.

1 medium cauliflower (roughly 600g)
50g butter
50g plain flour
½ tsp English mustard powder
500ml full-fat or semi-skimmed milk
75g Gruyère cheese, coarsely grated

75g mature Cheddar cheese, coarsely grated
1 thick slice of white or brown bread, crusts removed
flaked sea salt
freshly ground black pepper

To FREEZE (up to 2 months)
Assemble the cauliflower cheese in a shallow freezer and ovenproof dish. Line with foil first or use a silicone cake pan instead if you need your dish back once the cauliflower cheese has frozen. Cool then cover with foil, label and freeze.

To SERVE
Preheat the oven to 220°C/Fan 200°C/Gas 7. Unwrap the frozen cauliflower cheese and transfer it to an ovenproof dish if necessary. Cover the top with foil and bake for 30 minutes. Remove the foil and cook for a further 30–40 minutes until piping hot throughout.

Half-fill a large saucepan with water and bring it to the boil. Cut the cauliflower into small florets, halving or quartering any particularly large ones. You need them to be roughly the same size.

Add the cauliflower to the water and return to the boil. Cook for 4 minutes or until the cauliflower is almost tender but is fairly firm when prodded with the tip of a knife. (It will soften further when baked.) Drain in a colander, reserving the cooking water. Set aside.

Melt the butter in a large non-stick saucepan over a medium heat. Stir in the flour and mustard powder and cook for a few seconds before gradually adding the milk, stirring well after each addition. (Adding the milk slowly will stop your sauce going lumpy.)

Once all the milk is added, stir in 100ml of the reserved cauliflower water, then 50g of each of the grated cheeses. Season well with salt and pepper and cook for 3–4 minutes until the sauce is thick and smooth, stirring constantly.

Tip the cauliflower florets into an ovenproof dish and pour over the sauce. Break the bread into roughly 1cm pieces. Toss the remaining cheese with the bread pieces and scatter over the top of the cauliflower and sauce.

To cook now, place the dish on a baking tray and cook in a preheated oven at 200°C/Fan 180°C/Gas 6 for 25–30 minutes until golden brown and bubbling.

In this chapter there are lots of suggestions for freezing items that will save you time as you rush to put together midweek meals. Whether it's a Bolognese sauce that can be reheated from frozen, a spare pint of milk or pack of butter for emergencies, cheese ready for grating, a few croissants waiting to be warmed up or a crunchy crumble mix standing by; using your freezer efficiently makes everything so much easier.

With a good selection of sauces in the freezer and some dried pasta or rice in the cupboard, you need never be without a good meal. Breads, cakes and biscuits freeze very well too, while flavoured butters are easy to prepare and can dress up a simple steak or fillet of fish. With all of these, plus staples such as milk, cheese and pastry, you should always be able to come up with a great meal at a moment's notice.

Here I've given some recipes for basic standby foods that I like to freeze and find the most useful, but you can add your own favourites too. Just follow the tips and techniques in the Freezer Know-how chapter starting on page 210.

All of these foods freeze brilliantly:
* Stock
* Gravy
* Pasta sauces
* White sauce
* Milk
* Cheese
* Fromage frais
* Butter
* Bread
* Cakes
* Biscuits
* Pastry
* Crumble mix
* Dumplings
* Pancakes
* Yorkshire puddings

FREEZER STANDBYS

Stocks and sauces

Home-made stocks and sauces all work well in the freezer. They taste better and are less expensive than the shop-bought kind and since they are so quick to defrost, they're just as convenient. Sauces I couldn't be without include quick pasta sauces, rich ragùs, cheese sauce for vegetables and sweet sauces such as strawberry or chocolate for speedy puddings. I'll make a few big batches one weekend and use them over the months that follow. Use my flat freezing method (page 216) to freeze sauces easily and make the most of your freezer space.

I like to use both fresh stock and stock made from cubes. Fresh stock is best for making more subtly flavoured sauces and braises, but I like the beefy taste an Oxo cube gives to a meaty casserole or pie. It is possible to buy fresh stock in the supermarket but it is expensive. I prefer to make my own, knowing that it will store very well in the freezer for up to 6 months.

Making your own stock isn't complicated but it does take a little time. You don't need to spend hours slaving over a hot pan, just a couple of hours where you can watch it bubble away merrily on the hob. You can simmer all your stock ingredients from raw, but if the bones and veg are quickly roasted first, it will really help bring out all the flavours making it much better for gravies and sauces. If you don't have much space in your freezer, simmer the stock even further after straining so it is really concentrated. Add extra water when you come to use it.

I always ask my butcher for the leftover bones when I'm buying a rolled joint – I'll sometimes pick up a few chicken wings too; just enough to knock together a good chicken stock.

Bones left over from a family roast can also be used very easily, so don't bin them. Pop them in a saucepan with a few fresh vegetables instead. If you are short of time you can always freeze the bones and then make the stock another day.

Roasted chicken stock

Makes 500ml

I like to make stock using roasted bones because they will give it a richer flavour, but feel free to skip this step if you are short of time.

1kg chicken wings
1 medium onion, quartered
2 large carrots, cut into
   chunky pieces
2 celery sticks, cut into
   chunky pieces
1 small bunch, roughly 6–7
   sprigs, of fresh thyme
2 bay leaves
flaked sea salt
freshly ground black pepper

Preheat the oven to 200°C/Fan 180°C/Gas 6. Spread the chicken wings and vegetables over a large baking tray. Season with lots of ground black pepper. Roast for 30 minutes until well-coloured and a deep golden brown.

Transfer the chicken and vegetables to a large flameproof casserole or saucepan. Add the herbs and cover with 2 litres of cold water. Bring to a very gentle simmer and cook for one hour without covering. It is very important to simmer gently in order to keep the stock clear. Never allow it to boil at this point or your stock will be as murky as pond water.

Strain the stock through a colander into a large bowl and leave to cool for about 30 minutes. Skim off and discard any scum or fat that has floated to the surface. Pour the stock into a clean pan and bring to the boil.

Boil for 10–15 minutes or until the stock is reduced to around 500ml or further if you are short of freezer space. Cool.

To FREEZE (up to 6 months)
Pour the stock into one or 2 freezer-proof containers or labelled freezer food bags. Seal and freeze.

To USE
Transfer the stock to a large pan and heat through from frozen over a low heat until thawed. Add extra water if the stock is very reduced. Bring to the boil and cook for 5 minutes.

Great gravy

Makes 500ml

Use home-made stock to make a great gravy to serve with a roast dinner.

Transfer the roast meat (chicken, turkey, beef, lamb or pork) to a board or platter, cover with foil and a couple of dry teatowels and leave to rest. Spoon off all but one tablespoon of the fat from the roasting tin and place the tin on the hob over a medium heat. Stir in one tablespoon of plain flour and cook for a few seconds. Add 100ml of red or white wine and stir well with a wooden spoon to lift all the lovely meat juices and caramelised sediment from the bottom of the tin. Slowly stir in the warm thawed stock and bring to the boil, stirring constantly. Season well with salt and pepper.

Clever idea
Make stock with around a kilo of lamb, pork or beef bones instead. Even fish heads and bones (make sure the gills are removed first) or the shells from prawns, lobsters and crabs make good fish stock for the freezer. For flavours that work wonderfully with fish, add half a sliced fennel or a sliced leek to the other vegetables.

Time-saving tomato sauce

Makes 12 servings

This is a very simple basic tomato sauce, but one that I use at least twice a week to make quick meals from scratch. I make a large batch but freeze it in small portions which then only take a couple of minutes to heat from frozen. I sometimes add a little fresh or dried chilli, an extra splash of wine or even a slurp of cream depending on what I've got handy. It's a great sauce for stirring through freshly cooked pasta and gnocchi or for pouring over chicken breasts or fish fillets and then baking. It's also a great topping for bruschetta and canapés.

3 tbsp olive oil
3 medium onions, chopped
4 garlic cloves, finely chopped
2 tbsp plain flour
3 x 400g can chopped
   tomatoes
3 tbsp tomato purée

2 tsp caster sugar
2 tsp dried oregano or mixed
   dried herbs
2 bay leaves
1 tsp flaked sea salt
freshly ground black pepper

Heat the oil in a large saucepan or flameproof casserole over a medium heat and gently fry the onions and garlic for 15 minutes until softened and just beginning to colour, stirring regularly.

Stir in the flour and cook for another minute, stirring constantly. Add the chopped tomatoes, tomato purée, sugar, oregano and bay leaves. Season with salt and plenty of freshly ground black pepper.

Bring to the boil, then reduce the heat and simmer gently for 30 minutes, stirring occasionally until the sauce is thick. Remove from the heat and cool.

To FREEZE (up to 6 months)
Divide the sauce into labelled zip-seal bags. Squeeze out as much air as possible. Seal and flat freeze. Use my flat freeze portioning technique (see page 216) to divide it into larger or smaller portions, according to how you think you will use it.

To SERVE
Run the bag or bags under a hot tap for a few seconds, open and squeeze into a non-stick saucepan. Thaw over a low heat, stirring occasionally. Bring to a simmer and heat for 3 minutes, stirring regularly. You may need to add a little extra water if you find the sauce is a little thick after freezing.

Ridiculously good ragù

Makes 6 servings

Almost nothing beats a really good Bolognese and this recipe is one of the most used sauces in my freezer. The wonderful thing about this ragù is that it can also be used as the base for a delicious cottage pie, lasagne and for making a stew to top with dumplings.

500g lean minced beef
2 medium onions, chopped
2 garlic cloves, finely chopped
200g chestnut mushrooms,
   sliced (optional)
1 tbsp plain flour
150ml red wine or extra stock
400g can chopped tomatoes

2 tbsp tomato purée
500ml beef stock (made with
   1 stock cube)
1 tsp caster sugar
1 heaped tsp dried oregano
2 bay leaves
flaked sea salt
freshly ground black pepper

Place a large saucepan or flameproof casserole dish over a medium heat and cook the mince with the onion and garlic for 10 minutes until lightly browned. Use a couple of wooden spoons to break up the meat as it cooks, squishing it against the pan. Add the mushrooms, if using, and cook for 3 minutes more.

Stir in the flour followed by the wine, tomatoes, tomato purée, stock, sugar, oregano and bay leaves. Season with a good pinch of salt and plenty of freshly ground black pepper.

Bring to the boil, then reduce the heat and simmer gently for 40 minutes, stirring occasionally until the mince is tender and the sauce has thickened. Season with a little more salt and pepper to taste. Remove from the heat and cool completely.

To FREEZE (up to 4 months)
Divide the Bolognese into labelled zip-seal bags. Press out as much air as possible. Seal and flat freeze.

To SERVE
Run the bag or bags under a hot tap for a few seconds, open and squeeze into a non-stick saucepan. Thaw over a low heat, stirring occasionally. Bring to a simmer and heat for 5 minutes, stirring regularly. You may need to add some extra water if you find the sauce is a little thick after freezing.

Alternatively, transfer the contents to a large microwave-proof dish. Cover with plastic film. Reheat from frozen on HIGH for 6–9 minutes until piping hot. You'll need to open the microwave every 2 minutes and break up the sauce with a wooden spoon as it thaws.

Creamy bacon and chilli sauce

Makes 8 servings

This is a fabulous freezer standby and one my whole family loves. It is great tossed with pasta and gnocchi and also makes a good cooking sauce when combined with some frozen super-quick chicken strips.

2 tbsp olive oil
6 rashers smoked back bacon
   or 8 rashers smoked streaky
   bacon
2 medium onions, chopped
3 garlic cloves, finely chopped
1 tbsp plain flour
1–2 tsp dried chilli flakes

2 x 400g cans chopped
   tomatoes
2 tsp caster sugar
1 tsp dried oregano
2 bay leaves
4 heaped tbsp half-fat crème
   fraîche
flaked sea salt
freshly ground black pepper

Heat the oil in a large saucepan or flameproof casserole over a medium heat. Cut the bacon into roughly 2cm slices. Gently fry the bacon, onions and garlic for 15 minutes until the onions are softened and just beginning to colour, stirring regularly.

Stir in the flour and cook for about 30 seconds, stirring constantly. Add the chilli, tomatoes, sugar, oregano and bay leaves. Season with salt and ground black pepper.

Bring to the boil, then reduce the heat and simmer gently for 20 minutes, stirring occasionally until the sauce is thick. Remove from heat, stir in the crème fraîche and cool.

To FREEZE (up to 2 months)
Divide the sauce into labelled zip-seal bags. Squeeze out as much air as possible. Seal and flat freeze. Use my flat freeze portioning technique to divide it into larger or smaller portions, according to how you think you will use it.

To SERVE
Run the bag or bags under a hot tap for a few seconds and squeeze into a non-stick saucepan. Thaw over a low heat, stirring occasionally. Bring to a simmer and cook for 5 minutes, stirring regularly. You may need to add a little extra water if you find the sauce is a little thick after freezing.

Very versatile cheese sauce

Serves 4–6

This is enough for a lasagne or macaroni cheese for four or serves six poured over a vegetable accompaniment such as steamed broccoli or lightly boiled leeks.

50g butter
50g plain flour
600ml milk

100g mature Cheddar cheese,
   coarsely grated
flaked sea salt
freshly ground black pepper

To make the sauce, melt the butter in a large non-stick saucepan and stir in the flour. Cook over a low heat for about 30 seconds, while stirring. Gradually add the milk to the pan, stirring constantly. Increase the heat a little and bring to a gentle simmer. Cook for 5 minutes, stirring constantly. Stir in the cheese and simmer for 1–2 minutes more until melted, while stirring. Season with salt and pepper. Cool.

To FREEZE (up to 4 months)
Divide the sauce into labelled zip-seal bags. Seal and flat freeze. Use my flat freeze portioning technique to divide it into larger or smaller portions, according to how you think you will use it.

To SERVE
Run the bag or bags under a hot tap for a few seconds, open and squeeze into a non-stick saucepan. Thaw over a low heat, stirring occasionally. Bring to a simmer and cook for 3 minutes, stirring regularly. You may need to add some extra milk if you find the sauce is a little thick after freezing.

Cranberry sauce with clementines and apples

Serves 10–12

A delicious sauce to serve with roast chicken or turkey – perfect for a freeze-ahead Christmas.

2 clementines or satsumas	1 cinnamon stick
1 large eating apple	150g caster sugar
300g fresh cranberries, washed and drained	100ml cold water

Cut the clementines or satsumas (skin on) into fairly thick slices – 5 or 6 per fruit. Discard the end pieces and get rid of any obvious pips. Peel the apple, cut it into quarters and core and chop it into chunky pieces.

Tip the fruit slices and apple pieces into a saucepan with the cranberries, cinnamon, sugar and water. Cook over a medium-low heat for about 20 minutes, stirring occasionally until the cranberries soften and release their juice. When the sauce looks thick, remove it from the heat and adjust the sweetness to taste. Remove the cinnamon stick and cool.

To FREEZE (up to 6 months)
Spoon into a freezer container or bag. Seal, label and freeze.

To SERVE
Thaw at room temperature for 3–4 hours. Stir well and transfer it to a serving dish.

Decadent chocolate sauce

Serves 6–8

A rich chocolate sauce can turn even the most boring ice cream into an ice cream extravaganza. Pour the warm sauce into chunky sundae glasses or dessert dishes, layering with chunks of warm chocolate brownie (see page 138) or broken biscuits and generous scoops of ice cream.

Put 200g of plain, dark chocolate, broken into squares and 200ml of double cream in a heatproof bowl over a pan of gently simmering water. Heat until the chocolate is almost completely melted. Carefully remove the bowl with an oven cloth. Stir the sauce until smooth. Add a further 100ml of cream and stir until glossy.

To FREEZE (up to 2 months)
Pour the chocolate sauce into freezer-proof containers. Leave to cool. Cover, label and freeze.

To SERVE
Leave to thaw at room temperature for 2 hours or heat from frozen very gently in a large saucepan, add 2–3 tbsp of boiled water, stirring regularly.

Fresh strawberry sauce

Serves 4–6

Sometimes I get tempted by 'two for the price of one' offers and buy an extra punnet of strawberries. Strawberries aren't a fruit that freeze well; they are too full of water. Instead, make into a sauce and pour over ice cream or use as a fruity flavouring for strawberry fools and home-made yogurt or for drizzling over lemon tart or meringues.

To make the sauce, simply hull about 350g strawberries and cut them in half. Put them in a large non-stick saucepan with 100g caster sugar and place them over a low heat. Cook for 6–8 minutes, stirring until the strawberries have softened and released their juice and the sauce is bubbling gently. Tip the strawberries and juice into a fine sieve set over a bowl and press with the back of a ladle to extract as much juice and pulp as possible. Stir the sauce well and cool.

To FREEZE (up to 3 months)
Pour the sauce into a freezer-proof container. Cover, label and freeze.

To SERVE
Thaw at room temperature for 1–2 hours before serving.

Milk, cheese, cream and yogurt

Did you know that you can freeze milk, cheese, crème fraîche, butter and eggs? This is fantastic news as it can save you unnecessary trips to the shops and means you can freeze ingredients that you might otherwise throw away. I have found that some low- or reduced-fat products that contain natural stabilisers freeze best of all. You can also save money by buying dairy products in bulk and freezing anything you're not using straight away. And for sweet treats, if you keep a couple of tubs of ice cream in the freezer, you will never be without the main ingredients for a simple dessert or quick milk shake.

Milk

I always have a pint of milk handy in the freezer. Many supermarket milks, the ones in plastic containers, have been homogenised which means they freeze very well. I think that semi-skimmed milk has the best results and doesn't seem to suffer at all in terms of texture or taste.

Pour a little milk out of the container before freezing to allow for expansion if you can, but I often leave mine sealed. The plastic might balloon out as the liquid expands and although that doesn't look great, the frozen milk inside is fine. Milk looks fairly grey when frozen but soon returns to a creamy white when thawed. Either leave in the fridge overnight or thaw it at room temperature for 3–4 hours, popping it into the fridge as soon as it has defrosted. Milk should be used within 4–6 weeks of freezing so use and replace it regularly to ensure it doesn't remain in the freezer for longer. Never freeze milk in glass bottles as they could crack.

Cheese

Most supermarket cheeses will freeze pretty well. Often there is a slight change of texture when thawed but this is far outweighed by the convenience, especially if you use the cheese for cooking rather than taking centre stage on your cheese board. (I don't recommend freezing fine, artisan cheese as it won't maintain its unique texture and flavour and it could end up disappointingly crumbly.)

Hard cheese, such as Cheddar, Double Gloucester, Cheshire and Parmesan can be frozen successfully for up to 3 months. However, after a while they do become a little crumbly, so it is best to grate them before freezing. Store in a lidded container and use from frozen for cheese on toast, sauces, gratin toppings, stuffings and soufflés. Ready-grated cheese from the supermarket also freezes well and can be used directly from the bag.

Blue cheese freezes well for a few months. Wrap in foil and place the cheese in a freezer bag. Thaw and use as normal or crumble from frozen onto salads and over pasta or use for soups and blue cheese dressings.

I've also successfully frozen Camembert, Brie and other French cheeses. Thaw in the fridge for several hours and then return to room temperature before using if you have time. They maintain a good texture and are also excellent for topping bread for grilling or for using in salads. A whole Camembert can even be topped with cranberry sauce, wrapped loosely in foil and baked from frozen. Dip chunks of bread or vegetable sticks into the molten cheese for a simple starter or easy lunch. Goat's cheese also freezes well but won't taste as pungent on thawing. Try dribbling with a little runny honey and serving with wholegrain bread.

Mozzarella can be frozen without suffering too much. Vacuum-packed mozzarella freezes for up to 6 weeks just as it is and the balls for up to 4 weeks. I drain the mozzarella and re-wrap it in foil or tightly in a freezer bag. It won't have the same bouncy texture when thawed but will be perfectly good for topping pizzas and tossing through hot pasta. It can also freeze well when used in home-cooked dishes. For a simple and delicious meal, cover four chicken breasts with a rich pasta sauce and top with sliced mozzarella. Open freeze uncooked and then thaw before baking in a hot oven.

Full-fat soft cheese, such as Philadelphia, used for cream cheese frosting on frozen cakes has worked well as the sugar added to it helps to stabilise the cheese. Even so, I always serve the cake within one month, otherwise the top will begin to crack. Lower fat versions with the additions of various stabilisers will freeze better but as they will also last for several months unopened in the fridge, it is probably not worth using up freezer space for them.

Do not attempt to freeze cheeses with high water content such as ricotta or cottage cheese as they can become watery or have a grainy texture on thawing.

Cheesy gratin topping
The end of a loaf and a small block of cheese can be whizzed together to make a gratin topping for pressing onto fish fillets before freezing or for sprinkling onto savoury pie fillings. You can even add a few chopped herbs from the garden or leftover from another recipe. This makes enough to top six fish fillets, one family fish pie or four smaller pies. Toss 150g of fresh white breadcrumbs with 50g of coarsely grated hard cheese, such as Cheddar, and 1–2 tablespoons of roughly chopped fresh parsley (optional). Use immediately or pop it into a freezer bag. Seal, label and freeze for up to 2 months.

Cream
I have read that cream will freeze successfully if it contains over 40 per cent butterfat but I found that even the highest fat creams I tested were a disaster as all of them became grainy on thawing. Frozen cream is fine for enriching sauces but it won't whip or pour.

It is possible to whip double cream with a little caster sugar and pipe the cream in small rosettes onto a baking sheet before open freezing. These can then be used for decorating desserts. They do go a little stiff but still look fine on mousses and trifles. I use one tablespoon of caster sugar to each 150ml of whipped double cream and sometimes add a few drops of vanilla extract too. Keep the cream rosettes in a well-sealed bag or freezer-proof container as they will become tainted with other flavours very easily.

Crème fraîche
I love using crème fraîche in my recipes and I've found that most half-fat versions freeze brilliantly. This is because the stabilisers used to give the crème fraîche a creamy texture also help it freeze really well. I use it liberally instead of cream in sauces, quiches and pies and for topping canapés.

Yogurt
Many yogurts don't freeze well but those with stabilisers, often the lower fat versions, will freeze successfully. A few fruit yogurts make a handy addition to your freezer and can be popped into a lunchbox while frozen and should be thawed by lunchtime. An added bonus is that the icy yogurt will help keep your sandwich or salad nicely chilled.

Fromage frais
Sweetened fruit fromage frais freeze very well – the ones in small pots or tubes – are a brilliant standby for kids' packed lunches and can be served up instead of ice lollies. The plain low-fat fromage frais doesn't freeze well because it tends to become watery on thawing.

Butter
Butter can be frozen without unwrapping but I recommend popping it into a freezer food bag as all fats are easily affected by strong smells. Unsalted butter can be frozen for up to 6 months and salted butter for up to 3 months but I wouldn't leave it any longer than a couple of months as it will begin to slowly deteriorate.

Flavoured butters
To make a flavoured butter, always use butter that has been left at room temperature for about an hour so that it's soft enough to blend with your flavouring ingredients. If you can't wait that long, cut the butter into cubes, put it into a heatproof bowl and microwave on HIGH for 10–15 seconds. I always use slightly salted butter, even for sweet-flavoured butters, as I think the hint of salt helps bring out the flavours.

Flavoured butters can be frozen in a sausage-shape and then cut into discs straight from the freezer. Melt the butter onto hot-grilled or pan-fried meat, chicken and fish or toss through freshly boiled vegetables.

Eggs

Although they come from a bird, eggs are classified as dairy. Eggs in their shells cannot be frozen, either raw or hard-boiled.

I've found egg whites freeze well but that egg yolks solidify and are tough and sticky when thawed. If I have a couple of egg yolks left over from making meringues, I like to beat them with a little milk and freeze them in small containers to use as an egg wash for pastry at a later date.

You can also lightly beat whole eggs with salt or sugar or egg whites just as they are. Thaw slowly in the fridge for several hours and use as you would fresh. Don't forget to label the container well, so you know exactly how many eggs or egg whites it contains. Use immediately after thawing and cook thoroughly.

Ice cream

I love proper dairy ice cream and if you have an ice cream maker, you can enjoy making your own. Home-made ice cream is always best eaten within a few weeks, whereas shop-bought will last longer. Make your own sauces for ice cream or buy a jar of ready-made sauce, use what you need and then transfer the rest to a suitable container and freeze.

Ice cream sundaes

Scoop your favourite ice cream into wide tumblers or sundae glasses and have fun making your own ice cream sundaes. Here are a few variations that I love:

Chocolate fudge sundae Use chocolate or vanilla ice cream, Maltesers, chunks of chocolate brownie, broken Flake bars and lots of hot chocolate sauce.
Pavlova sundae Use vanilla or strawberry ice cream, fresh raspberries or strawberries, broken meringues and whipped cream.
Banana and butterscotch sundae Use vanilla ice cream, sliced bananas, chunks of dairy fudge, pecan nuts and maple syrup.

Chilli, coriander and lime butter

Makes enough for 16 slices

This is great with grilled or baked fish fillets and on barbecued chicken and lamb.

150g softened butter	3 tbsp finely chopped fresh
2 red chillies, deseeded	coriander leaves
and diced	finely grated zest of 1 lime

Put the butter in a bowl and with a fork or wooden spoon, beat in the chillies, coriander and lime zest.

Drop the butter onto a large sheet of foil and fold over one side to cover the butter. Roll into a fat sausage shape and twist the ends of the foil to seal. Label and freeze for up to 2 months.

To SERVE
Unwrap one end of the butter and place it on a chopping board. Using a large sharp knife, cut it into 1–2cm discs. Rewrap any unused butter and return it to the freezer.

Garlic and herb butter

Makes enough for 16 slices

This is perfect for making garlic bread, melting onto griddled steaks and tossing with freshly boiled green beans or peas.

150g softened butter	2 tbsp finely chopped fresh
4 garlic cloves, crushed	parsley leaves
	1 tbsp finely chopped fresh
	chives or parsley leaves

Put the butter in a bowl and beat in the garlic and herbs with a fork or wooden spoon.

Drop the butter onto a large sheet of foil and fold over one side to cover the butter. Roll into a fat sausage shape and twist the ends of the foil to seal. Label and freeze for up to 2 months.

To SERVE
Unwrap one end of the butter and place it on a chopping board. Using a large sharp knife, cut it into 1–2cm discs. Rewrap any unused butter and return it to the freezer.

Breads, buns, biscuits and cakes

The freezer is the perfect place to store emergency supplies of bread, rolls, breakfast standbys and cakes. They are changed very little by the freezing process and can be warmed or toasted from frozen very quickly. Because bread freezes so well, it also makes sense to prepare things that will come in handy later such as bruschetta, croutons and breadcrumbs. And when it comes to saving time later, make the most of bread's freeze friendliness and prepare seasonal accompaniments such as bread sauce and stuffing ahead of time and keep them in the freezer until needed.

White and brown bread, French loaves, rustic loaves, fruit loaves, rolls and buns can all be frozen.

Depending on the size of your freezer, you should be able to fit in 2–3 standard sized sliced loaves. If you have only a couple of drawers available, divide the loaf into useful portions instead. Four slices should fit into a small zip-seal freezer bag quite easily. Sliced bread can be toasted from frozen and will only take 10–15 minutes to thaw if the slices are separated.

Large unsliced loaves should be thawed at room temperature for 2–4 hours. You can heat bread rolls and baguettes from frozen if you leave them tightly wrapped in foil. Place the bread on a baking tray in a preheated oven at 200°C/Fan 180°C/Gas 6 for 15–30 minutes depending on size. Cool for a few minutes before removing the foil.

Breakfast pastries, buns and teatime treats

If your family loves croissants, Pain au chocolat and other French or Danish style pastries, it is definitely worth keeping a few in the freezer.

You will also save money by buying in bulk. Don't freeze them in the original packaging as it will allow too much air to reach the products and will ultimately cause them to become icy and unappetising. Instead, wrap each one tightly in foil or a small freezer bag. Seal and pop into a larger labelled bag so you know what is in there. Freeze for up to three months.

Doughnuts, scones, crumpets and muffins can also all be frozen. Wrap products that have a sugar or iced coating individually in foil. Other products can be frozen in freezer food bags.

Biscuits

Home-made, uncooked biscuits freezes very well and are perfect for break-time snacks. Roll the dough into a sausage shape so you can slice off and bake what you need from frozen. Sometimes the dough is a little hard to slice immediately, so let it stand at room temperature for a few minutes first. Baked biscuits can also be frozen, so why not cook a few batches and store them in well-washed ice cream tubs or other freezer containers, interleaving with squares of baking parchment between layers. Take out what you need and thaw for about 20–30 minutes before serving.

Cakes

All types of cakes freeze brilliantly and are great when you are expecting guests but have no time to bake. I also freeze portions of cakes for packed lunches and parties. Open freeze iced cakes for about an hour before wrapping them in foil. Single portions of cake take 30–60 minutes to thaw and larger cakes take 2–3 hours. Note that butter icings freeze better than glacé icing.

Garlic and herb bread

Makes 2 x ½ loaves (each one will serve 4–6)

Bought garlic bread can be expensive, so why not make your own instead? Use really fresh smelling, firm garlic. If it has green shoots forming inside the cloves the garlic will taste musty and spoil the flavour of the bread. And if you fancy fiery garlic bread, add a chopped fresh red chilli or dried chilli flakes to the butter mixture.

150g softened butter
4 large garlic cloves, crushed
2 tbsp finely chopped fresh
   flat-leaf parsley leaves

1 French loaf or baguette,
   2 French batons or a couple
   of part-baked ciabatta
   loaves
freshly ground black pepper

Put the butter in a bowl and use a wooden spoon to blend it with the garlic, parsley and lots of freshly ground black pepper.

Slice the bread almost all the way through at 2cm intervals all the way along its length, then cut it into 2 halves to make storage and cooking easier.

Spread the garlic and herb butter generously over one side of each slice. Wrap the bread in foil and place on a baking tray in a preheated oven at 200°C/Fan 180°C/Gas 6 for 10 minutes. Unwrap the foil and return to the oven for a further 5 minutes.

To FREEZE (up to 1 month)
Wrap the uncooked garlic and herb bread tightly in foil and place in freezer bags. Seal, label and freeze.

To SERVE
Preheat the oven to 200°C/Fan 180°C/Gas 6. Take the frozen bread out of the plastic bag and loosen the foil a little. Place it on a baking tray and cook for 15 minutes. Unwrap carefully and serve hot.

Bruschetta

Make delicious bruschetta using toasts from your freezer. Slice a baguette, baton or ciabatta into roughly 1cm slices. Place on a baking tray. Bake in a preheated oven at 200°C/Fan 180°C/Gas 6 for 8–10 minutes until crisp and pale golden brown. Cool on the tray then tip into a freezer bag or rigid container. Seal, label and freeze. Reheat from frozen on a baking tray in a hot oven. Drizzle with a little olive oil and top with fresh tomatoes, garlic and basil, sliced prosciutto or pâté.

Crisp croutons

Make croutons from leftover bread. Ciabatta and rustic French breads also work very well and even the end of a good farmhouse loaf can be used. Cut the bread into small squares and place on a baking tray. Bake in a preheated oven at 200°C/Fan 180°C/Gas 6 for 8–10 minutes until crisp and pale golden brown. Cool on the tray then tip into a freezer bag or rigid container. Seal, label and freeze. To use, toss in a small frying pan over a medium heat before using or thaw for 20 minutes before adding to soups and salads.

Breadcrumbs

Breadcrumbs are an excellent way to use up fresh bread before it goes stale. Cheesy crumbs make a great gratin topping for shaking straight from the freezer over pie fillings and onto fish and chicken fillets before baking. While plain breadcrumbs make a great coating for fresh chicken and fish pieces for home-made nuggets or goujons.

For cheesy crumbs, cut the crusts off the bread and whiz the bread in a food processor. Coarsely grate until you have about half the quantity of cheese to breadcrumbs. Combine the Cheddar cheese and put together in a freezer bag. Add some freshly chopped parsley or thyme leaves if you have some and season with freshly ground black pepper. Sometimes I'll also add some finely chopped sun-dried tomatoes or olives to the mix. Remove as much air as possible from the bag, seal, label and freeze for up to 3 months.

For a breadcrumb coating, cut the crusts off the bread and whiz the bread in a food processor. Dust the fresh chicken or fish pieces in plain flour and dip into beaten egg before rolling in the breadcrumbs. Slightly stale bread will work best as it is drier. Open freeze (see page 214) then pack them into rigid containers. Cover and freeze for up to 3 months. Cook on a baking tray from frozen in a preheated oven at 200°C/Fan 180°C/Gas 6 for 12–15 minutes until golden brown and cooked through.

Alternatively, just whizz the bread into crumbs and put it into a freezer bag. Remove as much of the air from the bag as possible, seal, label and freeze for up to 3 months.

Classic bread sauce

Serves 6–8

As well as being a make-ahead time-saver, bread sauce is also a brilliant use of bread that might otherwise spoil.

600ml full-fat or
    semi-skimmed milk
1 medium onion, cut into
    quarters
1 bay leaf
5 cloves
½ heaped tsp flaked sea salt
25g butter

100ml double cream
125g fresh white breadcrumbs
    or white bread torn into
    small pieces (remove the
    crusts first)
freshly grated nutmeg
    (to taste)
freshly ground black pepper

Pour the milk into a medium saucepan and add the onion, bay leaf and cloves. Place over a low heat and bring to a gentle simmer. Cook for 5 minutes then take off the heat and leave to stand for 30 minutes to allow all the flavours to infuse into the milk.

Strain the liquid through a sieve into a clean non-stick pan and add the butter and cream. Reheat gently until the butter melts, then add the bread and stir vigorously.

Bring to a very gentle simmer and cook for 2 minutes until thickened. Season to taste with a fine grating of nutmeg, more salt if necessary and plenty of freshly ground black pepper.

To FREEZE (up to 3 months)
Leave the sauce to cool, then transfer to a zip-seal bag or rigid container. Seal, label and freeze.

To SERVE
Either thaw overnight in the fridge or at room temperature for a couple of hours. Reheat in a large non-stick pan, stirring constantly. You may need to add a little extra milk or cream as the sauce tends to thicken a little more when frozen.

Apricot, leek and almond stuffing

Serves 8

This stuffing contains the perfect combination of colourful leeks, meaty sausage, chunky apricots and crunchy nuts. It goes particularly well with roast chicken, turkey and pork.

2 tbsp sunflower oil
2 medium leeks, trimmed and
    thinly sliced
450g good-quality pork
    sausage meat
100g fresh white or brown
    breadcrumbs
125g no-soak dried apricots,
    cut into quarters
75g blanched almonds,
    roughly chopped

finely grated zest of 1
    small lemon
1 tsp dried thyme or 1 tbsp
    finely chopped fresh
    thyme leaves
1 tsp dried sage or 1 tbsp
    finely chopped fresh sage
20g bunch of fresh parsley,
    leaves roughly chopped
1 tsp flaked sea salt
1 large or medium egg, beaten
freshly ground black pepper

Heat the oil in a large non-stick frying pan and fry the leeks gently for 4 minutes, stirring regularly until softened but not coloured. You want them to keep their vibrant green colour. Remove from the heat and tip into a large mixing bowl. Leave to cool.

Add the sausage meat, breadcrumbs, apricots, almonds, lemon zest, herbs, salt and egg to the bowl with the cooled leeks. Season with several twists of ground black pepper. Mix everything thoroughly together with clean hands.

Press the mixture into the base of a shallow foil or ceramic dish. It will need to be roughly 20 x 20 cm. To cook now, preheat the oven to 200°C/Fan 180°C/Gas 6. Cover with a piece of foil and place on a baking tray. Bake for 30–35 minutes, removing the foil after 15 minutes, until the stuffing is cooked and piping hot throughout.

To FREEZE (up to 3 months)
Cover the uncooked stuffing tightly with foil or a lid. Label and freeze.

To SERVE
Either thaw the stuffing in the fridge overnight and cook as above or bake from frozen in a preheated oven at 200°C/Fan 180°C/Gas 6 for 45–50 minutes or until thoroughly cooked and piping hot throughout. Cover loosely with foil for the first 20 minutes of the cooking time.

Pastry, crumbles and dumplings

I love making pastry and it never ceases to amaze me how even the humblest of ingredients can be transformed into something extra special simply by popping them into a rich shortcrust pastry case or by topping them with golden, flaky pastry. Luckily, pastry also freezes very well, so I always have a couple of blocks of bought puff pastry, a roll of filo pastry and some home-made shortcrust pastry in the freezer.

I also like to freeze unbaked pastry cases for making simple midweek tarts. These are great for using up leftovers such as cream and eggs, the odd rasher of bacon or assorted vegetables. Frozen shortcrust pastry cases can be blind baked from frozen with almost no shrinkage. I also have a stash of little pastry cases waiting to be filled and served as canapés with drinks, a bag of my own ready-mixed crumble topping for last-minute puddings and a bag of home-made dumplings ready to drop onto a bubbling stew.

I generally cook pastry tarts and small pies straight from frozen but thaw larger pies before baking. Larger pies need thawing first otherwise the pastry is liable to cook and brown before the filling is ready, although you can counteract this by covering the pie with a double layer of foil for at least half the cooking time. Filo and ready-rolled pastry must be thawed before using. I also find that puff pastry has a better rise if cooked once thawed.

Wrap home-made pastry blocks tightly with foil and they should freeze well for up to three months. Thaw in the fridge for several hours or overnight. Uncooked pastry lined tins can be baked blind from frozen and cooked pastry dishes either warmed through from frozen or thawed first. Use frozen crumble mix without thawing and add 5–10 minutes to your recipe.

I tend to use a food processor to save time, but these pastry recipes work equally as well made by hand using the traditional 'rubbing the fat into the flour' method.

Using frozen ready-made pastry

Most ready-made shortcrust and puff pastry are sold as a block. There are some excellent frozen all-butter and organic pastries available. Buy the ready-frozen pastry for the freezer if you can, although chilled pastry freezes well, it can discolour slightly or become a little sticky when defrosted. Thaw as directed on the packet or ideally thaw in the fridge for a few hours if using home-frozen pastry.

Rolling is much easier if you start by forming the pastry into the shape you want at the end. So if you're going to be covering a round or oval pie dish, shape the block into a round before rolling. You can do this easily by pressing in the corners with your hands.

When rolling ready-made puff pastry, always start by making three indentations across the block with your rolling pin. This makes it easier to roll the pastry out straight and flat without stretching it.

Puff pastry sometimes comes ready-rolled and interleaved with plastic sheets. Follow the packet instructions very carefully as it can become sticky if not defrosted properly.

Flaky freezer pastry

Makes enough to top a large family-sized top crust pie (roughly 30 x 20)

If you've run out of puff pastry in your freezer, this recipe makes a great alternative. It doesn't rise in quite the same way but is very easy to make and gives a delicious light, flaky crust. My granny was a wonderful pie maker and taught me the method. I like to use it best for top crust meat and fruit pies. If making a sweet pie, add two tablespoons of caster sugar to the flour before adding the butter.

400g plain flour, plus extra for rolling
½ tsp fine sea salt
250g frozen butter
125ml very cold water

Sift the flour into a large bowl and stir in the salt. Holding the butter with a folded piece of baking parchment to help prevent it melting, coarsely grate a third of it onto a board. Frozen butter can be brittle, so watch your fingers while grating.

Add the grated butter to the flour and toss lightly with a round-bladed knife. Repeat twice more, tossing the butter through the flour mixture until all the butter strands are lightly dusted with the flour. This will help ensure that the pastry bakes into flaky layers.

Slowly pour the very cold water into the flour mixture, stirring constantly until it all comes together and makes a light dough. Add a little extra water if necessary until the dough feels soft and pliable. Do not knead the dough. Shape into a ball or block and place on a floured surface ready to roll.

Clever idea

Whenever I make a pastry tart or pie, I gather up the trimmings, re-roll them and use them to line a 12-hole bun tin or mini quiche tin. Immediately put the tin in the freezer and freeze the cases until solid. Once solid, the little pastry cases can be stored in a rigid container or freezer bag for up to 3 months. When you need to make some little tarts or quiches, simply pop them back into the tin, fill as required and bake from frozen.

Another clever idea

You can freeze baked individual tart cases in cylindrical cardboard tubes, the ones used for party size Twiglets are especially good. The rigid container will protect the delicate pastry in the freezer. Pop into a freezer bag first so they can be removed easily. Seal, label and freeze for up to 3 months. Fill and bake from frozen or crisp up in a hot oven for a few minutes and then cool if adding an uncooked filling.

My shortcrust pastry

Makes enough to line a 23–25cm fluted tart tin

This is the pastry recipe I use 90 per cent of the time. It's light, buttery and short – just what a good shortcrust pastry should be. I finally settled on these measurements and the method after years of trial and error, so if you have never had much luck with pastry, give it a go.

250g plain flour, plus extra for rolling
150g fridge cold butter, cubed
1 large egg, beaten

Put the flour and butter in a food processor and pulse until the mixture resembles fine breadcrumbs. With the motor running, gradually add the beaten egg and blend until the mixture forms a rough ball.

Remove the blade and shape the dough into a flattened round. Wrap it in foil, place it in a labelled freezer bag, seal and freeze for up to 3 months. Thaw at room temperature for 1–2 hours before using. Do not allow the pastry to get warm. Roll out on a lightly floured surface.

Sweet shortcrust pastry

Makes enough to line a 23–25cm fluted tart tin

If you love making patisserie-style desserts, you will adore this pastry. Perfect for sweet pie crusts, it's particularly good for making tart cases. Line your tin before freezing and bake blind from frozen for the best results.

250g plain flour, plus extra for rolling
175g fridge cold unsalted butter, cubed
25g icing sugar
1 medium egg, beaten

Put the flour, butter and icing sugar in a food processor and pulse until the mixture resembles fine breadcrumbs. With the motor running, gradually add the beaten egg and blend until the mixture forms a rough ball.

Remove the blade and shape the dough into a flattened round. Roll out and prick the base with a fork. Open freeze then place in a labelled freezer bag for up to up to 3 months.

Basic crumble mix

Makes enough to top a shallow 1.7-litre pie dish

A great basic crumble mix that can be used to top any sweet crumble. It has that perfect combination of sweetness and crunch that everyone seems to love. Freeze it in a bag and shake over your fruit filling before baking.

175g plain flour
50g porridge oats
125g demerara sugar
125g cold butter, cubed

Put the flour, oats and sugar in a large bowl and add the butter. Rub the mixture together with your fingertips until it resembles coarse breadcrumbs. Tip the mixture into a labelled freezer bag, seal and freeze for up to 3 months.

Preheat the oven to 200°C/Fan 180°C/Gas 6. Shake the frozen crumble over your fruit filling and bake for 25–40 minutes until the topping is golden brown and the filling is bubbling.

Cheese twists

Makes 16

These flaky, golden pastry twists are great for dipping or nibbling with drinks.

320–375g sheet ready rolled puff pastry
2–3 tbsp beaten egg, thawed if frozen
50g finely grated Parmesan or Cheddar cheese

Preheat the oven to 220°C/Fan 200°C/Gas 7. Unroll the pastry onto a large baking tray lined with baking parchment. Brush lightly with the beaten egg.

Cut the pastry into 1.5cm wide strips with a large knife. Holding each end of a strip, twist fairly tightly. Press the ends firmly down onto the tray so the pastry remains twisted. Sprinkle with the cheese and bake for 15 minutes or until well risen and golden brown. Serve warm or cold.

Fluffy dumplings

Makes 20

My family loves dumplings and they are a great way of making a meal go so much further. They are easy to make and freeze, so I always have a batch to hand during the cold winter months.

200g self-raising flour, plus extra for rolling
100g shredded suet
2–3 tbsp finely chopped fresh parsley or 1 tsp freeze-dried
parsely, thyme or sage (optional)
150ml cold water
good pinch of flaked sea salt
freshly ground black pepper

In a large bowl, mix together the flour, suet, herbs if using, salt and some freshly ground black pepper. Slowly add the water, stirring constantly with a large spoon until the mixture comes together and forms a soft, spongy dough.

Roll the dough into 20 small balls and place them on a plate or tray lined with baking parchment. Dust your hands with a little flour if they become sticky. Open freeze for 1–2 hours until solid then put them into a freezer bag. Seal, label and freeze for up to 3 months.

Use the dumplings from frozen by gently dropping them directly into a simmering stew or soup. Cover with a lid and simmer for 20–25 minutes or until the dumplings are well risen, light and fluffy.

Better batter

All types of batters, whether for pancakes or Yorkshire puddings, freeze very well and it's well worth making double the quantity next time you are cooking some, just for the freezer. Batter can be made in a food processor, mixer or by hand and is a brilliant way of using up a few spare eggs or milk.

Pancakes can be knocked out pretty quickly following my simple recipe for Perfect Pancakes on page 192 and all you need are a few basic ingredients and a decent non-stick frying pan. Use a non-metal heat-proof spatula to turn the pancakes if you don't want to risk a toss. Pancakes are great for breakfast or a quick pudding served with freshly squeezed lemon and sugar. You could even make a few ahead ready for Shrove Tuesday as they store well in the freezer for a couple of months. Try filling them with a rich cheese sauce containing chunks of ham from the freezer for a cheap savoury supper.

I like to knock up a good stack and layer them with easy-leave film or squares of baking parchment. You can then pop them into a freezer bag, press out the air and seal. Just take out what you need then reseal the bag. When reheated from frozen in a hot frying pan they only take a couple of minutes each and are even quicker in the microwave.

American-style pancakes also freeze well, so check out the recipe on page 102. My kids love these for breakfast with sliced bananas and a dribble of maple syrup. They take less than five minutes to heat from frozen and make a nice change from cereal or toast. They are also perfect for a quick and easy dessert.

Yorkshire puddings are another handy addition to the freezer. I cook a couple of batches, serve one right away and freeze the rest. Much more delicious than the bought kind, they can be popped into the oven to reheat from frozen while your joint is resting. They can also be served with sausages and chops midweek. Don't forget to freeze gravy leftover from your weekend roast to serve with other meals.

Batters such as the Mole in the Hole (see recipe on page 62) that you want to rise into golden, puffy waves are best frozen before cooking and can even be put into a very hot oven straight from the freezer. And if you don't have time to cook a batch of pancakes or puddings, it's worth remembering that uncooked batter can also be frozen. Just make up the batter as described on pages 192 and 193, transfer it to a rigid container and seal, label and freeze for up to three months. Thaw it in the fridge, give a good stir and use as if it was freshly made, adding just a dash of extra milk or water if necessary. This will make your Sunday roasts a cinch.

Perfect pancakes

Makes 12 large or 16 small pancakes

Pancakes make a quick dessert. My kids often have pancakes for breakfast; it's an easy way of getting them to eat eggs and milk. Pancakes take just a couple of minutes to reheat from frozen and once you've started making them, it doesn't take that much longer to double the number, so you can always make extra for the freezer.

If you're making pancakes regularly, invest in a decent non-stick frying pan. A smallish one is ideal for pancakes and will only need a quick wipe around with a damp cloth once you've finished cooking. I also recommend buying a pack of baking parchment circles, the ones used to line cake tins, they're great for interleaving.

225g plain flour	25g butter
4 large eggs	2 tbsp sunflower oil
600ml semi-skimmed milk	

To make the pancakes, blitz the flour, eggs and milk in a food processor until smooth. If you haven't got a food processor, mix with a stick blender, electric whisk or large whisk instead. Pour into a jug.

Melt the butter and oil in a small saucepan then remove from the heat. Put a small non-stick frying pan over a medium-high heat. (I use a small frying pan because smaller pancakes are easier to stack and pack, but you can use a large one if you prefer.) Using a heatproof pastry brush, brush the pan with some of the melted fat.

Pour a little of the pancake batter into the pan and swirl around until the base is completely covered. Cook for 1–2 minutes or until the bottom of the pancake is golden. Loosen the sides with a palette knife and flip over. Cook the other side for 40–60 seconds until golden.

Continue making another 15 pancakes in exactly the same way, greasing the pan with a little melted fat each time.

To eat now, top with your favourite fillings, fold and serve.

To FREEZE (up to 2 months)
Stack the pancakes on a plate as they are prepared, separating them with easy-leave or baking parchment and leave to cool. Separate into stacks of 4 or 6 and wrap well in cling film. Pop into a freezer bag, seal, label and freeze.

To SERVE
Unwrap the pancakes and reheat one at a time from frozen in a lightly oiled frying pan over a medium heat, turning once. Alternatively, put the stack on a plate in the microwave and reheat on HIGH for 20–30 seconds. You can also wrap in foil and reheat in the oven at 150°C/Fan 130°C/Gas 2 for 10 minutes.

Pancake roll-ups

Pancakes can also be eaten as a filling on-the-move snack. Simply spread with your favourite filling, such as chocolate and hazlenut spread or jam, fold in the 2 sides and roll. Wrap in foil. Label and freeze for up to a month. To serve warm, remove the foil and reheat on a plate, covered loosely with cling film, in the microwave for a few seconds. Remember that very sugary fillings will heat very quickly so ensure it's the pancake rather than the filling that gets hot.

Foolproof Yorkshire puddings

Makes 12

This brilliant recipe came from my Mum and has been used in my family for over 50 years. I've adapted the imperial measurements to metric but I always find it's easiest to remember the quantities as 2, 4, 8. That is, 2 eggs, 4oz plain flour and 8fl oz of milk. In the past I used to make them with a combination of whole milk and water but now I've found that using semi-skimmed milk works even better.

Cook Yorkshire pudding when you have time and they will sit happily in your freezer for up to 2 months and are fantastically useful when you are expecting lots of people for Sunday lunch.

2 large eggs	½ tsp flaked sea salt
115g plain flour	2 tbsp sunflower oil
250ml semi-skimmed milk	

Break the eggs into a food processor and add the flour, milk and salt. Blitz until smooth. Alternatively, beat the eggs together in a bowl and add the flour, salt and half the milk. Beat until smooth then whisk in the remaining milk. Transfer to a jug and leave to stand for about 10 minutes.

Preheat the oven to 230°C/Fan 210°C/Gas 8. Pour a little of the sunflower oil into each of the cups of a 12-hole Yorkshire pudding or bun tin. Place in the preheated oven for 2 minutes.

Remove the hot tin from the oven using an oven cloth. Pour the batter into the 12 cups making sure you use roughly the same amount for each one.

Bake in the centre of the oven for 20–25 minutes or until the batter is very well risen and golden brown. Serve immediately before they have a chance to soften.

To FREEZE (up to 2 months)
Remove the puddings from the tin and leave to cool on a wire rack then put into a large, labelled freezer bag. Seal and freeze.

To SERVE
Scatter the number of frozen puddings you need over a baking tray. Reheat in a preheated oven at 200°C/Fan 180°C/Gas 6 for 5 minutes until hot and crisp. Serve at once.

Fluffy puffy fruit pudding

Sweeten the Yorkshire pudding batter with 50g caster sugar and one teaspoon of vanilla extract instead of the salt. Toss any prepared fruit, such as stoned cherries, sliced apples or peaches, gooseberries, plums or raspberries with 2–3 tablespoons of caster sugar and scatter over the base of a well-buttered, shallow freezer and ovenproof dish. Pour over the batter.

To FREEZE (up to 2 months)
Cover with foil, seal, label and freeze.

To SERVE
Cook from frozen at 220°C/Fan 200°C/Gas 7 for 30–35 minutes until puffed up and golden brown.

Herby batter

If you have lots of herbs in the garden or left over from preparing another dish, chop finely and stir into a batter. For herby pancakes add to pancake batter to use with savoury fillings. To make a fragrant Yorkshire pudding pour the batter into a well-greased baking tin.

To FREEZE (up to 2 months)
Cover with foil, seal, label and freeze.

To SERVE
Cook from frozen at 230°C/Fan 210°C/Gas 8 for 25–30 minutes until puffed up and golden brown.

There are some basic techniques that are well worth learning and particularly important if you are planning to freeze raw ingredients, such as meat, poultry and fish or fresh produce. By understanding how to freeze these items properly, you will be able to take advantage of price reductions and buy in bulk knowing that the food will freeze successfully for several months. You can also split your foods into the pack sizes most suited to your household and reduce food waste.

Freezing is also a great way of extending the home-grown vegetable and fruit season. Bear in mind how much space you have in your freezer though – you probably don't want bags and bags of runner beans and no room for a home-made lasagne.

Techniques are really important, it's not a matter of bunging it all into a freezer bag and hoping for the best. By applying the most appropriate method of freezing to individual raw and cooked ingredients, you will achieve much better results. For instance, nearly all fruit is best frozen in sugar or with a sugar syrup, most vegetables require blanching in boiling water before freezing, sausages can be frozen individually and mince should always be rewrapped before freezing.

All of these ingredients freeze beautifully:
* Beef, lamb, pork and poultry
* Game
* Sausages
* Mince
* Fish
* Shellfish
* Most vegetables
* Mushrooms
* Fruit
* Rice
* Pasta
* Potatoes

FREEZER
BASICS

Freezing meat, poultry and game

Meat, poultry and game freeze exceptionally well for fairly long periods of time and some tougher cuts can actually tenderise a little when frozen. It's worth noting, however, that buying a large quantity of meat for the freezer is only really a viable idea if you have lots of spare space. Having a chest freezer in the garage for large items, or infrequently used foods, and then an upright freezer in the kitchen for day-to-day cooking is perfect.

Plain, raw red meat, poultry and game can be safely frozen for up to 12 months, although I wouldn't recommend freezing for that long. Over a year, you will have opened your freezer hundreds of times, letting warm air in each time, and probably have defrosted it at least twice. It's not only flavour that could be affected, you may also find that the meat is less succulent and freezer burn becomes more of a problem.

I have a 6 month rule for large joints and 4 months for whole birds and recommend no more than 1–3 months for super-quick strips, mince, sausages and chops (see page 237).

Preparing meat for the freezer

It is best to unpack the meat, poultry or game and repackage it by wrapping it tightly in foil or small freezer bags and placing it in a larger freezer bag or rigid container. However, vacuum packed meats and fish do freeze well, so it's well worth buying vacuum packed and pre-frozen lamb or chicken breasts as freezer standbys.

Where possible, trim hard fat from cheaper cuts before you freeze, as it may develop a rancid flavour in the freezer. Cover any protruding bones with a double layer of foil before wrapping as they could otherwise tear the plastic or damage other foods and containers in the freezer.

If buying mince or other meats from the supermarket, it's best not to freeze them in the containers they come in for more than a week.

The protective air that preserves the colour of the meat will still allow moisture to settle and icy patches and freezer burn will occur.

If you buy sausages in a string from the butcher, cut between the links and wrap each sausage with interleaving film before putting them in a freezer bag or rigid container. Freeze for up to three months. Cook the sausages from frozen in a frying pan with a little oil for roughly 30–50 per cent longer than usual and until completely cooked in the middle. If you are only planning to freeze your sausages for up to a couple of weeks or so, try to buy them in the flat trays. That way, a quick tap on the work surface and the frozen sausages should separate and be ready to fry. The same goes for burgers and meatballs in trays. If you're freezing for longer, store the sausages in a freezer bag with as little air as possible around them.

Bacon and ham are best used within 2 months and if smoked, I suggest storing them in the freezer for no longer than one month. I've also tested cured sliced meats in my freezer and they easily last for up to a month.

I have cooked whole joints of meat from frozen in the past but I find even when cooked at a lower temperature and for longer, the meat tends to shrink back and release lots of liquid, so is rarely as tender and juicy as I would like it. You should never cook whole birds from frozen.

At all times, it is vital to prepare meat and poultry for freezing in extremely clean conditions.

Thawing meat can be a time consuming process so, if possible, pack into single portion sizes. If you are thawing before cooking, for safety reasons it is best to thaw overnight in the fridge. Defrost large joints thoroughly. A really big joint or a turkey can take a couple of days to thaw (see page 220 for tips on thawing). Always use meat within 24 hours of thawing.

Freezing fish and shellfish

I like to have a selection of fish and seafood in my freezer. It freezes brilliantly and can be cooked from frozen if necessary. A whole salmon can be frozen in April and still taste great served at a summer party in June. A creamy fish pie can be baked from frozen in under an hour and fillets of sea bass roasted from frozen to in just 15 minutes.

When you are freezing fish at home, it must be very fresh. Never freeze fish that is close to its use-by date or has been sitting in the fridge for a while. Fish that is already getting a bit whiffy will deteriorate very rapidly when thawed and will be pretty smelly when cooked too.

If freezing fresh fish bought from the supermarket, always ask which day it was delivered and only use fish that arrived that morning. This is especially important when you want to take advantage of a special offer or buy fish in bulk. It is also important to check that the fish hasn't previously been frozen and then thawed before selling. However, if the fish has been previously frozen, you can cook it immediately and then freeze the finished dish.

Preparing fish for the freezer

It is best to freeze fish as quickly as possible because this will help the texture remain firm when cooked. Fish can be frozen whole – gutted and any spiny fins and gills removed before freezing – but I think that fillets are the most convenient way to freeze and cook fish, both as sides of a whole smallish fish or in bite-size chunks. Try to keep the fish pieces roughly the same size so that they cook evenly.

Always wrap the fish really well; both to prevent the fish drying out and to stop fishy smells pervading the freezer. Either wrap individual fish or fillets in a double layer of foil before placing them in a freezer bag or open freeze them for a short while and then store them in a rigid container or freezer bag.

It is vital to use the fast freeze setting when freezing fish to speed up the freezing process (see page 212). Place the fish near the freezing coils or by the sides if you don't have a fast freeze setting. If the fish freezes slowly, large ice crystals will form and the delicate texture of the fish will be compromised.

The storage time for raw fish is quite short compared to meat or vegetables as fish will lose flavour and texture if frozen for too long. Oily fish such as mackerel may also develop a rancid flavour. For the best results, freeze white fish, such as cod and haddock for up to 3 months; oily fish like salmon, trout and mackerel for up to 2 months; smoked fish such as smoked salmon or kippers for 2 months and shellfish for up to 1 month.

Raw fish generally freezes better than cooked, although there are exceptions to this – a fish pie or bake where the fish is enveloped in a rich sauce or fish cakes where the fish is combined with mashed potato.

Shop bought frozen fish and shellfish also make good freezer standbys, especially prawns that can be thawed for salads or thrown into stir-fries and curries from frozen. Breaded and battered fish products such as scampi and fish fingers are handy additions that store well too.

Cooking raw fish, poultry or meat from frozen

Anything that makes life easier and more economical has to be a good thing and this includes cooking raw fish, poultry or meat from frozen.

I also cook other things such as fish fillets, chicken escalopes, lamb cutlets and minced beef from frozen. The wonderful thing about freezing your own raw ingredients is that you can flavour them before you freeze.

Don't be frightened of cooking raw meat from frozen. Just look along the aisles of your supermarket and you'll see you've been doing it for years. Fish fingers, chicken kievs, beef burgers are all raw and then cooked by you from frozen. As long as you follow a few very simple rules, you really can't go wrong.

The most essential thing to remember when cooking raw fish, poultry or meat from frozen is that it needs to have been properly prepared. This means cutting it into fairly small pieces or portions for freezing. A steak or pork chop is about as thick as I would recommend cooking without thawing first. When cooking from frozen, allow at least 50 per cent more time than for thawed food.

Super-quick strips

Among the most useful foods in my freezer are super-quick strips. These small slices or chunks of chicken, meat or fish are packed into rigid containers ready for me to grab by the handful and transform from frozen into a delicious stir-fry, risotto, curry or stew in minutes.

It is not surprising that a solid brick of frozen stewing beef is going to take longer to thaw and cook than a free-flowing pack of sliced beef. A chicken breast may take up to 30 minutes to cook right through to the centre from frozen, whereas sliced chicken breast can be pan-fried and ready to eat in 6–8 minutes.

To make super-quick strips

- Put your freezer on to fast freeze or turn to its lowest temperature setting.
- Line baking trays or small toughened plastic trays with easy-leave sheets, foil or baking parchment.
- Keep the work surfaces, your hands and any utensils extremely clean to prevent contamination by dirt or bacteria.
- Use boneless chicken breasts, pork tenderloin, lamb fillet and tender cuts of beef.
- Thinly slice, across the grain of the poultry or meat where possible. Slices should be 1.5–2cm thick. For fish, cut into fillets or chunky pieces for soups and stews.
- Toss with a little sunflower oil, chopped herbs and ground black pepper if you like.
- Arrange in a single layer on the prepared tray.
- Cover the tray with interleaving sheets or cling film and freeze for 1–3 hours or until solid. Freeze in the fast freezing compartment or shelf if you have one in your freezer.
- Take the tray out of the freezer and transfer the contents to rigid containers. Cover, label and return to the freezer. Discard the lining paper.
- Freeze for up to one month.
- Cook from frozen in a hot non-stick frying pan or wok with a little oil.
- Check that the food is piping hot throughout, that there is no pinkness remaining in poultry and that fish is opaque. Check the internal temperature with a digital food thermometer (probe) if in doubt.

Money-saving tip

Buy larger packs of chicken breasts and meat or whole fish when they are on offer. Use what you need immediately and then freeze the rest.

Freezing vegetables

Blanching is the best method for preparing vegetables for the freezer; it preserves flavour, texture and colour and can be stored in the freezer for up to 8–12 months in good conditions. Blanching also halts the loss of vitamins and minerals that occurs when fresh vegetables are stored at room temperature or even in the fridge. It is possible to freeze vegetables without blanching, but if you do, it's best to eat them within a week or 2.

Blanching time is crucial and varies with each vegetable and its size (see page 242). There is no need for special blanching equipment, as long as you have a big saucepan, a slotted spoon or tongs, a colander and a supply of freezer bags, you are set to go.

Only choose vegetables that are very fresh and in perfect condition. The only exception to this rule is if you have overbought or taken advantage of a special deal and you know you won't eat them within a day or 2.

To prepare vegetables for the freezer

❄ Prepare the vegetables as usual, so pod, shell, string, and trim as necessary. Each variety of vegetable should be roughly the same size. Wash well in cold water and drain.

❄ Weigh the vegetables and divide them into up to 500g portions. It's important to blanch the vegetables in small portions so the water can return to the boil within a minute of the vegetables being added. This prevents the vegetables softening and then spoiling when they are cooked later on.

❄ Fill a very large saucepan roughly two-thirds full of cold water and bring to a rapid boil over a high heat. As long as you have plenty of bubbling water and roughly 2 handfuls of veg in each portion, you will get good results. But as a guide, for a 500g portion of vegetables you will need 4.5 litres of water.

❄ Drop the vegetables into the water and return to the boil. If the water doesn't return to the boil within a minute, you are using too many vegetables for the amount of boiling water, so reduce the quantity next time.

❄ Start counting the blanching time as soon as the water returns to the boil. A digital kitchen timer is useful. Keep the heat high and follow the directions given for the vegetable you are freezing on pages 242–244.

❄ When the blanching time is complete, it is crucial to cool the vegetables as quickly as possible to stop the cooking process. I find it is best to remove them from the water with a slotted spoon or tongs and drop them into a colander over a bowl. Take directly to the sink and rinse under cold running water for a few minutes or plunge into a bowl of ice water until absolutely cold.

❄ As soon as the vegetables are completely cold, remove from the water and drain thoroughly in the colander. Extra moisture can cause loss of quality when freezing, so pat dry with a very clean tea towel if in doubt.

When the vegetables have been blanched, open freeze (see page 214) or pack directly into labelled freezer bags, seal and freeze at once. Don't forget to set your freezer to the fast freeze setting before you begin to blanch.

Cook frozen vegetables in a pan of fast boiling water, carefully breaking apart with a fork or wooden spoon so they cook quickly and evenly. Alternatively, cook small portions of vegetables in a saucepan with a couple of knobs of butter, stirring over a low heat until tender. If cooking in the microwave, put the vegetables in a suitable bowl and add a couple of tablespoons of water. Cover with cling film, pierce and microwave on HIGH.

Clever idea

If you are blanching vegetables such as artichokes, asparagus or celeriac, which tend to discolour when cooking, just add some fresh lemon juice to the blanching water to prevent this.

Freezing fruit

When I was growing up, it was nearly impossible to buy fresh summer berries, such as redcurrants and raspberries, out of the summer season. Nowadays, it's possible to buy most kinds of fruits all year round but they're expensive and unlikely to have been grown in the UK.

So, if your freezer is large enough, it is definitely worth freezing fruit in season when it is at its best – and cheapest, ready to enjoy later in the year. Frozen fruit isn't quite the same as fresh but the little changes that freezing makes to it are a small price to pay for the convenience and savings. And, if you grow your own fruit, freeze whatever you can't eat immediately and you'll be able to enjoy the fruits of your labour for months to come. Some fruit with a high water content, like strawberries, become very soft on thawing, some fruit skins may toughen but most seem to cope rather well if frozen. For those that don't freeze particularly well, such as strawberries, turn it into a dish that does.

Apples are an obvious choice for making pies and crumbles, but gooseberries, plums and pears also freeze well. Less obvious still, is freezing fruit salad. But my version, a combination of oranges, grapes and raspberries in a light sugar syrup is a lovely fresh fruit treat – delicious from the freezer. I also slice and freeze limes and lemons that would otherwise harden in the fruit bowl. Check the At a Glance chapter on pages 240–241 for more information on how to freeze particular fruits.

How to freeze fruit
Use fruit that is fully ripe. Pick through the fruit carefully and only freeze fresh fruit in perfect condition. Never freeze fruit that is damaged, blemished, mouldy or mushy. Any bruised tree fruits can be peeled, the damaged areas removed then cored or stoned and stewed with sugar before freezing.

For fruit that is to be frozen without peeling, wash in very cold water and dry carefully with kitchen paper or on a clean tea towel. Do not remove stalks before washing as they help to plug the fruit and stop water flooding inside.

For fruits that discolour on peeling, toss with lemon juice or cook quickly before they have a chance to start going brown.

Open freeze berries as soon as they are picked (unless you know they have been sprayed with chemicals or are very dirty, in which case, it is better to wash and carefully dry them first). If I've picked berries from my garden, I try to give them a quick rinse to get rid of any dust and bugs then drain them on kitchen paper before freezing. Handle as little as possible to prevent bruising.

Except for berries, most fresh fruits freeze better when mixed with sugar or a sugar syrup. Fresh fruit that is frozen without sugar should be used within 3 months as it tends to dehydrate during a longer storage. Thaw frozen uncooked fruits slowly in the fridge and use just before they are completely defrosted if you can. Thawing slowly will help the fruit retain as much of its original colour and texture as possible. A 500g pack of fruit in syrup will take about 6 hours to thaw.

If you are planning to cook the fruit, thaw it at room temperature just long enough for you to be able to separate the fruit pieces then cook as per usual.

Raw with sugar
This method is ideal for sliced rhubarb, peaches, apricots and nectarines. Make sure the fruit is clean and prepare if necessary. Place in a shallow tray and sprinkle with roughly 250g caster sugar per 1kg of prepared fruit. Toss lightly together until the sugar coats the fruit then pack into freezer bags or rigid containers and freeze. As the fruit thaws, the juices it releases will combine with the sugar to make a light syrup. Serve cold (except for rhubarb) with cream or ice cream or cook lightly and serve with custard or top with crumble and bake from frozen.

Raw in syrup

This method is great for plums, oranges, grapefruits, grapes and melons. Ensure the fruit is clean and prepared as necessary. Make a simple syrup by dissolving 250g caster sugar in every 600ml of cold water over a low heat. Simmer for a couple of minutes before leaving to cool. Pack the fruit into rigid containers and pour the syrup over so it is completely covered, leaving around 2cm of headroom to allow for expansion. Cover and freeze. Serve the fruit as fruit salads or use in cold, creamy desserts.

Stewed with sugar

This method is brilliant for apples, pears, gooseberries and also stone fruit such as plums and apricots. Cook lightly with a dash of water and sugar to taste. Cool thoroughly then pack into rigid containers or freezer bags. Seal, label and freeze. Use for pies, crumbles and sponges.

Fruit juice, purées and smoothies

Make according to your usual recipe then pour into rigid containers, leaving around 2cm of headroom to allow for expansion. Cover and freeze. Thaw slowly and serve as fresh.

Clever idea

Did you know you can freeze Seville oranges when they are in season and then make your marmalade when you are ready? Scrub the skins well before freezing.

Freezing rice, pasta and potatoes

It's all very well having a freezer packed with main meal dishes for you to pick from but unless you have a good selection of ready-cooked rice, pasta and even some potatoes to serve alongside, your meals could be pretty limited. Of course, pasta, rice and even potatoes don't take long to cook anyway, so you can always start from scratch while the main part of the meal is reheating, but there is definitely something very comforting about selecting the perfect accompaniment straight from the freezer, knowing it will be ready to serve in next to no time.

Rice

It's always best to cook rice for the freezer rather than freeze leftovers as cooked rice can lead to food poisoning if not handled carefully. Although this might sound a bit scary, all it means is that you must ensure your rice is cooked and then cooled very quickly before freezing. Cooked rice that has been left standing at room temperature – or even kept warm – for a while could cause problems. I always freeze easy-cook long-grain rice for the freezer as it heats up beautifully, but cooked brown is worth freezing too. Considering that brown rice takes a good 30 minutes to cook, having a stash in the freezer could really save you time.

Cooking your own rice for the freezer also means you can colour or flavour the rice with turmeric, spices or herbs. Boil the rice with a little ground turmeric, rinse in cold water and toss with chopped fresh coriander. Look for supermarket packs of frozen rice and paella-style meals too.

To freeze rice
* Half-fill a large saucepan with water and bring to the boil.
* Measure your rice. You will need around 60g of uncooked rice per serving.
* Add the rice to the water, stir well and return to the boil.
* Cook the rice for 10 minutes or according to the packet instructions until only just tender.
* Drain in a sieve and rinse under cold water until completely cooled. This will stop the rice cooking and cool it very quickly.
* Drain well and spread over a baking tray lined with easy-leave or baking parchment. Leave to stand for 10 minutes to dry out a little.
* Divide the rice between individually labelled press seal freezer bags.
* Lay each bag on the work surface and flatten the rice while pressing out most of the air and seal.
* Flat freeze until solid then stack the bags, either flat or on their sides.
* Freeze for up to 3 months.
* When ready to cook, simply take a portion of rice from the freezer, take out of the bag and put on a plate.
* Reheat in the microwave on HIGH for 1–2 minutes until piping hot. Fluff up with a fork and serve.

Alternatively, shake the rice out of the bag into a pan of boiling water. Stir well. Return to the boil and cook for 2 minutes or until piping hot. Drain and serve.

Pasta

Most pastas take less than 10 minutes to cook, so why bother to freeze it? I reckon frozen pasta makes a brilliant accompaniment to a range of dishes and a great freezer standby in its own right. You can cook a few batches when convenient and you'll always have single servings handy when you need them. When you are serving lots of people it makes sense to boil a big pan and cook dried pasta from scratch. As you are doing so, it's worth cooking a bit extra to freeze. You just need to rinse it in cold water then drain and flat freeze. I recently took a bag of penne from the freezer and grabbed some ham, cream and cheddar from the fridge. In less than 5 minutes I had a quick pasta carbonara for far less than a ready-meal would have cost and only one pan to wash. I think that small shapes freeze better than long spaghetti or tagliatelle which freeze more successfully when they are tossed through a sauce first. So next time you might think of binning that leftover spaghetti Bolognese, pop it into the freezer instead.

To freeze pasta

- Half-fill a large saucepan with water and bring to the boil.
- Measure your pasta. You will need around 75g of dry pasta shapes per serving.
- Add the pasta to the water, stir well and return to the boil.
- Cook the pasta for 2 minutes less than recommended on the pack, until only just tender.
- Drain in a colander and rinse under lots of cold water. This will stop the pasta cooking.
- Leave to stand for 10 minutes to dry out a bit.
- Divide the pasta between individual labelled press seal freezer bags.
- Lay each bag on the work surface and flatten the pasta into a single layer if possible while pressing out most of the air and seal.
- Flat freeze until solid then stack the bags, either flat or on their sides.
- Freeze for up to 3 months.
- When ready to cook, take a bag of the frozen pasta out of the freezer and separate the pieces with your fingers while still in the bag. This will help the pasta cook more quickly.
- Stir the pasta into a pan of boiling water. Return to the boil and cook for one minute or until piping hot. Drain and serve.

Potatoes

I've given recipes for a delicious mashed potato, roast spuds and fuss-free dauphinoise potatoes in this book. These can all be frozen in smaller portions to serve with single meals. I've found that new potatoes aren't suitable for freezing as they become water-logged and very soggy on thawing, however I've had great success with jacket potatoes. Next time you have the oven on for any length of time – or are cooking jacket spuds for another meal – add a few extras. They can be reheated from frozen in the microwave in little over 5 minutes and the results, surprisingly, are far better than if you cook fresh potatoes in the microwave. You can also reheat them in a hot oven for 40 minutes or so.

To freeze jacket potatoes

- Choose medium-sized floury potatoes such as King Edwards or Maris Piper.
- Wash well and pat dry with kitchen roll or a clean tea towel.
- Make a cross in one side of each potato with a sharp knife.
- Rub the potatoes with a little sunflower oil and season with flaked sea salt and freshly ground black pepper
- Put on a baking tray and bake in a preheated oven at 220°C/Fan 200°C/Gas 7 for 50–60 minutes until tender and lightly browned.
- Take out of the oven and leave to cool completely.
- Wrap each potato tightly in foil. Label and freeze for up to 3 months.
- When ready to serve, unwrap a potato and put on a microwavable plate. Cover with a second sheet of kitchen roll to absorb any moisture.
- Reheat in the microwave on HIGH for around 6½ minutes until hot throughout. Leave to stand for 2 minutes before serving. If you aren't sure whether the potato is hot, probe with a digital food thermometer.

If cooking 2 potatoes you'll need to almost double the cooking time.

Herbs, chillies, garlic and ginger

There will always be times when you've forked out for a few bags or pots of fresh herbs and have used about as much as you can. I can't bear watching them go limp and pale, so now I freeze any that I can't use immediately.

Frozen herbs work well when you are looking to inject some extra flavour into a dish. You'll never be able to use them for garnish as they go horribly soggy on freezing but a few tablespoons of frozen basil in a pasta sauce or some frozen mint added to a rich lamb gravy makes all the difference.

Some of the supermarkets also sell a good selection of ready-frozen herbs that make great freezer standbys. I also use freshly chopped herbs to liven up frozen rice and gratin-style toppings. The colour does deepen a little and the flavour isn't quite as intense but the dish still looks good when served and most people would never notice the difference.

You can freeze finely chopped herbs in ice-cube trays but I find the filling a bit of a fiddle, so prefer to use little plastic pots designed for baby food. I find the colour and flavour is preserved better if I freeze them under a little cold water or even a slurp of olive oil. Basil works particularly well frozen in a little olive oil. I've frozen herbs this way for 5–6 months, which means you can still be enjoying summer herbs from the garden at Christmas time and beyond.

When really rushed, I've also shoved bunches of fresh herbs into bags without chopping; then when I need to use them, I simply crumble the frozen leaves directly into my casserole or soup, or rub into my roast chicken before popping into the oven. For herbs such as thyme, it also means no fiddly removing from stems as the leaves will easily fall away once frozen. I have found that the herbs will keep in the freezer for a couple of months this way.

To freeze herbs

* Pick over the herbs and throw away any damaged or diseased parts.
* Quickly rinse under cold water then drain and pat dry gently but thoroughly with kitchen paper. If I'm taking herbs straight from my own garden I don't usually bother to wash them first but pick over them to dislodge any insects.
* Once the herbs are dry, you can place on a board and chop with your sharpest kitchen knife. Make sure your knife is sharp or the herbs will bruise.
* Divide between small plastic containers and cover with a little cold water or oil.
* Freeze until solid.
* Fill a bowl with just-boiled water.
* Dip the base of each of the frozen herb pots in the water for a few seconds then turn out. Your pots can then be washed and used again.
* Transfer the frozen blocks of herbs to a freezer-proof container or freezer bag. Seal, label and freeze.

Other aromatic ingredients such as garlic, fresh root ginger and especially chillies all freeze brilliantly and can be used from frozen. I have read that they can either become more pungent or taste musty after a couple of months in the freezer. I have yet to find any evidence from my own cooking, so I think that as long as you choose top-quality produce, it will freeze well for a few months without suffering. Definitely avoid using garlic with green stems.

It's also worth freezing fresh lemongrass, kaffir lime leaves and curry leaves. As with any strongly smelling foods, always double wrap to prevent their aromas pervading the freezer and perhaps tainting other more delicate foods.

Some cooks crush their garlic or grate quantities of ginger then form them into sausage shapes and wrap in foil. A little can then be broken off each time it is needed and the rest returned to the freezer. You can also store large quantities in small tubs ready for the next time you want to cook a curry.

I finely chop or slice chillies for freezing although occasionally I'll also freeze them whole, especially scotch bonnet chillies that I add to curries whole. If you prefer to deseed chillies before cooking, then prepare them this way for the freezer too. If you are freezing chillies whole and need them chopped for a recipe, it is best to chop them while still frozen as they will soften on thawing.

To freeze garlic and ginger
- Peel firm whole cloves of garlic and knobs of ginger.
- Finely chop, grate or crush.
- Transfer to small freezer-proof pots or wrap in foil.
- Double wrap in freezer bags.
- Seal, label and freeze for up to 3 months.
- Use from frozen.

To freeze fresh chillies
- Wash and pat dry with kitchen paper.
- Finely chop or slice, discarding the seeds if you prefer, although I tend to keep them.
- Transfer to freezer-proof containers.
- Double wrap in freezer bags.
- Seal, label and freeze for up to 3 months.
- Use from frozen.

Freezing is a quick, easy and natural way of preserving food. If you freeze food correctly and use it within a sensible time span, it will be just as good as fresh.

In this chapter you'll find all the information you need to know to freeze food safely and with perfect results. I've briefly explained the importance of freezing food quickly – and thawing it slowly – and have also explained terms such as *fast freezing* and *open freezing* that you'll find in the recipes. One particular eureka moment for me was when I discovered flat freezing. This method of freezing soups, sauces and even home-made ready meals not only ensures that the food freezes quickly and can be cooked from frozen, but also saves space, as the flat packs stack up so neatly in a freezer drawer (see page 216).

From bitter experience, I would also like to emphasise the importance of being organised. You might think that you will remember that bag of brownish lumps is a delicious beef stew but a few months later on you'd be surprised how unrecognisable it could become. Follow my tips for choosing the right freezer bags, wraps and containers for each dish and always label and date everything carefully to make sure you know what you have and when

it needs to be used by, adding cooking or reheating instructions if applicable. It doesn't take long to label your food and you'll get the very best from your freezer.

Rules for successful freezing:
* Freeze food when it is at its best and freshest.
* Cool cooked foods quickly and thoroughly before freezing.
* Open freeze delicate items or foods that could stick together when frozen.
* Wrap food very well and remove as much air as possible from bags.
* Allow a little room for expansion when freezing liquids.
* Use shallow rather than deep containers if you want to cook from frozen.
* Label food clearly.
* Freeze food quickly using the fast freeze button on your freezer if it has one.
* Don't overload the freezer when adding fresh food.
* Keep to the recommended storage times.
* When possible, thaw food in the fridge where it will defrost slowly and remain cold.
* Cook or reheat frozen food to a high enough temperature to ensure it is safe to eat (see page 223).
* Thoroughly cook thawed raw ingredients before freezing again. Once thawed and reheated, do not refreeze.

FREEZER KNOW-HOW

Benefits of freezing food

Freezing is a natural way of preserving food. It is one of the simplest methods for ensuring food maintains its quality and texture, remaining as close as possible to its natural state. Freezing food is like pressing the pause button; foods in perfect condition, frozen at -18°C or less cannot rot or become mouldy. At this low temperature, bacteria, moulds and ripening enzymes are no longer active. However, it is also important to remember that food will not improve in the freezer and will quickly continue to deteriorate when thawed.

Please note that it is vital that foods are cooled quickly after cooking and before being placed in the freezer. Foods should be removed from the cooking pan and spread out thinly or cooled by standing in a pan or bowl in iced water. I transfer a cooked casserole to a large clean roasting tin or large, shallow ovenproof dish to cool. Dividing between freezer containers from the hot pan is also a good way to ensure foods are cooled quickly. I spread vegetable dishes and chunky sauces onto trays. Cooked vegetables, rice, pasta, etc., are rinsed under running water until cold.

Rapid cooling is important for food safety reasons. Hot food shouldn't be put in the fridge or freezer as it will cause the internal temperature to rise too quickly. Food that is cooling before being placed in the freezer should be covered very lightly to prevent contamination by insects, etc.

The importance of fast freezing

When food is frozen quickly the water content will form into tiny ice crystals. However, slower freezing allows larger crystals to form. These will break down the cell structure of the food as they expand which adversely affects the colour, flavour and texture of the food when it is thawed. So fast-freezing is much better for the quality of the food.

To help ensure that fresh food can be frozen solid quickly and without raising the temperature of the existing frozen food, many freezers have a fast freeze switch that enables the motor to override the thermostat – the control that regulates the temperature in the freezer – to allow the temperature to continue to fall until the newly added food is frozen.

Some freezers have a separate compartment for fast freezing. Its size dictates how much fresh food can be added without affecting the temperature of the food elsewhere in the freezer. Other, more advanced freezers have an automatic fast freeze that cuts in if the temperature in the freezer becomes too warm and turns off again when food is frozen.

Fast freeze know-how

- Set the fast freeze control or reduce the freezer temperature for 2–5 hours before adding fresh food.
- Put well-wrapped and labelled packages in the fast freeze compartment.
- If you don't have a special fast freeze compartment, put food in the coldest part of the freezer and away from already frozen foods.
- Times for fast freezing will vary according to the size, density, shape of package, type of food and how much food is already contained within the freezer.
- Don't overfill the freezer with fresh food at any one time as your freezer might be unable to maintain the extra low temperature.
- If buying in bulk, keep foods in the fridge and add to the freezer when you are sure that the previous additions are solid. It takes roughly 1–2 hours for a 500g food package to freeze. Try not to use more than about 10 per cent of the freezer's total capacity for freezing fresh food every 24 hours.
- As soon as all the food has frozen, turn off the fast freeze switch or turn up the thermostat so the freezer can return to its normal setting. This will help preserve the quality of the food, perhaps prevent the motor overheating and save electricity.

Open freezing

Open freezing is a method of pre-freezing foods that need to remain separate when they are frozen. This applies to the super-quick strips, fillets of fish and chicken and smaller cuts of meat, decorated cakes and tarts, plus some vegetables and lots of fruit, especially the soft berry fruits. By open freezing these items in a single layer on a baking tray before packing them into bags or containers, they should remain free-flowing and easy to use.

You'll need to use trays that fit in your freezer and line them with foil or easy-leave before using.

To open freeze
- Put your freezer on to fast freeze or turn it to its lowest temperature setting.
- Line baking trays or small, plastic trays with foil or easy-leave.
- Select good quality fresh foods and wash or prepare as necessary. Keep the work surfaces, your hands and any utensils extremely clean to prevent contamination by dirt or bacteria.
- Divide food into single elements, whether lamb cutlets or fresh raspberries, and place them on the tray, spaced slightly apart. Very small items such as berries, peas, podded beans or sprouts should be as close as possible but dont allow to touch. Cakes and tarts can be placed in the centre of the tray.
- Keep raw fish, poultry and meat on separate trays from cooked foods, raw vegetables and fruit.
- Brush fish pieces, poultry and meat with sunflower oil to help prevent freezer burn.

- If you have more than one tray to freeze at a time, put a shallow cake tin – a small Victoria sandwich tin is ideal – in between the trays.
- Cover the tray of food with cling film and freeze for 1–3 hours or until solid. Freeze in the fast freezing compartment or shelf if you have one in your freezer.
- Take the tray out of the freezer and transfer the contents to freezer bags or rigid containers. Seal, label and return to the freezer.
- Discard the lining paper.

Pre-seasoning saves me time when I come to cook and helps use up fresh herbs and other ingredients that would otherwise go off in the fridge. I put gratin toppings on fish fillets, chicken is sometimes seasoned with fine slivers of garlic and chilli before I open freeze. Lamb chops are coated with a delicious herb rub and I marinate meats for stir-fries. Not only does brushing or tossing meat, poultry and fish with a little oil help prevent freezer burn, it also helps seasoning stick.

Open freezing is also perfect for freezing fruit and berries such as redcurrants, raspberries, blackcurrants and blueberries. Rinse carefully in cold water and drain extremely well. Open freeze on a tray until solid then transfer to rigid containers. Use the thawed fruit for pavlovas and Eton mess or trifles and ice cream sundaes. Buy lemons and limes when they are on offer and slice thickly. Open freeze, then pack into freezer bags or rigid containers. Perfect to use for cold drinks.

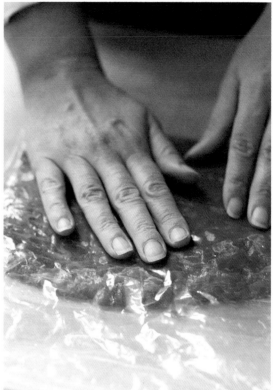

Flat freezing

I'd been pondering freezer space and how to make the most of it, when it struck me that freezing foods completely flat would not only save valuable space but would also ensure food would freeze quickly and then thaw super fast.

In addition, it turned out that finding things in the freezer is much easier when they are flat frozen. Just flick through the stack and pick out what you want and because the zip-seal bags are clear – I always use transparent bags – the food looks much more appetising too.

Flat freezing works best for foods such as thick soups, sauces, stews and curries, puréed vegetables, fruit and rice. You can even divide the food into portions and then break off a section whenever you need it. A portion of pasta sauce cooked from frozen is ready to eat in just 3–4 minutes.

Stack it and see

Filled, flattened and frozen zip-seal bags stack brilliantly in the freezer. In just one drawer, I have the following home-made foods – many more than I could ever fit in before:

- 4 servings of mushroom soup
- 3 servings of carrot and coriander soup
- 4 large servings of time-saving tomato sauce
- 3 single servings of tomato and chilli pasta sauce
- 2 family-sized portions of Bolognese sauce
- 1 family-sized portion of beef stew
- 1 family-sized portion of chicken and leek pie filling
- 1 small serving of chicken gravy
- 4 portions of cooked rice
- cheese sauce to serve 6
- apple sauce to serve 6

To flat freeze

- Make sure the food to be frozen is cold.
- Choose your bag or bags.
- Label the bag or bags before you fill.
- Place the bag in a jug to help hold it open and spoon or ladle the required number of servings inside.
- Transfer the bag to a small metal baking sheet. Using a baking sheet to transport the bag to the freezer and supporting the food while it is freezing helps maintain its flatness.
- Tip the bag on its side and press the food with the palms of your hands to flatten it until it is just 1–2cm thick, leaving the top of the bag open for air to escape. Try to keep the zip area clean and free from food to ensure a good seal.
- If the bag contains several servings, divide into even portions using a ruler or the side of your hand.
- Leave about 2cm of space at the open end to allow for expansion and zip the bag closed.
- Continue filling bags as needed, piling up to 4 on top of each other on the baking sheet and put the sheet and bags into the freezer.
- Freeze the filled bags until solid, then remove the baking sheet and stack and store the flat frozen bags in the freezer.

Reheating food that has been flat frozen is easy too. Simply run water from the hot tap over the unopened bag for a few seconds, unzip the bag and drop the contents directly into a pan or dish for reheating. Because it is only a couple of centimetres thick, it is super quick to heat from frozen, which means you can have spaghetti Bolognese ready to serve the family in less than 15 minutes.

Flat freezing can also be used for bought foods or leftover sauces. Buy pasta sauces, canned tomatoes and cooking sauces in catering sized packs. Use what you need and flat freeze the rest. Try to use heavy gauge zip-seal bags as they can be washed thoroughly and reused several times.

Flexible freezing

In the past few years silicone bakeware has become increasingly popular for it's non-stick qualities. I tend to rely on my metal cake tins but I have found a new use for these rubbery, ovenproof containers. I've discovered that they are perfect for fast-freezing prepared dishes too. Their flexibility means that hard-frozen foods are simple to pop out and then can be wrapped in foil or dropped into a plastic bag and returned to the freezer.

Pre-freezing in this way saves space in the freezer, as wrapped foods can be easily stacked, and saves money reducing the need for a continuous supply of new freezer containers.

I match my silicone cake pans to the oven-proof dishes, casseroles or tins in my kitchen so the frozen foods can be unwrapped directly into a suitable dish and then either thawed or cooked from frozen. I never lose my dishes for weeks in the freezer, the food cooks more quickly as it isn't contained in a freezing cold dish to start with and I don't have problems with frozen dishes cracking when placed in the oven. My round silicone cake pans are exactly the same size as the base of my favourite casserole dish and the rectangle ones marry perfectly with my most useful lasagne dish. I even freeze small portions of sauce and stocks in silicone muffin tins and then transfer to freezer bags once frozen.

I've frozen everything from beef stew, to dauphinoise potatoes, uncooked cake batter, broth-style soups, cauliflower cheese and lasagne in mine.

And don't forget, silicone bakeware can also be used in the oven up to certain temperatures, so even if you don't have quite the right-sized dish to transfer your frozen food into, you can always pop it back into the silicone container. (Always place silicone bakeware on a baking tray to keep it stable when cooking and moving.)

To flexible freeze

- Put your freezer on to fast freeze or turn it to its lowest temperature setting.
- Wash and dry silicone containers thoroughly.
- Place containers on flat trays to keep the rubber stable.
- Keep the work surfaces, your hands and any utensils extremely clean to prevent contamination by dirt or bacteria.
- Keep raw fish, poultry and meat away from cooked foods, raw vegetables and fruit until ready to freeze.
- Make sure the food that will be frozen is completely cold.
- Arrange the food in the silicone containers, keeping larger pieces, such as chicken pieces or braised steaks, spaced apart to allow them to freeze and cook more quickly.
- Cover the containers with plastic wrap and fast freeze for 5–8 hours or until solid. Freeze in the fast freezing compartment or shelf if you have one in your freezer.
- Take the trays out of the freezer and pop the frozen food straight out of the silicone bakeware.
- Double wrap the food tightly in foil or transfer to freezer bags and suck out the air. Seal, label and return to the freezer.

Before you start your silicone bakeware collection, you can also line freezer-proof dishes with foil and pre-freeze foods for re-wrapping. It works well but the foil is more difficult to remove and can't be used again.

Thawing food from the freezer

Although I much prefer the convenience of cooking food from frozen, there are many times when thawing first is preferable. Don't forget, thawed food should be cooked and eaten quickly and not refrozen, unless initially raw and then cooked completely before returning to the freezer.

There are four ways I like to thaw frozen food, depending on what it is.

Thawing food in the fridge

Anything that must be stored in the fridge when fresh or freshly prepared should also be thawed there; so high risk foods such as anything meaty, fishy or containing dairy products or eggs. Best suited to joints of meat, fish or game, plus deep-filled pies, very chunky casseroles, creamy puddings and precooked dishes to be eaten cold.

Thawing in the fridge gives a chance for the ice crystals to melt slowly and reduces the chance of toughening or drying. It does take several hours to thaw food thoroughly in the fridge, so you need to be able to plan your meals ahead. As a general rule, take the food out of the freezer and place in the fridge 18–24 hours before it needs to be cooked or reheated.

Make sure the food, especially whole poultry birds, is completely thawed in the middle before cooking or reheating as it could end up cooked on the outside and raw or cold in the centre.

Thawing at room temperature

I thaw high risk foods at room temperature if I am certain that I will be cooking, reheating or eating them within an hour. It's not a good idea to leave foods at room temperature for more than an hour as at some point they will no longer be frozen and will slowly begin to rise to room temperature – way above the 5°C recommended. Exceptions to this are cakes, pastries and breads that are generally suited to storing without refrigeration.

Thawing in the microwave

Very occasionally I thaw raw food in the microwave before cooking. This does need to be done with care as some foods, especially meat or chicken pieces, can begin to cook before they are thoroughly defrosted. I do reheat some precooked foods directly from frozen in the microwave as it saves heaps of time. You will need to remove any metal ties from bags and transfer foods frozen in foil into microwavable dishes or bowls.

Thaw in short bursts, break up the food or stir to prevent the outside of the food beginning to cook. You'll need to check your microwave manufacturer's guidelines for the best results.

Thawing by cooking from frozen

All frozen vegetables, pre-cooked pasta and rice are best prepared this way. Precooked dishes that need extra cooking or are to be eaten hot, such as shallow pies or bakes and servings of pasta sauce, are also ideal for cooking from frozen. You will need to add around 50 per cent to the usual cooking time.

To thaw food from the freezer

* Food should be left in its original wrappings. The exceptions to this are cakes and decorated puddings, which could soften and stick.
* Raw frozen meat and fish will produce water as they thaw, so should be kept wrapped to prevent cross contamination.
* Place the food in a bowl or on a tray to collect any water that does seep out. Bags should be thawed upright. If you are worried that your food hasn't been properly wrapped, thaw instead in a plastic container.
* Put at the bottom of the fridge to stop any drips landing on other food.
* Allow between 2 and 48 hours for food to thoroughly defrost, depending on size.
* Unwrap and drain off any liquid. You may need to pat meat or fish dry with kitchen paper before cooking.
* Cook or eat as soon as possible. Do not refreeze foods that have completely thawed.

Organising your freezer

Having an organised freezer means you can find foods easily and ensure that, as far as possible, foods are used in rotation.

It is very irritating to make or buy foods for your freezer only to discover a stash of exactly the same thing hidden away at the bottom. By using foods in rotation, you'll be much more likely to eat foods when they are looking and tasting their best.

If you want to get super-organised, it is well worth keeping a small notebook listing all the items in the freezer, so you know exactly what is in there and when it should be used. Keep the notebook close to your freezer, with a pen attached. Cross items off as you use them and jot down the newest additions as you go along. On one of my smaller freezers, I have stuck an adhesive blackboard on which I write the contents with a white chalkboard pen. That way I can see at a glance exactly how many portions of lasagne or chocolate mousse it contains

How you stack your freezer depends on the types of foods you are most likely to freeze and which type of freezer you are using, but it is definitely best to freeze foods of the same type in the same section. For instance, having all the frozen vegetables in one section and the home-cooked meals in another. It's also a good idea to let other members of the family know your system, so there is less chance of them throwing a heavy bag of ice into the freezer right on top of your delicate pavlova.

If you have an upright freezer, try to allocate whole or parts of drawers to one type of food. Stick labels on the front of the drawers to remind yourself of the sections. If you don't have solid fronts to your drawers, tie luggage labels written with a permanent marker instead.

For chest freezers, I use the stacking plastic boxes you find in hardware or pound shops and department stores. Buy those made from the toughest plastic as they will be less likely to crack in the freezer and they should last for years. Wash well before using.

The plastic boxes come in different sizes and can be colour coded for various food types. I keep my frozen vegetables in a green box, puddings, cakes and cookies in purple and fish and meat in blue and red. If you don't want to use plastic boxes, sturdy cardboard boxes can be used instead, although you will need to replace them fairly often.

The hanging baskets that are sold with the freezer can be used for small items that you are likely to use more often or have a shorter freezer life, such as super-quick strips, sandwiches, pasta sauces, leftover chunks of cheese, tubs of wine, filled pasta, etc.

How I organise my freezer

- Handy standbys, such as butter, breadcrumbs, cheese, filled rolls, filled pasta, frozen herbs, chopped chillies, garlic and ginger
- Super-quick strips and small cuts of meat or fish
- Ready prepared family meals
- Ready prepared individual meals
- Larger joints of meat
- Puddings, ice cream, cakes and cookies
- Sauces, stock and soups
- Frozen vegetables and fruit
- Bread, breakfast pastries, pancakes, Yorkshire puddings.

Freezer essentials

The good news is that food can be stored and covered in a variety of easily obtainable bags, wraps and containers that you can pick up in any supermarket, hardware shop or department store.

Freezer bags are something which I keep a wide variety of in various sizes in the kitchen, although I definitely have my favourites. The most often used are the zip-seal bags with their efficient plastic slide mechanism. They are more expensive than other kinds, so I tend to keep them for flat freezing – the technique I've developed for freezing thicker soups, sauces, rice, puréed vegetables and fruit, where the zip seal is crucial. Press-seal bags can come undone during prolonged freezing, so I use them for things like sandwiches or small cakes that I'm not planning to freeze for over a week or so. Soup 'n' sauce bags are handy for freezing thin liquids such as stocks and gravies when the flat freezing method cannot be used. Don't forget to leave room for the liquid to expand.

Basic larger polythene bags are good for freezing bulky or oddly shaped items like croissants, buns or home-frozen vegetables or fruit. They are also perfect for holding foods that are wrapped in foil or cling film such as portions of fish and poultry and joints of meat that need to be stored together so they don't get lost in the freezer. Double wrapping will also help prevent smells and moisture penetrating frozen foods.

Always choose bags that are suitable for freezing as the polythene is thicker and designed to withstand very cold temperatures.

Plastic bag ties are one item that doesn't seem to have changed much for decades. Plastic covered wire ties are used for sealing bags and are particularly useful for bulky foods where zip-seal or press-seal bags can't close properly.

Freezer-proof labels are essential for helping ensure the correct identification of all of your frozen foods. You can buy ones that peel off after use so that you can reuse the bag or container.

Permanent freezer markers are special freezer pens with permanent ink that will not run or

To freeze food successfully it is essential to make sure it is properly wrapped. Air and moisture are the enemies when freezing. Both can adversely affect the quality of frozen food and cut the storage times drastically.

Freezer burn is the term used to describe the unappetising dry white patches that appear on the surface of meat, poultry and fish when they have been poorly wrapped. It is caused by cool air affecting the surface. Although it doesn't make the food unsafe to eat, the eating quality is greatly reduced.

If you have a large joint that has areas affected by freezer burn, it is possible to slice off the patches once the meat has thawed. Smaller fillets of fish and poultry are probably not worth attempting to save.

fade in the freezer. Use them to write on labels, or directly onto plastic bags and the tops of foil cartons.

Aluminium foil is brilliant for lining tins for open freezing, wrapping individual portions of fish, poultry and meat and covering dishes, protecting delicate desserts, wrapping sandwiches and wraps and covering cakes and tray bakes.

Foil can also be used to line a ceramic dish before filling with a lasagne, stew or cottage pie. Once frozen the meal can be removed in a solid block, double wrapped in more foil and returned to the freezer, freeing up your dish. Remove the foil and return to the dish when you are ready to cook.

For the best results, choose a good-quality, fairly wide foil without perforations and avoid using foil with acidic foods such as citrus fruit or vinegars or pickles which can corrode the aluminium.

Clingy plastic film is very useful for covering food while open freezing and wrapping cakes, sandwiches and wraps. I always choose a multi-purpose cling film that is suitable for freezing. I find that plastic film can become brittle and tear easily once it has been in the freezer for a while, so I tend to use it for items that I'm planning to freeze for under a month.

Baking parchment is something I use lots of in my kitchen, mainly for lining tins for baking. It is also useful for the short-term lining of trays for open freezing or interleaving pancakes. Baking parchment is coated with a special non-stick coating, and although it isn't moisture-proof, it can be used in the freezer for a few weeks. It is also cheaper than foil if you are open freezing lots of foods.

Plastic interleaving (easy-leave) sheets are handy for placing in between individual items such as fillets of fish or chicken or burgers and chops to stop them freezing together into a solid block. This means that you can remove portions as you need them and thaw or cook from frozen with the minimum of fuss. Store the interleaved individual items together in a rigid container or freezer bag.

Drinking straws are handy for sucking the air out of freezer bags before sealing. Simply gather the freezer bag together in one hand, just above the food to be frozen, and insert the straw. Suck as much air as possible out of the bag and then seal with a knot or tightly twisted wire tie. Do not inhale the air or blow it back out again on the food.

An electric vacuum packer will give even better results than a straw, although I've found that only the more expensive models seal the food sufficiently well to justify the cost.

A digital food thermometer is one kitchen gadget that I couldn't do without. Available from some cookware shops, catering suppliers and online, you can get hold of a good digital thermometer for under £15. A decent digital thermometer is a brilliant way of ensuring that your food is cooked or reheated thoroughly and safely before serving.

I like the simplest battery operated variety with a large digital display. Turn the probe on, insert into your food and wait for a few seconds while the temperature gauge climbs and then reveals the internal temperature of the food. I take the temperature in at least 3 different places, wiping the probe with a clean, damp piece of kitchen paper in between readings. It is also possible to buy special wipes for cleaning the probe.

It is particularly important to push the probe into denser areas of the food and thicker pieces of meat, especially in pies, stews and curries, as the saucy parts will heat more quickly. You need to make sure the food reaches over 75°C and holds the temperature for 30 seconds to get a true reading.

While most freezers have accurate thermostats that keep them running at suitable temperatures for freezing, it is well worth being doubly sure by checking the internal temperature with a freezer thermometer. They aren't expensive and will help you gauge whether your freezer is cold enough to freeze fresh foods quickly and efficiently, essential if you don't have a fast freeze setting. If foods are frozen from fresh too slowly, large ice crystals will form and spoil the texture when thawed.

Measuring spoons and digital scales will help ensure all the recipes in this book work as well for you as they do in my own kitchen. This is especially important for baking recipes, where a slight variation in an ingredient can make a huge difference to the final result.

Freezer containers

The main considerations for choosing containers for freezing food in are: food safety, size, shape, what the container is made from, what length of time the food will be stored for and whether you want to be able to cook or reheat the food in the same container as it was frozen in.

It is important that all containers used in the freezer are easy to clean. Be sure to always thoroughly wash and dry containers before putting food in them to freeze. I use a mix of rigid containers including lidded plastic containers, foil, ceramic and enamel dishes and glass Pyrex dishes with plastic lids. Containers should definitely not be porous; wooden dishes and unglazed pottery are definitely not suitable for freezing, and only toughened glass should be used as thinner glass can crack in the freezer.

Lidded plastic containers

If made from extra tough freezer-proof plastic, lidded containers are perfect for freezing a variety of foods.

Lidded plastic boxes, bowls, basins and containers are available in a variety of sizes. So select the container that most snugly holds your food to ensure that air within the container is kept to a minimum – not forgetting to leave space for liquids to expand. Rectangle and square dishes are useful for curries, stews, Bolognese sauce and storing leftovers. Round plastic basins are great for freezing puddings ready for steaming or microwaving. They are also great for holding liquids such as egg whites or beaten eggs and for storing sweet and savoury sauces and batters. Use baby or toddler food-freezing pots for freezing small portions of leftovers or foods such as chopped herbs, grated Parmesan, crème fraîche and yogurt.

Cheaper lidded containers or those designed for takeaway meals cope less well with freezer conditions and may crack at very cold temperatures. Look on the pack and check they are suitable for freezing before buying.

Foil containers

Foil containers are useful if you want to freeze foods for a fairly long period of time and are fantastic for reheating and cooking food in the oven from frozen as the aluminium conducts heat quickly. Choose between foil or cardboard lids. Both types can only be used once and cardboard lids will need to be removed and replaced with kitchen foil when you come to cook or reheat the dish. Once the food is in the dish and the lid is on, you can't see what's in the container so labelling is especially essential. Foil dishes are not suitable for acidic – vinegar or citric – dishes.

Choose the thicker, more durable foil dishes as they are less likely to get damaged and can be used again. Although the foil lids can only be used once, they can be bought separately. Individual and family-sized dishes are brilliant for freezing a huge variety of foods. Placing larger dishes on a thin metal baking tray when filling and freezing will provide extra stability until solid. I find foil flan tins useful but thin and bendy, so double up to get round this.

Pyrex dishes

Toughened glass Pyrex dishes have become one of my favourite freezer containers. Not only can I see what's in the dish, which immediately makes it more appetising, but the dishes also come with decent plastic lids that create a good seal around the edge.

They are great for packed lunches and picnics as I can thaw and serve the food from the same container in which it has been frozen, perfect for saving on time and washing up. They are also good for freezing fruit salads and desserts. Pyrex is fairly pricy but should last for years and is very versatile as some of their dishes are designed to go straight from the freezer to the oven (check the label). As Pyrex mixing bowls are made from toughened glass, they can also be used to store food in the freezer.

Silicone bakeware

Silicone bakeware is perfect for freezing food using my flexibile freezing method (see page 218). Silicone pans aren't expensive, are completely leak-proof, will last for years and can be used again and again. Choose the best quality and build up a collection of different sizes to freeze all types of dishes.

Ceramic dishes

Ceramic pie and flan dishes can be used in the freezer and help protect more delicate foods such as heavily decorated pies or quiches made with thin, rich pastry while larger rectangular ceramic dishes are great for lasagnes and potato-topped pies. Ceramic dishes conduct heat fairly slowly, so I tend to thaw thoroughly before reheating or cooking for the best results. They are also useful for heating food in the microwave where you can't use foil.

For more sturdy foods, you can always line the ceramic dish with foil first, remove the food once frozen, double wrap it in foil, return to the freezer, then unwrap and pop back in the dish when you are ready to reheat or cook.

Enamel dishes

Enamel-coated tin dishes are inexpensive and great for freezing food. I particularly like to use them for pies as they conduct heat well and look good enough to serve from. If planning to cook from frozen use individual or shallow dishes as the heat will travel through the food more quickly. But make sure your dishes are new rather than vintage. Cracks and chips in the paint can cause dishes to rust and become rather unsavoury looking, not to mention unhygienic.

Baking trays

I use baking trays for open freezing (page 214) foods that I need to remain separate when frozen. This applies to the super-quick strips, fillets of fish and chicken, smaller cuts of meat, cakes and tarts, plus some vegetables and a lot of fruits. Use

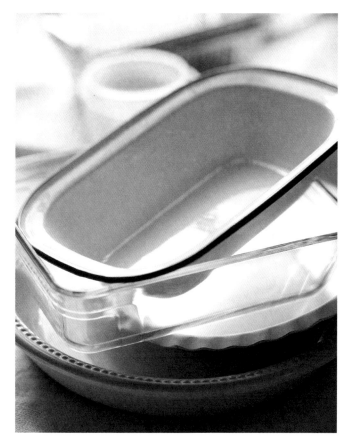

trays that fit in your freezer and line them with foil or baking parchment before using them in the freezer.

Ice-cube trays

I'm not a huge fan of using ice-cube trays for freezing as they never seem to hold enough. For small quantities of food, I find baby or toddler food pots more useful. However ice-cube trays can be useful for freezing tiny portions of leftover curry paste, crushed garlic and finely chopped chillies. Stock can also be boiled and reduced to an almost syrupy glaze, then frozen in an ice-cube tray to save space in the freezer. Once a food has frozen solid, don't leave it the tray but transfer it to a well-sealed bag or container to avoid smells permeating your freezer.

Types of freezer

Chest freezers are usually kept in a garage or utility room because of their size and bulk. They have a lockable top-opening lid, offer the most storage space and come in a range of sizes. Chest freezers are great for holding large joints of meat and food packages and are supplied with removable baskets to aid storage. However, it can be difficult to locate food towards the bottom of the freezer, so I use toughened plastic boxes in mine that I can lift out easily.

Upright freezers take up less floor space and are front opening. Food is stored either directly on shelves with plastic flaps or drawers mounted onto the shelves. The flaps at the front help the freezer retain cold air when the door is open. Many upright freezers have fixed shelves between all the drawers, which makes it impossible to store very large items such as a decent sized turkey or ham. Some have a very shallow freezer drawer for ice cubes or open freezing. Transparent compartments are useful as they allow you to find foods more easily.

Fridge freezers combine a fridge and a freezer and are perfect if you have little floor space available in your kitchen but plenty of height. Some have a single thermostat for both the fridge and the freezer and others have a separate thermostat for each. The one-control models tend to be cheaper but there is always a risk that the right temperature for your fridge might adversely affect the temperature of the freezer. Dual controls have the added advantage of allowing you to maintain the coldness of the fridge while the freezer is being defrosted.

Built-in freezers are integrated into a kitchen cabinet. They are usually a little more expensive to buy and to run as they have to work in confined spaces with reduced flow of air.

American-style fridge freezers are designed with the fridge and freezer compartments side by side. They look good but take up lots of space and I find the freezer part a little on the small side. They usually have ice and chilled water dispensers that take up room in the freezer compartment and

Freezer star ratings

✳✳✳✳ −18°C and above, freezes fresh food for up to 3–12 months or longer

✳✳✳ −18°C, stores pre-frozen food for up to 3 months

✳✳ −12°C, stores pre-frozen food for up to 1 month

✳ −6°C, stores pre-frozen food for up to 1 week

will need to be plumbed into the water supply. They also tend to create more noise.

Fridges with a small freezer at the top can be a full 4* rated freezer or not much more than a basic ice box. A small freezer in the kitchen can be useful if you have a larger freezer but I strongly recommend buying one with a high star rating as it will be able to store frozen food safely for longer and to also freeze fresh food reasonably fast. Fridges with ice boxes are only useful for keeping ice and storing small quantities of already frozen food.

Special features

Frost-free freezers shouldn't need defrosting. They work by forcing air through the freezer cabinet which gets rid of the moisture that would otherwise freeze and build up as frost or ice over time. It is important to allow more space around food for air to circulate in frost-free freezers.

Door alarms and warning lights let you know when you haven't closed the door properly. Keeping the door firmly shut not only stops food partially thawing and allowing large ice crystals to form, it also saves energy by stopping the freezer going into overdrive trying to keep food frozen.

Choosing the right freezer

If you want to freeze lots of garden produce, buy in bulk to save money or batch cook to save time, you are best investing in the largest freezer you have space for and can afford. Look out for chest models. If you want to store a few standbys, some family meals and desserts, a tall upright freezer should suit you. If you only want to hold a selection of prepared meals and a couple of packs of frozen vegetables, a combined fridge freezer will be fine.

Capacities claimed by manufacturers can be misleading and unrealistically large, so check the freezer out for yourself. There are guidelines to how much freezer space will be required,

according the size of the household, but I think a good look inside will give you a much better idea.

Pick a freezer with a good rating for energy consumption. Although not hideously expensive to run (£20–£40 a year), a freezer with an energy efficient A, A+ or A++ rating could save you pounds each year.

Every freezer has a climate class that tells you the range of room temperature with which it can cope. This is particularly important if you want to keep your freezer in a building outside.

It's also worth checking out how much noise is made by the motor. Manufacturers should be able to give an indication in decibels measured during use.

Looking after your freezer

All manufacturers will recommend how to care for your freezer after purchase and will include information on how to defrost if required. Chest freezers will need to be defrosted once or twice a year and upright models probably more often. A thorough defrost should take less than 2 hours.

Why defrosting is important

Defrosting is necessary because frost will build up on the walls, shelves and doors as it is used. This will stop the freezer working effectively and make it difficult to remove the baskets and open drawers. The capacity will also be reduced and the motor will need to work harder to keep food frozen if the door seals are iced over.

How to defrost your freezer

* Get together as many bags or boxes as you can find. Cardboard and plastic boxes can be used.
* Wrap food in several sheets of newspaper and pack tightly into the bags or boxes. This will help them remain cold. Cover with heavy blankets or towels for further insulation.
* Switch off the freezer and place bowls of hot water in the bottom of the freezer, close the door and leave for 15 minutes.
* Remove the bowls and spread dry towels or newspaper over the bottom of the cabinet to absorb the water.
* Leave the freezer open to allow warm air to circulate.
* Protect your hands from the cold by putting on waterproof gloves and remove as much frost and ice as possible by scraping down the sides of the freezer with a wooden or plastic spatula. Never use a sharp knife or metal tool as the interior walls could get damaged.
* Collect large pieces of ice and transfer them to a sink to drain away. Use a clean dustpan for collecting smaller pieces of ice as you scrape.
* Some chest freezers have a drain at the bottom that can be used to remove excess water.
* As soon as the cabinet is free from frost, remove towels and newspaper.

* Wipe out the freezer with lukewarm water and dry thoroughly with kitchen paper or a clean towel.
* Wash and dry baskets or shelves and return them to the freezer.
* Restart the freezer and leave for one hour before returning the food.
* If any of the food has started to thaw, pop it into the fridge and use within a day.

Power failure

If you have a power cut, keep the freezer door tightly closed and the food should remain frozen for several hours. Most power cuts are for less than an hour, so no action needs to be taken. If it lasts longer than 18 hours, the food will need to be carefully checked.

If you know that the power failure is likely to last several hours or days, try and move food to a friend's freezer. If well wrapped, most of it should remain frozen for up to 2 hours. If the freezer has been inadvertently switched off or if the freezer door has been left open for even a short time, food will also start to thaw. Switch back on at once and check all the contents using the guidelines below.

* If thawing is complete but the food is still very cold, raw foods such as fish, poultry and meat can be refrozen as long as they are cooked first.
* All pre-cooked dishes, such as cottage pie, beef stew and fish cakes, and raw or cooked vegetables should not be frozen but kept chilled in the fridge and eaten within 24 hours.
* Ice cream and creamy desserts should be thrown away.
* Bread and cakes can be refrozen if partially thawed but the texture may be altered.
* Fruit can be refrozen but will have become soft and flabby, so you are better off cooking it quickly and then using it for pie fillings.
* Any thawed foods that do not feel very cold or that have an unpleasant appearance or smell should be immediately discarded.

In this chapter, I have selected a few foods that I think will be most useful when you are new to freezing and explain how you prepare and use them from the freezer. It's also well worth buying a book listing A–Z of hundreds of foods and how you freeze them for something more in-depth.

If you can't find a particular item here, you can follow the tips for freezing on pages 202 and 204, which will apply to most vegetables and fruits. Also make sure you are familiar with the Know-how chapter, starting on page 210. If in any doubt, keep storage time in the freezer to a minimum.

Many foods will freeze for several months more than I've stated in this guide, but this book is about eating well, not storing foods for years on end. I've given suggestions for what I feel is the maximum time foods should remain in the freezer so they remain both appetising and delicious.

Some foods freeze more successfully than others so it's best to either avoid those that don't freeze well or transform them into something that does.

* Salad ingredients such as lettuce, cucumber and tomatoes become limp due to their high water content. Instead of freezing them raw, make into soups or sauces.
* Strawberries become soft on thawing but can be made into fruit purée before freezing or jam from frozen.
* Cheese with less than 40 per cent fat can become grainy and watery. Instead, use for enriching roux-style sauces or blend into stuffings. Lower fat soft cheese can be made into cheesecake and ricotta cheese mixed with cooked spinach and onions for a veggie pie filling
* Avoid egg emulsion-style sauces, such as mayonnaise, hollandaise and béarnaise, as they will separate when thawed.
* Eggs in their shells will crack when frozen as the liquid inside expands.
* Plain yogurt will separate when frozen but can be used in cooked dishes. Yogurt containing stablisers, especially fruit yogurts, will freeze more successfully and can be thawed for packed lunches.
* Some spices, especially cinnamon, become more pungent when frozen, so reduce quantities slightly when adapting favourite recipes.
* Boiled potatoes become soft and watery when thawed, so mash them with butter and cream before freezing instead. Alternatively, sauté chunks of boiled potatoes in a frying pan until dry and crisp, then cool before freezing. Reheat from frozen in a hot pan.

AT A
GLANCE

Bread

Food	Prepare	Wrap	Use	Best before (months)
Fresh baked bread, unsliced, sliced, packaged and rolls freeze well but do need to be well wrapped. Crusty loaves or rolls don't freeze as well as others and tend to break up within a week or 2 of freezing.		Wrap in freezer bags or foil, or keep in original packaging for a week or 2. Place in a large freezer bag if necessary.	Thaw at room temperature for 2–6 hours. Once thawed, can be reheated in a hot oven at 200°C / Fan oven 180°C/Gas 6 for 5 minutes to recrisp crusty breads. Serve immediately.	**4** **2 weeks (crusty breads)**
Bread dough	Cut into usable portions.	Place in freezer bags, remove air and seal.	Thaw overnight in fridge. Shape and allow to rise in a warm place before baking as usual.	**1**
Breadcrumbs		Place in freezer bags or a rigid container.	Thaw at room temperature for 30 minutes, or use from frozen for cooked dishes.	**3**
Croissants		Best placed in rigid containers or wrapped in individual freezer bags.	Thaw overnight in fridge, or at room temperature for 2 hours, or heat from frozen at 200°C /Fan 180°C/Gas 6 for 15 minutes.	**3**
Pita, naan and speciality breads		Wrap in freezer bags or foil, or keep in original packaging for a week or 2. Place in a large freezer bag if necessary.	Thaw at room temperature for 1 hour or toast/grill/microwave from frozen.	**4**
Sandwiches	Avoid fillings that don't freeze well such as hard-boiled eggs, mayonnaise, salad stuffs. Do not use thawed prawns or other seafood.	Wrap in freezer bags or foil. Place in a large freezer bag if necessary.	Thaw at room temperature for 1–2 hours or in the fridge overnight.	**2 weeks**
Buns and pastries Currant and hot cross buns freeze well. Pastries freeze best without icing.		Place in freezer bags or rigid containers.	Thaw at room temperature for 2–3 hours.	**3**

Cakes and biscuits

Food	Prepare	Wrap	Use	Best before (months)
Uncooked cake batter Uncooked whisked sponge batters don't freeze well.	Prepare as usual.	Open freeze in foil-lined cake tin until firm. Transfer to a freezer bag, or place into rigid container.	Unwrap and return to original tin. Allow to thaw at room temperature for 2–3 hours, or thaw batter and use as usual.	2
Baked sponges, fairy cakes, muffins, Swiss rolls and light fruit cakes.	Prepare as usual.	Wrap undecorated cakes in foil and place in freezer bags. Decorated cakes should be open frozen on a tray until solid then wrapped in foil and freezer bags. Delicate cakes should be placed in rigid containers.	Unwrap cakes while frozen and thaw at room temperature for 1–3 hours.	**4 (undecorated)** **3 (decorated)**
Biscuit mixture or cookie dough	Prepare as usual and shape into rolls.	Wrap in cling film or foil and place in freezer bags.	Leave dough in wrapping until it softens. Unwrap and cut into slices then bake.	4

Eggs

Food	Prepare	Wrap	Use	Best before (months)
Do not freeze in their shells or as hard-boiled.				
Whole	Lightly whisk adding ½ tsp of salt or sugar to 6 eggs for savoury or sweet to prevent coagulation.	Place in a small rigid container or open freeze in silicone bakeware then transfer to a freezer bag.	Thaw in fridge or at room temperature and use immediately. One egg equals 3 tbsp.	1
Whites	Separate eggs and lightly whisk.	Place in a small rigid container or open freeze in silicone bakeware then transfer to a freezer bag.	Thaw in fridge or at room temperature and use immediately. One egg equals 3 tbsp.	1

Food	Prepare	Wrap	Use	Best before (months)
Most products keep for some time in the fridge, but can be frozen. Good for emergency supplies or unexpected gluts.				
Butter		Leave in original packaging and wrap in foil or a freezer bag.	Best thawed in fridge overnight.	**3 (salted)** **6 (unsalted)**
Savoury butters	Prepare as usual. Shape into a roll 3cm in diameter.	Wrap in foil.	Unwrap and slice using a knife dipped in hot water for use on hot dishes.	**2**
Double cream	Softly whip adding 2 tsp caster sugar per 100ml.	Spoon into a rigid container and seal. Or pipe into rosettes and open freeze before placing in a rigid container or freezer bag.	Best thawed overnight in fridge. Frozen cream rosettes can be placed directly on puddings and cakes; allow 10 minutes to thaw.	**3**
Cheese Hard, soft and blue cheeses all freeze well. Hard cheese may crumble on thawing but can be grated. Soft cheese should be frozen at the desired ripeness.				
Hard cheese	Cut into usable portions if necessary, or grate.	Wrap in foil and place in a freezer bag or transfer grated cheese to freezer bags.	Portions are best thawed for several hours or overnight in fridge. Grated cheese can be used from frozen.	**3**
Soft cheese Brie, Camembert, goat's cheese.	Cut into usable portions if necessary.	Keep in original packaging (if applicable) then overwrap in foil. Or doublewrap individual portions in foil.	Best thawed for several hours or overnight in fridge. Return to room temperature 30 minutes before serving.	**3**
Shop-bought yogurts containing natural stabilisers		Freeze in unopened sealed pot.	Best thawed overnight in fridge. If thawed at room temperature use immediately.	**1**

Pastry and pies

Food	Prepare	Wrap	Use	Best before (months)
Pastry Can be frozen raw or baked. Filo and puff pastry damage easily and should be well packaged.	Prepare as usual and cut in usable portions, or roll into sheets.	Wrap in foil and place in a freezer bag. Sheets can be rolled around clingfilm and covered in foil.	Thaw raw pastry overnight in fridge or at room temperature for 3–4 hours.	**3**
Tarts	For unbaked tarts, make pastry as usual and use to line tart tin. Prep the base. For baked tarts, make and bake as usual.	Open freeze in foil dishes then wrap in foil and place in freezer bags.	Unbaked tarts can be baked blind from frozen and filled as required. Baked tarts can be thawed in the fridge or at room temperature or reheated from frozen in a moderate oven at 180°C /Fan 160°C/Gas 4 until hot.	**3 (meat or fish)** **6 (fruit and sweet)**
Pies Cover pastry with foil if the pie begins to over-brown before the filling is piping hot.	For both unbaked pies and baked pies, prepare as usual.	Open freeze then wrap in foil and place in freezer bags, taking care to protect the top.	Thaw overnight in fridge or at room temperature if thoroughly cooked before freezing. Thaw overnight in the fridge to cook from raw. To cook or reheat from frozen bake in a moderate oven at 180°C /Fan 160°C/ Gas 4 until piping hot throughout.	**3 (meat or fish)** **6 (fruit and sweet)**
Crumble	Prepare as usual in a freezer and ovenproof dish or in a flexbile freezer container (see page 219). Prebake or freeze uncooked.	Wrap in foil.	Prebaked crumbles can be thawed overnight in fridge or for 3–4 hours at room temperature. Bake as usual. Uncooked crumbles can be baked from thawed or from frozen by adding 50 per cent extra cooking time.	**6**

Fish and seafood

Food	Prepare	Wrap	Use	Best before (months)
Only very fresh fish should be frozen. It's essential to use the fastest freezing process possible. Never freeze fish or seafood that has been previously frozen. Freezing battered, cooked or uncooked, fresh fish is not recommended unless bought commercially.	Whole fish should be gutted, washed and dried. Round fish – remove head, fins and tail. Flat fish – remove fins and trim. Fillets or steaks may be skinned, washed and dried. Seafood should only be frozen if very fresh, raw or just cooked. A lot of seafood is sold ready cooked and should be frozen on the day of purchase. Do not freeze if it has been frozen before – always refer to packaging or retailer.	Fillets or steaks should be separated using cling film before freezing. Transfer whole fish, fillets or steaks to freezer bags. Make sure as much air as possible is removed from the bags before sealing. Vacuum packed fish can be frozen without any further preperation.	Fish and shellfish should not be thawed at room temperature. Small whole fish, steaks and fillets may be cooked from frozen, allowing 3–5 minutes extra cooking time or thawed for 4–6 hours or overnight in the fridge. Large whole or thick pieces of fish are best thawed, in their wrapping, in the fridge. Under 2kg overnight Over 2kg 24–36 hours. Shellfish is best thawed in the fridge and used immediately or cooked from frozen.	
Oily fish Salmon, trout, herring, mackerel etc.	Prepare whole fish or divide it into usable fillets or steaks.	Wrap in cling film and place in a freezer bag.	See general fish use to thaw or cook from frozen.	2
Smoked fresh fish	Divide into usable portions.	Wrap in cling film and place in a freezer bag.	See general fish use to thaw or cook from frozen.	2
White fish Cod, whiting, plaice, sole, etc.		Wrap in cling film and place in a freezer bag.	See general fish use to thaw or cook from frozen.	3
Seafood can be frozen raw or cooked. Do not refreeze any seafood that has already been frozen.	Prepare whole, shelled or for serving e.g. crab meat should be removed, shredded and returned to shell.	Wrap in cling film and place in a freezer bag.	Thaw overnight in fridge in its wrappings. Raw product may be cooked from frozen.	1

Meat

Food	Prepare	Wrap	Use	Best before (months)
Choose good-quality meat, which has been cut into usable joints, chops or pieces before freezing. Note weight of meat before freezing.	Refer to freezing meat guidelines on page 196.	Chops or steaks should be separated using a double layer of waxed paper or cling film before freezing. Vacuum packed meat can be frozen without any further preperation.	Raw meat is best thawed slowly in its wrapping in the fridge. Allow 5 hours per 500g	
Bacon, gammon steaks, gammon joints.	Non pre-packed should be divided into usable portions.	Wrap tightly in cling film, cover in foil and place in a freezer bag.	Salty bacon joints are best thawed overnight in the fridge.	**2** **4 (if vacuum packed or according to supplier's instructions)**
Uncooked chops, steaks and cubed meats		Open freeze with cling film or foil. Transfer to a freezer bag or rigid container.	See general meat use to thaw, or cook from frozen (see page 196)	**4 (chops and steaks)** **3 (cubed)** **1 (super-quick strips)**
Cooked meats	Cool quickly after cooking. May also be frozen with gravy or sauce.	Wrap well in foil or freeze in a rigid container with gravy or sauce.	Thaw overnight in fridge If packed with gravy, warm through thoroughly over a gentle heat.	**2**
Deli meats		Keep in original packaging (if applicable). Or wrap in cling film and place in freezer bags.	Thaw in fridge overnight or cook from frozen. Best used in cooked dishes once thawed.	**1**
Uncooked joints		Wrap in foil then place in a freezer bag.	See general meat use to thaw. Joints should thawed according to guidelines on page 220.	**6**
Mince, burgers, meatballs	Divide into usable portions.	Open freeze burgers and meatballs and transfer to freezer bags. Flat freeze mince (see page 217)	Thaw in fridge overnight, or cook from frozen. Burgers must reach a core temperature of 75°C using the thermometer.	**3**
Sausages and sausage meat	Divide into usable portions.	Wrap in cling film or foil and place in freezer bags.	Thaw overnight for several hours in fridge and use immediately or cook from frozen. Make sure the sausage meat is fully cooked throughout.	**2**

Poultry

Food	Prepare	Wrap	Use	Best before (months)
	Do not stuff whole poultry before freezing. Keep work surfaces scrupulously clean at all times.	Portions should be separated using cling film or waxed paper before freezing.	All whole birds must be thawed completely in the fridge before cooking. Approximate thawing times for poultry: Up to 2kg: 12 hours 2–6kg: 24–36 hours Over 6kg: 36–72hours	
Chicken and duck	For whole birds, remove giblets if necessary. Remove portions from original packaging before freezing.	Doublewrap whole birds in freezer bags. Wrap portions in individual freezer bags or foil before overwrapping in a large freezer bag or placing in a rigid container.	Thaw as according to guidelines on page 220.	4
Turkey	For whole birds, remove giblets if necessary.	Doublewrap whole birds in freezer bags or foil. Freeze giblets separately in small freezer bags.	Thaw in fridge according to weight.	4

Herbs

Food	Prepare	Wrap	Use	Best before (months)
Freeze well and are convenient for cooking but not suitable for garnishing. May lose flavour on freezing. See page 208 for more information on herbs.				
Basil, chives, mint, parsley	Leave whole or chop finely.	Place in small rigid containers or small freezer bags.	Use from frozen in cooked or prepared dishes.	6
Rosemary, thyme	Strip leaves from woody stalks.	Place in small rigid containers or small freezer bags.	Use from frozen in cooked dishes.	6

Rice and pasta

Food	Prepare	Wrap	Use	Best before (months)
Rice	Cook as usual. Cut the cooking time by roughly 20 per cent. Rinse in a sieve under running water until completely cold; drain.	Place in usable quantities in freezer bags as soon as drained.	Cook from frozen, stirring well.	3
Spaghetti, macaroni, etc. Can be frozen, although this does not save much preparation time, but is useful to save waste.	Cook as usual. Rinse in a colander under running water until completely cold; drain. If cooking for the freezer, reduce intial cooking time by 20 per cent.	Place in freezer bags.	Cook from frozen, stirring well. Drain and serve.	2
Composite dishes such as lasagne, cannelloni, macaroni cheese	Prepare as usual in a freezer and ovenproof dish, foil-lined dish or silicone baking pan. Do not bake.	Open freeze until firm, cover dish with foil and place in a freezer bag. Alternatively, remove from dish or baking pan, wrap in foil and place in freezer bag.	Thaw overnight in fridge and cook as usual or reheat from frozen at 190°C/Fan 170°C, Gas 5, increasing the cooking time by around 50 per cent.	3

Fruit

Food	Prepare	Wrap	Use	Best before (months)
Home-grown fruit should be picked and frozen within 2 hours. Shop bought should be fully ripe and undamaged. See freezing fruit section on page 204.	Blanching will make most fruit become mushy on thawing. Other freezing methods are generally used instead.	Dependent on fruit type and end use, there are a number of freezing methods suitable for making the most of fruit. Allow 2cm of headroom when freezing in rigid containers. 1. Open freeze 2. Raw with sugar 3. Raw with syrup 4. Stewed with sugar	Fruits are best thawed in the fridge or at room temperature. Served at the point of thawing for use as raw. Fruit frozen in sugar or syrup is best thawed in the container, turned upside down, so the fruit is immersed in the syrup. Fruits that are to be further prepared, cooked in pies or stewed can be used from frozen and warmed gently.	
Apples	Peel, core, slice or chop. Steep in water with juice of one lemon to prevent discolouring or stew in minimum water with/without sugar then purée.	1. Open freeze 2. Raw with syrup 3. Stewed with sugar	See general fruit use to thaw or to use from frozen.	**6 (dry)** **10 (in syrup/stewed)**
Avocado Do not freeze whole	Skin and stone fruit, mash flesh with lemon juice. Use 1 tbsp per avocado.	Store in rigid containers or flat freeze in usable portions.	Thaw at room temperature.	**2**
Banana Do not freeze whole	Skin and mash flesh with lemon juice and sugar. Use 3 tbsp of lemon juice and 100g caster sugar for every 6–8 bananas.	Store in rigid containers or flat freeze in usable portions.	Thaw in the fridge. Use immediately.	**6**
Berries Blackcurrants/redcurrants, blueberries, blackberries, cranberries, gooseberries	Prepare fruit, remove stems or stew in minimum water with/without sugar then purée. Sieve if necessary.	1. Open freeze 2. Raw with sugar 3. Raw with syrup 4. Stewed with sugar	See general fruit use to thaw or to use from frozen.	**4 (dry)** **10 (in syrup/stewed)**

Food	Prepare	Wrap	Use	Best before (months)
Grapes	Half and de-pip seeded grapes, seedless may be halved or left whole.	Raw with syrup.	Thaw in container at room temperature.	6
Lemons/Limes/Oranges	Wipe over fruit, leave whole or cut into slices, or grate, peel or extract juice or segment. Seville oranges may be frozen whole for making marmalade.	Wrap whole fruit in freezer bag. Open freeze slices. Place rind and juice in separate rigid containers.	Thaw in wrapping/container at room temperature and use as required. Slices can be used frozen in drinks.	10
Peaches, nectarines	Peel, halve and remove stone.	Raw with syrup.	Thaw at room temperature.	5
Pears Choose just ripe pears	Peel and core; halve or slice. Best poached.	Stewed with sugar. Place in rigid containers.	Thaw at room temperature.	10
Rhubarb	Wash and cut to required lengths. Blanch for 1 minute to retain colour.	1. Open freeze 2. Raw with sugar 3. Raw with syrup 4. Stewed with sugar	See general fruit use to thaw or to use from frozen.	4 (dry) 10 (in syrup/stewed)
Soft fruit Strawberries, raspberries	Wash in iced water and gently dry in kitchen towel.	1. Open freeze 2. Raw with sugar 3. Raw with syrup 4. Stewed with sugar	See general fruit use to thaw or to use from frozen. Strawberries tend to lose texture and flavour on thawing.	4 (dry) 10 (in syrup/stewed)
Stoned fruit Apricots, plums, damsons	Wash, halve and remove stone.	1. Open freeze 2. Raw with sugar 3. Raw with syrup 4. Stewed with sugar	See general fruit use to thaw or to use from frozen.	4 (dry) 10 (in syrup/stewed)

Food	Prepare	Wrap	Use	Best before (months)
Most vegetables can be frozen raw, however to maintain quality beyond 2 weeks, they should be blanched to stop enzymes working, which make the vegetables deteriorate, even when frozen. Do not freeze: Salad vegetables/greens or raw tomatoes See freezing vegetable section on page 204.	Vegetables should be prepared as normal, blanched and frozen. Best blanched in up to 500g batches. Cool in cold iced water for the same time as blanched. If freezing mixed batches of vegetables, blanch according to kind before freezing. Vegetables can also be cooked as usual, puréed and frozen. This works particularly well for asparagus, carrots, peas and spinach.	Place vegetables in rigid containers or freezer bags. Puréed vegetables can be frozen in silicone bakeware or ice-cube trays. Allow headspace in rigid containers for purées.	All vegetables can be cooked from frozen, plunging the vegetables in boiling salted water. Blanching partially cooks the vegetables. Reducing the time you would cook from fresh.	8 (for most vegetables once blanched)
Artichokes, Globe	Remove outer leaves, trim and wash. Blanch with lemon juice for 7 minutes.	Wrap in foil before placing in a freezer bag, or in a rigid container.	Cook from frozen for about 5 minutes or until centres are tender or thaw overnight in fridge. Or thaw at room temperature.	6
Artichoke, Jerusalem	Scrub, peel, simmer until tender and purée.	Place in rigid containers or silicone bakeware.	Reheat gently from frozen, adding a little milk or butter.	3
Asparagus	Prepare as usual, cut to fit container. Blanch for 2–4 minutes or simmer until tender and purée.	Open freeze unpuréed asparagus. Place in rigid containers.	Cook from frozen for 3–5 minutes.	8
Beans, broad, French and green	Shell beans if necessary. Blanch for 2 minutes.	Open freeze then place in freezer bags.	Cook from frozen for 6–8 minutes.	8
Broccoli	Prepare as usual, cut into florets of equal size. Blanch for 2 minutes.	Open freeze then place in freezer bags.	Cook from frozen for 6–8 minutes.	6
Brussels Sprouts	Prepare as usual.	Open freeze then place in freezer bags.	Cook from frozen for 6–8 minutes.	8
Butternut squash and marrow	Peel, slice and dice. Blanch for 2 minutes.	Place in freezer bags in usable quantities.	Cook from frozen for 5 minutes until tender.	8
Cabbage, green, red or white	Prepare as usual. Blanch for one minute.	Flat freeze	Cook from frozen for 3–4 minutes.	8

Food	Prepare	Wrap	Use	Best before (months)
Carrots	Prepare as usual. Small, young carrots freeze best. Slice or dice larger carrots. Blanch for 3–5 minutes dependent on size.	Open freeze then place into freezer bags.	Cook from frozen for 5–7 minutes.	**10**
Cauliflower	Prepare as usual, cut into florets of equal size. Blanch for 2 minutes.	Open freeze then place into freezer bags.	Cook from frozen for 6–8 minutes.	**8**
Celery	Scrub and cut into even lengths. Blanch for 5 minutes.	Place in freezer bags.	Cook from frozen as recipe suggests.	**6**
Corn on the cob	Remove husk and silk. Blanch for 4–8 minutes according to size.	Place whole in freezer bags or scrape off kernels, open freeze and place into freezer bags.	Cook whole from frozen for 15 minutes or cook kernels for 5 minutes.	**8**
Courgettes	Prepare as usual, cut into sticks or thick slices. Blanch for 1 minute.	Open freeze then place into freezer bags or rigid containers.	Cook from frozen or thaw at room temperature and sauté in butter.	**8**
Leeks	Prepare as usual, wash well. Leave whole or slice. Small and medium sizes are best. Blanch for 2 minutes.	Place in freezer bags.	Cook from frozen for 6–10 minutes or thaw at room temperature and sauté in butter.	**6**
Mushrooms	Prepare as usual. Leave whole or slice. May be frozen raw or sautéed in butter for 2 minutes, cooled and frozen.	Open freeze sliced raw mushrooms, place in freezer bags. Place cooked mushrooms in rigid containers.	Use from frozen in dishes.	**3**
Onions	Prepare as usual. Leave whole, chop or slice. May be frozen blanched for 1–3 minutes according to size or unblanched for short-term freezing.	Open freeze then place into freezer bags.	Add frozen while cooking dishes or thaw at room temperature for 2 hours.	**6** **1 (unblanched)**
Parsnips	Prepare as usual, slice or dice. Blanch for 2 minutes or boil and purée.	Open freeze then place into freezer bags. Flat freeze for purée.	Cook from frozen. Reheat purée gently.	**8**

Food	Prepare	Wrap	Use	Best before (months)
Peas	Shell and blanch for 1 minute.	Open freeze then place into freezer bags.	Cook from frozen.	6
Potatoes Must be cooked before freezing.	Mash: prepare as usual. Chipped: blanch for one minute and toss with oil. Roast: par-boil and toss with oil. Jacket: rub with oil and fully bake in oven.	Mash: flat freeze Chipped: open freeze then place into freezer bags. Roast: open freeze then place into freezer bags. Jacket: wrap individually in foil and place into freezer bags.	Mash: reheat gently from frozen. Chipped: fry or bake as usual. Roast: place in oven as usual. Jacket: reheat in the microwave until hot throughout.	3
Spinach Select young fresh leaves.	Wash thoroughly and remove tough stalks. Blanch for 2 minutes.	Drain very well, squeezing out excess liquid then flat freeze.	Reheat from frozen.	6
Turnips	Prepare as usual, slice or dice. Blanch for 2 minutes or boil and purée.	Open freeze then place into freezer bags. For purée place in rigid container or flat freeze.	Cook from frozen or add frozen while cooking.	8
Tomatoes Use only in cooked dishes.	Raw: wash and pat dry. Cooked: remove skins and roughly chop flesh.	Raw: place in freezer bags. Cooked: cook in a saucepan over a medium heat for 5 minutes until softened. Cool quickly and flat freeze or place in rigid containers.	Raw: rinse under hot water from frozen to remove skin. Thaw at room temperature until soft enough to chop. Cooked: use from frozen.	2 weeks (raw) 4 (cooked)

Prepared foods

Food	Prepare	Wrap	Use	Best before (months)
Casseroles, chilli con carne, curries	Cook in usual way. Cool quickly.	Freeze in foil container or silicone bakeware. Doublewrap in foil if necessary.	Thaw overnight in fridge. Dishes can be reheated from frozen using a gentle heat.	3
Ready-made foods Make sure the product does not defrost on its journey to the freezer.		Store in freezer according to manufacturer's instructions.	Thaw or use from frozen as per manufacturer's instructions.	**According to manufacturer's instructions**
Leftovers Do not freeze leftovers that have been frozen before.	Divide into usable portions.	Place in rigid container or freezer bags.	Thaw overnight in fridge. Dishes can be reheated from frozen using a gentle heat.	3
Meringues	Prepare as usual until crisp and dry.	Place carefully in rigid containers interleaving with baking parchment or cling film.	Thaw at room temperature for 5 minutes, fill and serve.	4
Mousses	Prepare as usual but do not garnish or decorate.	Wrap in foil and place in a freezer bag.	Defrost overnight in fridge.	3
Soups, stocks and sauces Most freeze well. Do not freeze egg-based sauces.	Prepare as usual. If adding eggs do this after thawing and reheating.	Pour into rigid containers or flat freeze (see page 216).	Thaw overnight in fridge or at room temperature or gently reheat from frozen in a saucepan, stirring regularly.	4–6

Index

Recipe list

Acknowledgements

This book has been a real labour of love over the past two years. Discovering more about freezing food than I thought possible and freezer testing hundreds of recipes. During this time my family has had to put up with two huge freezers in the dining room, one in the garage and another in the utility room. Thank you John for not complaining too much when we had to have our Christmas lunch in the kitchen. And thank you Jess and Emily for trying all the new dishes and for your confidence at all times that there would always be something worth eating in the freezer. I'm sorry that you had to spend months eyeing up all the cakes before you had a chance to try them.

Massive thanks to my brilliant assistants, Jane Gwillim, Gileng Salter, Lauren Brignell and Kirsty Thomas. I honestly don't know what I would have done without you all. Thank you for humouring me through every recipe tweak and donning rubber gloves, coats and hats for the frequent freezer reshuffles. Also, thanks my wonderful PA Fran Brown for keeping everything superbly organized and Sadie Homer for helping me assemble the information for the At A Glance guide at the back of the book.

A huge thank you to the very talented photographer Cristian Barnett for making frozen food look great and for letting me squeeze a ridiculously large number of recipes into each day. Also, Cristian's assistant, the ever hungry, Roy Baron for always showing his appreciation of the dishes. Thanks to our stylist, Claire Bignell for choosing the perfect props and welcoming us into her home for some of the shoot days.

A special thank you to the fantastic Sally Coleman who helped me make sense of the words and content. Your words of wisdom ring in my ears.

At Orion, I would like to thank the amazing Amanda Harris for her unfailing encouragement ... and flexible deadlines. Also Jillian Young for all her enthusiasm and for being so good at what she does. A big thank you to the lovely Lucie Stericker, Loulou Clark and Andy Campling for their superb creative skills and innovative design solutions. And thank you also to Jinny Johnson for all her valuable advice.

I'm very grateful to my lawyer, Sarah Staines, and accountant, Susan Boardman, for looking after the business side of things while I concentrate on the cooking. And an extra thank you to John and Joan at Smeg UK for kindly lending me additional freezers and ovens for testing all the recipes. And to Charlotte for all her positive feedback.

And a final thank you to my mum – the only person I know who owns more freezers than me – for proving that solid bundles of unidentifiable 3 year old meat from the freezer won't kill you and can actually be turned into something rather nice. (Not recommended but perfectly possible.)